HISTORY THROUGH HEADLINES

HISTORY THROUGH HEADLINES

igloo

igloo

Published in 2012

by Igloo Books Ltd

Cottage Farm

Sywell

NN6 0BJ

www.igloo-books.com

2 4 6 8 10 9 7 5 3

B044 0312

ISBN: 978-1-84817-398-9

Printed and manufactured in China

The news stories featured here reflect the social attitudes of the day
and do not reflect the opinions of the publisher.

Contents

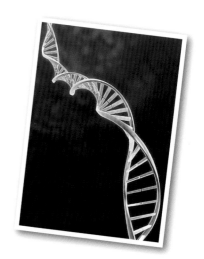

Introduction

Read all about it! The past 100 years of world history are portrayed here, through dramatic newspaper headlines, vivid front-page images, detailed explanatory stories and timelines with important events, from atomic bombs and the sinking of the Titanic, to the fall of the Berlin Wall and the election of President Obama.

Events that shaped the 20th Century and, therefore, life as we know it, from major experiences such as the assassination of President John F. Kennedy, to the less crucial but life-changing flight of Charles Lindbergh, the first person to fly solo across the Atlantic, are chronicled here, by decade and by year.

This comprehensive reflection of the past 100 years encapsulates history from 1900 up to the present.

Right: Ethiopian refugees rest as they reach a camp in Sudan in 1985, having been forced out of their country by famine.

*Crowds gather outside the
New York Stock Exchange
on Wall Street following
news of the stock market
crash on October 24, 1929.*

American astronaut Bruce McCandless uses the
Manned Maneuvering Unit to move around the
space shuttle Challenger *in 1984.*

The wreck of the oil tanker Amoco Cadiz sinks off the coast of Brittany, France, in March 1978 releasing what was, at the time, the largest oil slick ever spilled.

1900–1909

1900
SIEGE OF MAFEKING

The Second Boer War was fought between the British Empire, of which South Africa was a part, and two independent Boer republics within South Africa. In May 1900, the Siege of Mafeking in South Africa ended in an overwhelming British victory against the Boers. Colonel Robert Baden-Powell, who later founded the Scouting movement, made his name by raising two regiments in Cape Colony and taking up a defensive position in the town of Mafeking. Although Baden-Powell's troops were greatly outnumbered, they managed to resist Boer forces. This was largely due to Baden-Powell's employment of skillful deceptions, including laying fake landmines and telling his troops to climb over imaginary barbed wire.

'The Siege of Mafeking in South Africa ended in an overwhelming British victory against the Boers.'

1901
QUEEN VICTORIA DIES

Queen Victoria reigned for 63 years, overseeing an expanding British Empire, the technological advances of the Industrial Revolution, and increased literary and artistic output. She died of a cerebral hemorrhage on January 22, 1901, at the age of 82. Since the death of her husband, Prince Albert, in 1861, Victoria had taken on somber mourning, both in her dress and in her manner, an attitude that was reflected in national habits where mourning became lavish, ornate, and drawn out. Her death was to mark the end of such a somber fashion. Her funeral took place on February 2, 1901, and she was laid beside the body of her husband at the mausoleum in Great Windsor Park.

Above: The Albert Memorial was commissioned by Queen Victoria (right) in 1861.

1900
New Quantum Physics
German physicist Max Planck formulates new laws of physics, showing that energy comes in tiny packets called 'quanta.'

September 6, 1901
McKinley Assassinated
U.S. President William McKinley is shot as he meets the public in Buffalo, New York. He dies of his injuries a week later.

December 10, 1901
First Nobel Prizes Awarded
At a ceremony in Sweden the first annual nobel prizes, for Chemistry, Physics, Medicine, Literature, and Peace, are awarded. They were set up according to the will of the Swedish inventor Alfred Nobel.

February 23, 1903
U.S. Lease Guantanamo Bay
Cuba leases Guantanamo Bay, an area in the east of the island, to the U.S.A.

1900–1909

1904
JAPAN AND RUSSIA AT WAR

In 1904, war broke out between Russia and Japan over control of Korea and Manchuria. In 1896, Russia had formed an alliance with China that allowed the country to extend the Trans-Siberian Railway across Chinese-held Manchuria to the Russian port of Vladivostock. The Japanese demanded that the Russians withdraw from Manchuria and threatened military action. On February 8, 1904, the Japanese fleet launched a surprise attack on the Russian Navy at Port Arthur in Southern Manchuria. On land, the two armies were fairly evenly matched, and despite mounting casualties, neither side was able to claim a victory. At sea, however, the Japanese had the upper hand, and when the Japanese Navy destroyed the entire Russian Baltic Fleet at the Battle of Tsushima in May 1905, the Russians were forced to sue for peace. The resultant deal saw the Russians withdraw from Southern Manchuria, which was returned to the Chinese, while Japan took control of the rest of Manchuria and Korea.

1906
SAN FRANCISCO DEVASTATED BY EARTHQUAKE AND FIRE

The earthquake that struck northern California on April 18, 1906 was one of the most severe in America's history. The quake itself caused significant loss of life, and started a fire in the city of San Francisco that raged out of control. At the time, it was estimated that 700 people were killed, but it is now thought that there were many more fatalities. The 1906 Californian earthquake also taught geologists a good deal about earthquake patterns. The tremor along the San Andreas Fault was 296 miles (480 km) long, and its horizontal displacements over such a large area baffled scientists of the day. In the years before the discovery of plate tectonics, analysts developed a theory of elastic-rebound at the quake's source, which today still stands as the clearest explanation of earthquake cycles.

December 1, 1903
First Feature Film
The first full-length silent movie, *The Great Train Robbery*, goes on general release in the U.S.A.

1905
E=MC²
Albert Einstein publishes his Special Theory of Relativity, in which he formulates the relationship between energy and matter: $E = mc^2$.

February 19, 1906
Kellogg's Founded
Will Keith Kellogg founds the Toasted Corn Flake Company to sell the new breakfast cereal he developed with his brother John Harvey Kellogg.

1906
Finnish Women Granted the Vote
Finland is the first European country to give women the vote.

July 25, 1909
Plane Flown Across the English Channel
Frenchman Louis Bleriot is the first person to fly a heavier-than-air craft (as opposed to a hot-air balloon) across any large body of water as he crosses the English Channel.

1910–1919

1912
TITANIC HITS ICEBERG

Four days into its maiden voyage across the Atlantic Ocean, and with 2,200 people on board, the ocean liner R.M.S. *Titanic* hit an iceberg. The ship had been designed to be 'unsinkable' because its hull was divided into sixteen 'watertight' compartments, up to four of which could safely fill with water before the ship lost its buoyancy. However, when the ship hit an iceberg just before midnight on April 14, 1912, it tore through the hull, filling five of the compartments with water, and the ship began to sink. The *Titanic* did not have adequate emergency measures in place. A shortage of lifeboats meant that, although around 700 passengers were saved, the remaining 1,500 people on board drowned or froze to death in the ice-cold waters of the Atlantic. It took little more than two hours for the ship to sink.

1914–1918
U.S.A. JOINS THE WAR

U.S. President Woodrow Wilson kept America out of the war for three years. U.S. isolationism and a significant German and Austrian population in the U.S. prevented their direct involvement. The German government had already announced their intention to strike any vessels traveling between Great Britain and America, so when a new German submarine offensive was announced in January 1917, the U.S. broke off diplomatic ties with Germany. The U.S. public was angered when it was revealed that the German government had offered to help Mexico regain territory in Arizona and Texas. On April 2, 1917, President Wilson sought Senate approval for war against Germany, and this was granted on April 4. The U.S. was still not officially taking sides: it was declaring a separate war against Germany. However, in reality the U.S. had joined the Allies.

'Although around 700 passengers were saved, the remaining 1,500 people on board drowned or froze to death'

'The U.S. public was angered when it was revealed that the German government had offered to help Mexico regain territory in Arizona and Texas'

November 20, 1910
Call to Arms in Mexico
Opposition leader Francisco Madero issues a statement declaring the re-election of Mexican president Porfirio Dias null and void. His call for armed resistance marks the start of the Mexican Revolution.

July 24, 1911
'Lost City' Rediscovered
American explorer Hiram Bingham rediscovers the abandoned Inca city Machu Picchu high in the Andes mountains.

November 5, 1912
Wilson New U.S. President
Democratic challenger Woodrow Wilson defeats the incumbent William Taft in the U.S. election, as the Republican vote is split between Taft and a third candidate, former president Theodore Roosevelt.

December 20, 1912
Fossil Hoax
The discovery of the remains of a form of early human is announced in the U.K. Known as Piltdown Man, it is later exposed as a hoax.

1910–1919

1914–1918
FIRST WORLD WAR ENDS

On November 11, 1918, at 5 a.m. the Allies and Central Powers agreed to end hostilities, signing an armistice that signaled the end of the war. The armistice came into effect six hours later at 11 a.m. – the eleventh hour of the eleventh day of the eleventh month of the year. Germany had first sued for a peace agreement in October, eager that U.S. President Wilson's 'Fourteen Points', which included an end to secret treaties and general military disarmament, should be implemented. Great Britain and France objected to various points, but they were persuaded by Wilson to agree to them. The armistice, which was signed in a railway carriage in France, demanded that Germany withdraw from all territories that it had occupied, while the Allies would occupy parts of Germany. The Germans were also instructed to give up the majority of their military equipment and the German Kaiser Wilhelm II was to abdicate. The exact nature of reparation payments to be made by Germany was not agreed in detail – the Treaty of Versailles in early 1919 would settle that.

1919
TREATY OF VERSAILLES SETS TERMS OF PEACE

The treaty that officially tied up the loose ends of the First World War was signed in the vast palace of Versailles near Paris. France, represented by Georges Clemenceau, pushed for harsher treatment of Germany, while Great Britain, represented by British Prime Minister David Lloyd George, urged caution. U.S. President Woodrow Wilson was also in favor of reconciliation, but Clemenceau reflected both French public opinion and his own feelings when he demanded the highest price possible. Germany's new leader, Friedrich Ebert, accepted responsibility for the war on behalf of his country and agreed to the terms outlined, which included the loss of German territories outside Germany, the occupation of Germany by the Allies, military disarmament, and heavy financial penalties. Russia, which had fought on the side of the Allies, had made peace with Germany separately in 1918.

December 15, 1914
Mine Explosion in Japan
A gas explosion in a coal mine on Kyushu island kills 687 people, the worst coal mine disaster ever in Japan.

September 6, 1915
New Tank Tested
A prototype tank is tested by the British army. Tanks are used in battle for the first time by the British during the Battle of Flers-Courcellette a year later.

October 25, 1917
Revolution in Russia
The October Revolution in Russia, a series of events that will eventually lead to the overthrow of old Tsarist order and the establishment of a Communist regime, begins in earnest, as the Winter Palace in Petrograd, official residence of the Tsar, is captured by revolutionaries. The Bolsheviks, led by Lenin, quickly seize power, but a civil war rages in Russia for the next six years.

October 28, 1919
Alcohol Outlawed
Prohibition begins in the United States as the sale of alcohol is banned by the Volstead Act.

1920–1929

TUTANKHAMUN'S TOMB DISCOVERED

After searching for several years, on November 5, 1922, British archaeologist Howard Carter discovered the tomb of Pharaoh Tutankhamun in Egypt's Valley of the Kings. King Tutankhamun had only ruled for a short time as a boy king and had died at the age of 18. Given that most of the tombs in the area had already been discovered and looted, it was generally assumed that his had met a similar fate. But on November 26, Carter broke through to the inner section that had been closed by the tomb-builders 3,000 years earlier – their footprints were still visible in the dust on the ground. There he discovered, besides thousands of precious artefacts, the intact and mummified body of the boy king lying in his solid-gold coffin. The full excavation of the four-roomed tomb took several years, and in the process Carter unearthed countless objects, including a fleet of miniature ships intended to aid the king on his journey to the next world.

Above: The Tutankhamun gold mask at the British Museum in London.

MUSSOLINI BECOMES PRIME MINISTER OF ITALY

Italy felt that it had been given a raw deal at the Paris Peace Conference that followed the First World War. The general complaint was that the other Allied Powers were preventing Italy from becoming a great power by denying it the territorial advantages allowed to others. Post-war Italy was crippled by poverty and unemployment, which led to social unrest and a rise in organized crime. Benito Mussolini exploited this volatile situation and harnessed discontent by forming a paramilitary group called the Blackshirts. The Italian government, fearing a Communist revolution, welcomed Mussolini's strong-arm tactics, despite their profoundly undemocratic nature, and so the leader of the Fascist Party joined mainstream politics. The democratic government was viewed as weak and ineffective, and many of the Fascist party's proposals, which included a minimum wage, an eight-hour working day, and votes for women, were popular. The party had aligned itself with national pride, and appeared to represent both a strong economy and a return to law and order for those who feared revolution. In March 1922, Mussolini organized a march on Rome and forced King Victor Emmanuel III to make him Prime Minister. At first, under Mussolini's rule, Italy experienced economic revival while extensive public works provided much needed employment.

Above: Benito Mussolini taking his morning ride at the Villa Torlonia near Rome with his youngest son.

May 17, 1920
France and Belgium Leave Germany
French and Belgian troops leave the German cities they have been occupying since the end of the First World War.

July 27, 1921
Insulin Hormone Discovered
Discovery of the hormone insulin, the only successful treatment of diabetes, is announced by researchers at the University of Toronto.

June 28, 1922
Civil War Breaks Out
The Irish Civil War, involving a dispute over the Anglo-Irish Treaty, begins.

October 16, 1923
Cartoon Studio Founded
Roy and Walt Disney found the Disney Brothers' Cartoon Studio, which later becomes the Walt Disney Company.

FIRST NON-STOP SOLO FLIGHT ACROSS ATLANTIC

In 1927, Charles Lindbergh, a Minnesota mail pilot, became the first person to fly a plane non-stop from New York to Paris. As soon as Lindbergh heard about a competition to cross the Atlantic with a prize of $25,000, he secured sponsorship and set about having a plane built to his own specifications. The result was the *Spirit of St. Louis*. Lindbergh set out from Long Island on the morning of May 20, 1927, carrying on board four sandwiches and two canteens of water.

'Lindbergh set out from Long Island on the morning of May 20, 1927, carrying on board four sandwiches and two canteens of water.'

Around 33 hours later, on the evening of May 21, he touched down in Paris to be met by thousands upon thousands of well-wishers. Lindbergh's achievement sparked an overnight enthusiasm for aviation and the man himself became a hero. There was something in his spirit of adventure and endeavor that captured the hearts of the American people. On his return home, he was treated to parade after parade, and lauded in high places wherever he went. Charles Lindbergh then embarked on tours all over America, and devoted the rest of his life to advancing aviation – a mission which he fulfilled ably. He received a number of accolades in the course of his career, culminating in the Congressional Medal of Honor, the highest honor the U.S.A. awards its people.

FRENCH PRESIDENT'S DECORATION FOR LINDBERGH

AIR HERO'S GREAT WELCOME HOME   BOROTRA'S WIN

Above: Today, thousands of people cross the Atlantic daily on passenger air liners.

April 6, 1924
First Round-the-World Flight
Four planes from the Douglas Aircraft Company leave Seattle, Washington, on the first round-the-world flight, which takes 175 days.

December 26, 1925
Sphinx is Uncovered
The Great Sphinx of Giza in Egypt is revealed after extensive excavation work.

January 26, 1926
Television Demonstration
Scottish inventor John Logie Baird demonstrates a television system.

September 25, 1927
Slavery Abolished
A treaty signed at the League of Nations Slavery Convention abolishes all types of slavery.

September 28, 1928
Penicillin Discovered
Alexander Fleming makes the first breakthrough in his discovery of penicillin.

1920–1929

WALL STREET CRASH HERALDS THE GREAT DEPRESSION

On Thursday October 24, 1929 (known thereafter as Black Thursday), a massive slide in the price of shares on the New York Stock Exchange prompted a complete loss of confidence in the value of stocks, which in turn led to an unprecedented collapse in the U.S. financial market, known as the Wall Street Crash. The crash came at the end of the 1920s, which in America had been a decade of prosperity, excess, and extravagance. The feel-good factor was so high that President Hoover felt moved to comment in 1928: 'We in America today are nearer to the final triumph over poverty than ever before in the history of any land.' The crash followed a period of ever-rising stock prices, when everyone wanted a piece of the pie. More people than ever bought stock, assuming that it would continue to rise, and this forced prices up even higher. The problem was that much of the money used to buy stock was borrowed, so the situation was entirely false. All it took for the bubble to burst was a moment of doubt. As soon as prices dropped, worried investors sold up, which created a sense of panic as more investors sold up and prices continued to fall. The Wall Street Crash forced the closure of around 100,000 businesses across America. The consequent unemployment meant that consumers could not afford to spend, and this led to more business closures and further unemployment. Thus began the Great Depression of the 1930s.

Left: Crowds take to the streets outside Wall Street on hearing news of the crash.

January 15, 1929
Future Pioneer
Martin Luther King Jr. is born in Atlanta, Georgia.

February 18, 1930
New Planet Discovered
Clyde Tombaugh discovers Pluto while studying photographs. Pluto is considered a planet until 2006. Pluto is now considered to be a dwarf planet.

March 19, 1931
Gambling Legalized
Nevada legalizes gambling as a way of lifting the state out of the hard times of the Great Depression.

May 1, 1931
Empire State Building Opened
Construction of the Empire State Building in New York is completed and it is officially opened.

April 4, 1932
Vitamin C Isolated
Chemist C.C. King isolates vitamin C.

ADOLF HITLER MADE FÜHRER OF GERMANY

The death of President Hindenburg on August 2, 1934 cleared the way for Hitler's assumption of absolute power in Germany. Hitherto, Hindenburg's popularity had kept a check on Hitler's actions, but as soon as he was out of the way, Hitler prepared a referendum asking the German people to vote him in as leader of the country. On the eve of the referendum, Rudolf Hess delivered a speech broadcast to the German people which he opened by declaring, 'It is a challenge to attempt to prove the good of something as obvious as Hitler's assumption of Hindenburg's position,' and ended: 'To you, our Führer, we pledge our loyalty – Adolf Hitler, we believe in you.' In his assumption of Hindenburg's position, Hitler combined the roles of Chancellor and President in one new title, Führer, or absolute ruler. As a result of the overwhelming propaganda, including a forged letter from Hindenburg recommending Hitler, 90% of German voters agreed to Hitler's succession as Führer. The army subsequently swore an oath of allegiance, not to the nation but to Hitler himself, making it in effect Hitler's personal army.

> **'Hitler combined the roles of Chancellor and President in one new title, Führer, or absolute ruler.'**

Right: Hitler's home in the Obersalzberg of the Bavarian Alps, renamed the Berghof in 1935.

June, 1932
Polaroid Photography Invented
Edwin Herbert Land and George Wheelwright drop out of university in June to work on their production of the 'polarizer' – a material to eliminate glare which is now known as Polaroid film. They successfully complete the invention in August.

March 20, 1933
Concentration Camp
The first Nazi concentration camp is opened in Dachau, Germany.

December 26, 1933
FM Radio Invented
Edwin Howard Armstrong receives a patent for Wideband Frequency Modulation (FM). This enables much clearer radio broadcasting with less static.

September 18, 1933
U.S.S.R. in League
The U.S.S.R. joins the League of Nations.

SPAIN PLUNGES INTO CIVIL WAR

BRITON KILLED, WIFE INJURED WHEN REBELS SHELL YACHT

Destroyer Races to Rescue of Vessel After Bombardment

A BRITON killed and his wife seriously injured when a shell from a rebel warship hit their yacht off the north coast of Spain, and an attack on the United States Consul in Barcelona threatened an international flare-up in the Spanish civil war last night.

Captain Rupert Savile, a former R.A.F. officer, of Fowey, Cornwall, left England with his wife on a health cruise in their yacht, the **Blue Shadow**, last autumn.

BRITONS MUST LEAVE, OR—

Urgent appeal to all British subjects in Madrid to leave the capital as soon as possible has been issued, following the receipt of a cable from London last night from the British Foreign Office, says Reuter.

The appeal, which has been distributed to all the hundred or so members of the British colony who still remain at their posts contains these paragraphs:—

" I am willing to be evacuated at once. (Space for signature).

" I do not wish to be evacuated and hereby absolve his Britannic Majesty's Government of any responsibility for the safety of myself, my wife, family or property in Spain. (Space for signature).

Yesterday as they sailed near Gijon, in North Spain, a shell from the cruiser Almirante Cervera, which has been bombarding the town for several days, hit the yacht.

Captain Savile was killed outright and his wife was wounded in the legs. The yacht, although badly damaged, remained afloat.

First news of the incident reached the British Consul at Bayonne, and H.M.S. destroyer Comet, on its way from Gijon, raced to the scene and picked up Mrs. Savile with her husband's body.

Tried to Escape

The story was told to the *Daily Mirror* last night by an official of the British Embassy, which moved from Spain to Hendaye, on the Franco-Spanish frontier, last week.

" Captain Savile, with his wife and three members of the crew had put into Gijon after the Blue Shadow had been aground off the harbour on a sandbank.

" Apparently this was to inspect possible damage to the vessel.

" Warned, however, that the Almirante Cervera was approaching and had threatened to bombard the town, it was decided to put out again to sea as quickly as possible in the hope of escaping before the bombing started.

" It seems that as she approached the mouth of the harbour the rebel cruiser, which had been firing at everything entering and leaving the harbour, dropped a shell just on to the yacht, killing Captain Savile and wounding his wife.

Flying Blue Ensign

" The Spanish Government authorities immediately sent a doctor on board, and then the Comet, which was on its way to St. Jean de Luz, took off the dead man and Mrs. Savile and the crew.

" The Blue Shadow was flying the Blue Ensign at the time, but visibility was very poor—about a mile.

" Sir Henry Chilton, the British Ambassador, who was near St. Jean de Luz at the time, was

(Continued on back page)

Bicycle Made for Two . . .
. . . new style is this strange craft of the road seen in a Lincolnshire lane.

The Sermon on Wings . . . bare heads and bare backs were prominent among ... Rev. Cecil Boulton, curate of ...

THE KING TRAVELS TO ... YACHT IN YUGOSLA...

FROM OUR SPECIAL CORRESPONDENT
JESSENICE, Sunday.

KING Edward reached the Yugoslav frontier this evening at six o'clock more than two hours behind scheduled time, after his journey across Europe.

On arrival at this little frontier station, he was greeted by Prince Paul, Senior Regent of Yugoslavia, and brother-in-law of the Duchess of Kent, and Mr. J. Balfour, British Chargé d'Affaires at Belgrade.

Prince Paul and the King—they were at Oxford together—chatted smilingly.

In the meantime the King's party transferred from the special Austrian train to the luxurious Yugoslav royal train, which had been waiting, with steam up, for several hours for the King's journey to the coast.

Right: A church bombed during the Spanish Civil War.

On July 17, 1936, rebel groups within the Spanish army rose against the Republican government, instigating a civil war which was to last for the next three years. The war was politically motivated: the Nationalists, as the rebels were termed, had the support of Fascist Italy, Nazi Germany, and Portugal, while the Republic was backed by Communist Russia and Mexico. In this sense, it was seen as a clash of ideologies which prefigured the Second World War. Spain had already undergone years of wrangling between conservatives and reformists, which had led to the abolition of the absolute monarchy. The anti-religious Constitution of 1931 had created much discontent and failed to please either side in the struggle for a church-state balance. The outcome of the civil war was the installation of General Franco as fascist dictator.

> **'Spain had already undergone years of wrangling between conservatives and reformists, which had led to the abolition of the absolute monarchy.'**

June 1, 1935
Drivers Tested
Compulsory driving tests are introduced in the U.K.

November 22, 1935
China Clipper Delivers
The Pan-Am *China Clipper* takes off from California and delivers the first airmail cargo across the Pacific Ocean.

March 1, 1936
Hoover Dam Completed
The construction of the Hoover Dam is completed, creating Lake Mead, the largest reservoir in the world.

October 1, 1936
Broadcasts Become Regular
The BBC launches the world's first regular television broadcasts.

1930-1939

GERMANY INVADES POLAND

In planning Germany's territorial expansion, Hitler made the assumption that, if he headed east towards the Soviet Union, the Western powers would leave him alone. Following his successful takeover of Czechoslovakia, therefore, he moved towards Poland, claming right of access through Poland to East Prussia, which was part of Germany. British Prime Minster Neville Chamberlain, however, had already lost face over the breaking of the Munich Agreement, and he was determined not to appear helpless a second time. As a warning to Hitler that he could not do as he pleased, Chamberlain declared in the House of Commons that Britain would support Poland if the Nazis invaded, and France agreed. When Hitler falsified an invasion of Germany by Polish soldiers, he had his pretext and invaded Poland on September 1, 1939 – the day that the Second World War is held to have begun. On September 3, Britain and France presented a united front and demanded that Hitler withdraw his troops from Poland immediately. Hitler did not consider the demand worthy of a response and continued as planned. British Prime Minister Neville Chamberlain had up until this point been pursuing a policy of appeasement, which involved giving in to Hitler's territorial demands in Eastern Europe in the hope that he would be satisfied. The overriding aim had been to avoid war with Germany at all costs, but the policy of appeasement did not take into account the sheer magnitude of Hitler's ambitions. For Poland, Western intervention came too late, however. The Soviet army had joined the invasion, and old-fashioned Polish cavalry horses had little hope against modern tanks. On September 27, Poland had no choice but to surrender to its invaders.

> '[Britain's] aim had been to avoid war ... but the policy of appeasement did not take into account the sheer magnitude of Hitler's ambitions.'

1937
Toyota Motor Company Launches in Japan
The Toyota Motor Company is established as an independent company. The founding family name was 'Toyoda,' but to mark the company's beginning and simplify pronunciation the new company is given a different name.

1937
Jet Engine Built
The first jet engine is built by Frank Whittle.

November 9, 1938
Kristallnacht in Germany
'The night of broken glass' begins in Germany as troops loot and burn Jewish businesses. Around 7,000 businesses and 200 synagogues are destroyed, and about 91 Jews are killed.

April 1, 1939
Spanish Civil War Ends
The Spanish Civil War ends when the last Republican forces surrender.

1940

FRANCE SURRENDERS TO GERMAN OCCUPATION

Hitler's invasion of Belgium and the Netherlands on May 10, 1940 marked the first major offensive since the Western powers had declared war in September 1939. Now referred to as the Battle of France, this invasion meant that the war had started in earnest after months of uncertainty and hesitation.

Ever since the German invasion of Poland, France and Britain had been waiting to see what would happen next. Although the German Army was worn down after the invasion of Poland and resources were low, Hitler decided that an early attack on France might catch the Allied Powers unawares and allow the Germans a swift victory. The German plan was to advance through the Ardennes, the thickly forested region running through Luxembourg and Belgium that was thought to be impassable, making it look as if Belgium were the main target. The real purpose was to draw Allied forces north toward Belgium in order to surround and isolate them. Belgium and the Netherlands had both declared themselves neutral countries, and were unprepared to counter such an attack, so France reacted as expected and sent forces to their aid. Approaching via the Ardennes enabled German forces to bypass the Maginot line, the lengthy defensive line in which the French put all their faith and hope of safety. The plan was successful, and by the end of June, France had surrendered to German occupation.

> **'The invasion of Belgium meant that the war had started in earnest after months of uncertainty and hesitation.'**

May 15
New Fashion Item
Nylons go on sale for the first time in New York stores.

June 4
Churchill's Speech
Winston Churchill tells the House of Commons, 'We shall fight on the beaches, we shall fight on the landing grounds, we shall fight in the fields and in the streets, we shall fight in the hills; we shall never surrender.'

June 10
Norway Surrenders
After two months of desperate resistance, Norway surrenders to German forces.

June 14
Auschwitz Opens
A group of 728 Polish political prisoners from Tarnów become the first residents of the Auschwitz concentration camp.

CHURCHILL TAKES OVER

The German invasions of France and the Netherlands had further consequences in Britain. Prime Minister Neville Chamberlain, having adopted a policy of appeasement with Hitler in an attempt to avoid war at all costs, now came under attack for his inaction and was forced to resign. It was felt that if the British government had acted earlier, instead of holding back and hoping for the best, Hitler might never have got this far. There were two possible candidates waiting in the wings to replace Chamberlain: Lord Halifax, who refused to take office, and Winston Churchill, who accepted. In his first address as prime minister, Churchill told a packed House of Commons, 'I have nothing to offer you but blood, toil, tears, and sweat.'

'I have nothing to offer you but blood, toil, tears, and sweat.'

June 22
France Surrenders
Charles de Gaulle, the French leader, flees to Britain after France surrenders to Germany.

July–October
Battle of Britain
A major campaign between Britain and Germany is fought entirely by their air forces.

August 20
Churchill Praises R.A.F.
Winston Churchill pays tribute in the House of Commons to the Royal Air Force: 'Never in the field of human conflict was so much owed by so many to so few.'

August 21
Trotsky Assassinated
Russian revolutionary Leon Trotsky is assassinated with an ice axe by a Soviet agent in Mexico.

1940

EVACUATION FROM DUNKIRK

Once German troops had broken through French defensive lines, they cornered British and French troops by forcing them toward the sea at Dunkirk. So it was that in June 1940 an estimated 300,000 men found themselves trapped between the sea and the German Army. In order to prevent their complete annihilation, it was essential to evacuate these troops from the beaches of Dunkirk. However, the water was shallow and no sizeable vessels could get anywhere near the shore. The solution was Operation Dynamo, a mission that involved dispatching around 800 small boats from Britain to rescue soldiers off the beach and deliver them to larger ships waiting farther out at sea. The evacuation operation was completely successful: Winston Churchill called it a 'miracle' that so many had been rescued in such a short time.

Above: British army helmet left on the beach at Dunkirk after the retreat from the Germans.

NAZI ARMY INVADES SOVIET UNION

Despite having signed a non-aggression pact with the U.S.S.R. in 1939, on June 22, 1941, Hitler ordered his troops to invade the country from the south, the west, and the north. The pact had been signed just before Hitler invaded Poland, and for both parties it was a means of securing short-term safety. Nazi Germany and the communist U.S.S.R. could not have been more opposed to each other in terms of ideology, but they both needed security against the Western European powers, so they decided to unite for the time being. The attack, which Hitler boasted on national radio would be the greatest the world had ever seen, took Joseph Stalin completely by surprise. Although Hitler had only 3,000,000 men compared to the Red Army's 9,000,000, German military skill was the more impressive. In Britain, Prime Minister Winston Churchill, who had always been an outspoken opponent of Communism, nevertheless declared: 'The Russian danger is our danger, and the danger of the United States, just as the danger of any Russian fighting for his hearth and home is the cause of free men and free peoples in every quarter of the globe.' Operation Barbarossa, as it was known, lasted for six months, during which time millions were killed on both sides.

September 12
Prehistoric Paintings Discovered
In Lascaux, France, 17,000-year-old cave paintings are discovered by a group of young French hikers. The paintings depict animals and date from the Stone Age.

September 27
Tripartite Pact
Germany, Italy, and Japan sign a pact that forms a military alliance against the Allied Powers.

October 28
Italian Troops Invade Greece
Italy's invasion begins the Balkans Campaign.

November 13
Fantasia Released
The Walt Disney film *Fantasia* is released, but is initially unsuccessful at the box office.

BISMARCK SUNK BY BRITISH

The German ship *Bismarck* had been launched in 1939 and was the pride of the newly rebuilt German fleet. Britain's best hope in the war was her naval superiority, and consequently the Allies were determined to dominate the Atlantic. In May 1941, when the Germans decided to set the *Bismarck* loose in the Atlantic, the German aim was to cause as much damage as possible to the British fleet, and the Allies were determined to catch her.

> **'All possible resources were targeted at the one aim of capturing the Bismarck.'**

All possible resources were targeted at the one aim of capturing the *Bismarck*, and on May 24, two British ships, the *Hood* and the *Prince of Wales*, sighted the *Bismarck* and attacked. There followed a ferocious battle, during which the *Hood* exploded, losing her entire crew of 1,421 men. However, the two British ships had done enough damage between them to cause a fuel leak in the *Bismarck*. She fled toward the coast of France, but, once identified, became a target of Allied guns. The *Bismarck* was eventually sunk under the combined fire of aircraft and warships on May 27, 1941.

U-BOAT THREAT THEIR DOOM

BISMARCK MEN STRUGGLE IN SEA

THE MIGHTY BISMARCK SUNK BY THE GUNS OF THE ROYAL NAVY, NAZI SEAMEN SCRAMBLE FOR LIFE IN THE SEA. THEY CLING DESPERATELY TO THE ROPES THROWN FROM THE DECKS OF A BRITISH WARSHIP. MORE WOULD HAVE BEEN SAVED BUT THE WARNING THAT A U-BOAT MIGHT BE NEAR PUT AN END TO THE RESCUE WORK.

More Pictures— Page 5

By KENNETH HORD AND ARCHER BROOKS

BISMARCK, Germany's "unsinkable" pride, split in two, flaming like a torch from stem to stern, heeled over and sank with the flag of Nazi Germany trailing in the water from her broken mast.

BISMARCK HIT— NAVY RACE FOR THE KILL

BAYONETS IN CRETE

LONDON PRIDE

HITLER HAS AN IDEA

U.S. CALLS MORE MEN

LESS THAN PRE-WAR PRICE

January
M&Ms Give Taste of Home
American soldiers are given the candy by the U.S. Army.

February 9
Plea for Arms
Winston Churchill, in a worldwide broadcast, pleads with the U.S. to show its support by sending arms to the British: 'Give us the tools and we will finish the job.'

March 28
Sinatra Makes Film Debut
Frank Sinatra appears in his first film, *Las Vegas Nights*.

April 6
Germany Invades Greece
Nazis occupy Greece. The British forces are evacuated.

1941

JAPANESE ATTACK PEARL HARBOR

On November 17, 1941, the U.S. Ambassador to Japan, radioed a warning to Washington, D.C. He feared that Japan might suddenly and unexpectedly attack the U.S. The aim of such an attack would be to disable the American military presence in the Pacific so that the Japanese could go ahead with their planned invasions of the Malay Peninsula and the Philippines. On November 26, a fleet of six Japanese aircraft carriers headed for Pearl Harbor on the Hawaiian island of Oahu, where the bulk of the U.S. Pacific fleet was stationed. They traveled under strict radio silence and remained completely undetected. Then, on December 2, they received a coded message to carry out the planned attack. Their combined force of 30 ships, 20 submarines, and 360 aircraft hit Pearl Harbor on December 7, 1941. The attack lasted only about three hours, but the Japanese achieved their aim of crippling the U.S. Pacific fleet. They also destroyed most of the aircraft on the Pearl Harbor airfield, making an effective counterattack almost impossible. Around 2,500 American personnel were killed, while the Japanese lost fewer than 100 lives. The day after the attacks, President Franklin D. Roosevelt addressed Congress, which immediately declared that the U.S. was at war with Japan. Two days later, Germany and Italy declared war on the U.S. Thus was America drawn into the Second World War.

U.S. PROMISES TO HELP FEED AND ARM BRITAIN

President Roosevelt persuaded the U.S. government that it should lend aid to Britain. To achieve this he used the comparison of one neighbor lending another a garden hose to put out a fire in his house. The neighbor with the hose, he argued, would not demand the $15 he paid for the hose as payment, but would ask that the hose be returned when the job was finished. With the consent of Congress, F.D.R. signed a 'Lend-Lease' agreement by which the U.S. would loan Britain food and military supplies. Over the next four years, the U.S. lent Britain today's equivalent of $700 billion worth of supplies in food, equipment, and ammunition.

May 1
Citizen Kane
The film *Citizen Kane*, directed by 26-year-old Orson Welles, premieres in New York.

May 9
Secret Code Breakthrough
The German submarine *U-110* is captured by the British Royal Navy. On board is the latest Enigma cryptography machine, which Allied cryptographers later use to break coded German messages.

May 10
Hess Crashes in Scotland
Rudolf Hess, deputy leader of the Nazi Party, crash-lands in Scotland in a Messerschmitt 110, claiming that he wants to meet with King George VI to discuss peace terms.

September 1
Yellow Star Introduced
Jews in Germany are instructed to wear a yellow star with the word *Jude* by the Nazi Party.

1941

SOVIET ARMY HITS BACK AT GERMAN INVASION

Although Stalin received a warning about it from his intelligence services, the German invasion had succeeded in taking the Red Army completely by surprise. The Germans mustered massive numbers of infantry, cavalry, tanks, and aircraft for their three-pronged attack on the U.S.S.R. The Baltic states fell first, and, meeting little resistance, the Germans anticipated a swift victory. Initially, both Stalin and his army were so stunned by the German turnaround that they were paralyzed. But the fact that army officers feared being shot for cowardice if they went on the defensive made them resourceful, and they began to regroup. The Red Army refused to give in, and under Stalin's orders, burned villages to the ground as they retreated, leaving nothing behind for the Germans.

Right: The German military combined tanks, infantry, and aircraft in a tactic known as Blitzkrieg, *or 'lightning war.'*

GERMANS REACH MOSCOW'S OUTER DEFENSES

By the time the Germans approached Moscow, the bitter Russian winter and the torrential rains that turned everything to mud were strongly against them. Tipped off that the Japanese were busy planning an attack on the U.S., Stalin felt free to relocate his most experienced fighters from the Far Eastern borders. When the punishing winter had all but finished off the German Army, the Russians mounted a successful counterattack in December. Although Hitler had at first refused to allow his generals to retreat, on January 15, 1942 he was forced to withdraw. This move marked the first defeat for Hitler since the beginning of his rampage across Europe. However, it was by no means over. By this time, both totalitarian leaders had taken personal command of their armies, and Hitler chose to redirect the attack in the direction of the Caucasus oil fields around Stalingrad. His aim was not only to replenish German supplies, but to use up the last strength of the Red Army, who would rush to defend the oil fields.

October 23
Elephants Might Fly
Walt Disney's *Dumbo* is released and proves to be one of his best cartoons. Its star is a flying elephant with huge ears.

December 4
Women Join War Effort
Churchill calls up women for war service.

December 12
India at War
India declares war on Japan.

Freeze-drying Takes Off
The technique of freeze-drying food is developed commercially during the war years.

1942

BATTLE FOR STALINGRAD RAGES

The Battle of Stalingrad, which raged from August 1942 to January 1943, marked the first instance where Hitler's obstinate refusal to give in lost him an entire army. The Sixth Army had been at the forefront of the bid to seize Stalingrad, but the Russians had held firm for three months. By November 19, 1942, the Red Army had succeeded in its plan to encircle the Sixth Army. Hit by this reality just as the harsh Russian winter set in, Commander Friedrich Paulus requested permission to withdraw. Hitler refused and insisted that Paulus should hold firm and fight to the last man. The battle for Stalingrad was fiercely fought on both sides, with hand-to-hand combat in the streets, but the Russians were determined that the city named after their leader should not be taken. When, on January 31, 1943, Commander Paulus's final 91,000 men were captured by the Russians, he surrendered along with them, a move that infuriated Hitler.

> 'The battle for Stalingrad was fiercely fought on both sides, with hand-to-hand combat in the streets.'

January 1
U.N. Comes into Being
The 'Declaration of United Nations' is signed by 26 Allied Nations in Washington.

January 15
New Leader in India
Mahatma Gandhi appoints Jawaharlal Nehru as his successor.

January 20
Nazis Decide on the 'Final Solution'
Nazis at a conference in Berlin decide that the 'final solution' to the 'Jewish problem' is to move them to camps to die.

1942

JAPAN TAKES SINGAPORE

On February 14, 1942, the island city of Singapore, which had been a British colony since the 19th century, fell into Japanese hands. The battle for the Malay Peninsula had begun in December 1941 – in fact, part of Japan's reason for attacking Pearl Harbor was to handicap U.S. forces and prevent them coming to the aid of Malaya. The battle between the British and the Japanese was fought mainly from the air, and hundreds of civilians were killed in the process. When, on February 8, some 5,000 Japanese soldiers landed in Singapore, the British defenses proved ineffective at withstanding them, and the British general Arthur Percival was forced to surrender. In the process, 62,000 Allied soldiers were taken prisoner, more than half of whom did not survive their captivity. The loss of Singapore meant that Britain no longer held any military position in the east.

Right: British troops surrendering to Japanese soldiers during the fall of Singapore.

ALLIED FORCES WIN VICTORY AT EL ALAMEIN

In 1942, El Alamein, west of Cairo in Egypt, became the focus of the war between the Allies and the German-led 'Axis' powers. The loss of Singapore had done much to weaken British morale, and Prime Minister Winston Churchill was determined that the Allies would win in North Africa. The Afrika Korps, led by German general Erwin Rommel, was aiming for control of the Suez Canal, which would enable them to cut off the major British supply route. Desperate to achieve victory, Churchill sacked his own general, Claude Auchinleck, and replaced him with General Bernard Montgomery ('Monty', as he became known). Helped by the code-breakers at Bletchley Park, Montgomery found out not only Rommel's battle plans, but also his lines of supply, so was able to sabotage them. Despite his consequent shortages, Rommel went ahead and attacked the British at El Alamein, but Montgomery knew that that his rival couldn't hold out long. Monty also had another card to play: Sherman tanks that could wipe out the German Panzer tanks. Partly by outwitting Rommel, and partly by outnumbering the German tanks, the British, Australian, and New Zealand forces under Montgomery managed to crush the Germans and Italians. By November 1942, they were able to declare themselves the victors. The loss of life on both sides was massive: 32,000 Germans and Italians to 13,000 Allies.

June
Gas Chambers
The first mass killing by gas takes place at Auschwitz death camp.

June 7
U.S. Attack on Japan
The U.S. hits Japanese ships poised to attack American carriers at the Pacific island of Midway.

July 14
De Gaulle Renames his Resistance Fighters
General de Gaulle, French leader in exile, states that all the forces resisting his country's occupation will be known as 'Fighting France.'

August 9
Gandhi Arrested
Gandhi and all the other All-India Congress Party leaders are arrested.

1942

BATTLE FOR THE ATLANTIC REACHES CRISIS POINT

Right: An Allied aircraft attacks a German U-boat on the surface of the Atlantic Ocean.

The naval battle for control of the Atlantic lasted for the duration of the war, involving a series of military campaigns rather than a single battle. However, when Winston Churchill coined the phrase 'the Battle of the Atlantic' in 1941, he was referring to the ongoing struggle between German U-boats (submarines) and the British fleet, which reached its height in 1942. German U-boats had been wreaking havoc on the British fleet in the Atlantic since the beginning of the war, seeming to attack any Allied vessel without differentiating between military and non-military. But by 1941, U-boat production had been increased, and they started attacking in 'wolf packs'. Since Britain relied so heavily on imports, the chief aim of the Germans was to cut off supplies and starve Britain out of the war, so their main targets were merchant vessels. Throughout the early part of the war, Britain had focused intelligence efforts on decoding planned German U-boat routes, so British ships were frequently able to evade attack. However, a change in cipher around the time the U.S. entered the war meant that the Allies were failing to anticipate attacks and suffering significant losses as a result. In the winter of 1942–3, the Germans launched a major offensive. When the Americans entered the war, the German U-boats turned their attention to the East Coast of America, causing mayhem within the unprepared U.S. Navy. Even before entering the war, U.S. ships had been escorting Allied convoys carrying supplies, and in early 1942 the German U-boat commander Admiral Karl Dönitz targeted these ships mercilessly, sinking around 88 per month. Now the American ships that had previously been escorting Allied supply vessels were engaged in transporting U.S. troops to Western Europe. Consequently, with a further 480 Allied ships sunk in the second half of 1942, the naval situation had reached crisis point.

> 'German U-boats had been wreaking havoc on the British fleet in the Atlantic asince the beginning of the war.'

August 22
Brazil at War
Brazil declares war on Germany and Italy.

October 5
Oxfam Founded
Gilbert Murray founds Oxfam, initially named the Oxford Committee for Famine Relief.

October 16
Deadly Cyclone
A cyclone in Bengal (now Bangladesh) kills 40,000 people.

December 2
First Nuclear Chain Reaction
The world's first nuclear reactor is built in Chicago, and Enrico Fermi and a team of scientists achieve the first nuclear chain reaction.

ITALIANS JOIN FORCES WITH THE ALLIES

The newspaper front page shown includes the following headlines and articles:

RAF crew seized Fleet by accident

BIG BATTLE IN ITALY

Twin naval bases ours

RUSSIANS IN NOVOROSSISK

Italians offered to fight with us

FULL STORY OF HOW ARMISTICE CAME

Stiff Air Resistance

FASCIST CHIEFS FREED BY GERMANS

MUSSO. FREED HUNS CLAIM

GERMAN GUN LAW IN ITALY

Infants taught 'give thanks to Hitler'

FINNS' TERMS

DANES BLOW UP CITROEN WORKS

By May 1943, with the German Army halted in North Africa, the balance of power had altered in the Mediterranean and the three-year Italian and German siege of Malta had come to an end. The Axis defeats in the Balkans and North Africa had destroyed Italian confidence in Benito Mussolini as a military leader, and in July 1943 he was successfully ousted by a group of senior military and political figures backed by the king, Victor Emmanuel III. Pietro Badoglio, the new prime minister, then set about extracting Italy from the war and came to a secret agreement with U.S. General Dwight D. Eisenhower, who commanded Allied troops in the Mediterranean. It was announced on September 8, 1943 that the Italians had signed a peace agreement with the Allies, effectively changing sides and therefore committing themselves to the expulsion from Western Europe of their former ally, Germany. Eisenhower went on Algiers radio to announce: 'All Italians who now act to help eject the German aggressor from Italian soil will have the assistance and support of the United Nations.'

> 'Italy signed a peace agreement with the Allies, effectively changing sides and committing to the expulsion of Germany.'

Left: The flag of the Italian Navy.

January 15
Pentagon Dedicated
The Pentagon, the world's largest office building and the headquarters of the U.S. Department of Defense, is dedicated.

April 19
Jewish Uprising in Warsaw Ghetto
When Waffen-SS (combat troops) move into Warsaw's Jewish ghetto for a final 'clear-up', the surviving Jews make an armed stand.

April 19
Chemist Discovers Effects of LSD
Albert Hofmann, a Swiss chemist, reveals the effects of LSD after experimenting on himself.

May 14
Australian Hospital Ship Torpedoed
The Australian hospital ship *Centaur* is sunk off the coast of Queensland after being hit by a torpedo from a Japanese submarine. The *Centaur*, a motor passenger ship converted into a hospital, carries wounded soldiers home from the front.

1943

BRITISH INVADE ITALY: GERMANS OCCUPY ROME

Following the British invasion of mainland Italy on September 3, 1943, Germany occupied Rome, allegedly to ensure the safety of the Vatican. Pietro Badoglio, as the new prime minister of Italy, left Rome just before it was occupied by German forces. The Germans acted swiftly as soon as they heard of the Italian surrender, and immediately disarmed the Italian Army. The Germans also sank a fleeing Italian battleship and rescued the deposed Mussolini in order to set him up as leader of a puppet government in Rome. Meanwhile, Badoglio set up temporary government, first in Brindisi and then in Palermo.

Right: Pietro Badoglio

RED ARMY DRIVES THE NAZIS OUT OF SOVIET UNION

Following its surrender at Stalingrad, the German army began to retreat and the Soviets went on the offensive, retaking cities that had been captured by the Nazis. By the time the Germans made their final stand at Kursk, the Red Army had had enough time to prepare, and Stalin's plan to exhaust the German troops by allowing them to do their worst before attacking had been successful. Between them, they had 6,000 tanks, and during the hard-fought battle, each side lost around 2,000 of these tanks. But in the end, the Soviets had superior air forces. Between the summer of 1943 and the spring of 1944, the Red Army fought back with great determination, regaining more cities that had been captured by the Germans. However, progress was slow for both sides, and neither was prepared to give in. As an indication of how closely fought the battle was, the town of Kharkov was taken and retaken four times before the Soviets finally secured it. Eventually, the Red Army succeeded in driving the Nazis out of their country, three years after they had first invaded.

'The town of Kharkov was taken and retaken four times before the Russians finally secured it.'

May 17
R.A.F. Smashes Three Dams
The R.A.F. bombs the Möhne, Sorpe, and Eder dams in the industrial heartland of Germany's Ruhr Valley.

June 1
Passenger Plane Shot Down
A scheduled passenger flight is shot down over the Bay of Biscay by a German Junkers Ju 88. All 17 people on board are killed.

June 1
Frank Sinatra Solo
Frank Sinatra officially starts his solo career when he signs with Columbia Records after leaving Harry James's band. He releases his first hit, *All or Nothing at All*, later that year.

July 25
Mussolini Steps Down
Fascist leader Benito Mussolini resigns as head of the armed forces and the government.

U.S. HALTS JAPANESE ADVANCE IN THE PACIFIC

Between August 1942 and February 1943 the U.S. fought an intense battle for control of the Pacific island of Guadalcanal in a bid to break Japan's naval superiority in the Pacific. It was their first significant campaign since becoming involved in the Second World War. Originally, the agreement between the Allies and the U.S. had been to concentrate first on stopping Germany before addressing the issue of Japanese territorial expansion. However, it was essential for the Allies that they keep supply lines from Australia and New Zealand open, so Japanese domination of the Pacific began to pose a real threat. The island of Guadalcanal was closest to Australia and provided a natural 'camp' from which to conduct Allied offensives in the Pacific. In July 1942, Japanese forces invaded the island, intending to use it as a vantage point in the Pacific. A month later, American forces landed with the intention of recapturing it. During the campaign for control of the island, the Japanese proved weaker on the ground due to the superiority of the U.S. Air Force. However, the Japanese made up for this weakness with their strength at sea, where they showed themselves to be masters of torpedo combat. However, after suffering almost daily bombardment from the air, the Japanese Navy was getting worn down. In the conclusive naval battle in November 1942, the Japanese gave up their attempts to recapture Guadalcanal, and began to evacuate their troops from the island. By February 1943, the Americans were in control of the island.

'It was essential for the Allies to keep supply lines from Australia and New Zealand open.'

Left: The flag of the Japanese Navy.

July 24–August 2
Operation Gomorrah
In a planned joint attack, the British bomb Hamburg by night and the Americans bomb it by day for a full week.

October 13
Italian Reversal
Italy declares war on Germany.

November 28
Big Three Meet
Churchill, Roosevelt, and Stalin meet in Tehran, Iran, to plan the defeat of Germany.

December 3
Radio Audience Along for the Ride
Edward R. Murrow, a newsman for American network C.B.S., tags along with an air crew making a strike on Berlin. The next day he broadcasts his experience on the radio to the American people and the piece becomes known as 'Orchestrated Hell'.

1944

D-DAY: ALLIED FORCES LAND IN NORMANDY

4,000 ships and 11,000 planes take part in attack • **German shore guns are quelled—Churchill!**

WE HOLD BEACHHEAD

WITHIN a few hours of the mightiest assault in history Allied troops established a beachhead on the Normandy coast yesterday.

Airborne troops are fighting some miles inland. More than 640 naval guns—from 4 to 16 inches—had practically silenced the German coastal batteries. The Allied air force was in absolute control.

All through the day, from the 7 a.m. landings until dusk, Allied fighter-bombers were dive-bombing, glide-bombing and strafing German defences and communications. They flew into the mouths of guns and dived within feet of the bridges.

EISENHOWER HAD 11,000 PLANES FOR THE JOB, AND HIS EXPERTS FORESAW 20,000 SORTIES IN THE DAY.

20,000 SORTIES

CHANNEL ISLAND ATTACK
—German Report

Scaled the Cliffs

Berlin provided the only place-names in the news. They said they were fighting Allied troops on an eighty-mile front between Trouville and Barfleur, on the Cherbourg peninsula.

They spoke of hard fighting around Caen, and of landings in the Seine Bay area.

Tanks, they said, were landed at Aromanches, fifteen miles from Caen, nine hours after the main landings.

In this landing there were 200 boats, and Berlin spoke of :

"THE ENEMY TRYING TO SCALE THE STEEP COAST WITH THE AID OF SPECIAL LADDERS."

Other landings were being made under strong air protection at Ouistreham and Marcoeurf, and Berlin added: "the landing parties were once engaged in extremely costly battles."

There is no word at all from the Allied side to support the German statement that we have landed paratroops on Guernsey and Jersey, which lie off the coast.

Mass airborne landings had been successfully effected. The fire of the shore batteries had been largely quelled and landing on the beaches was proceeding.

THE ANGLO - AMERICAN ALLIES ARE (Continued on Back Page)

What the Huns said

The German radio made the first announcement to the world yesterday morning and throughout the day their military commentators and experts never stopped talking.

"They are coming. They are coming," shouted Captain Sertorius, and Lieutenant-Colonel von Olberg more dignified, then and Cherbourg, said: "D-Day has dawned—the invasion has begun. There is every indication that the present Allied question is a big amphibious offensive which MUST BE TAKEN VERY SERIOUSLY INDEED."

The enemy radio said the invasion began with the landing of airborne troops near the mouth of the Seine and the period that the operations extended from Le Havre to Caen to Cherbourg.

Their early reports said that

"First British prisoner"

Private James Griffith, of Newcastle, was one of the first prisoners to be captured by the Germans, said German radio. He had been fighting in the Caen and Cherbourg areas.

"The fighting was tough," he said.

"FIGHTING ALONG 80 MILES"

Sky troops sweep in

MINEFIELD HAZARDS OVERCOME

"What a Plan!"

Mr. Churchill gave the House the facts at noon. "This is the first of a series of landings," he emphasised.

BEFORE SUNRISE YESTERDAY AN ARMADA OF 4,000 SHIPS, WITH SEVERAL THOUSAND SMALLER CRAFT, HAD CROSSED THE CHANNEL—WHICH WAS NOT TOO KIND AND SMOOTH.

Right: Beach at St-Laurent-sur-Mer, Normandy, better known as Omaha, one of the five D-Day landing sites.

June 6, 1944, now referred to as D-Day, saw Allied forces land in Normandy in a bid to liberate France from Nazi occupation. These landings marked the start of the Battle of Normandy. Operation Overlord, as it was called, was coordinated by British General Montgomery and U.S. General Eisenhower and involved landing more than 150,000 men on the beaches of northern France while further reinforcements arrived by air. In scale, it was the largest sea-borne assault in history. The sheer numbers involved overwhelmed the German defenses along the coast of France, and as German tanks rolled toward the coast to provide backup, they were attacked by Allied planes. The massive operation also involved a complex web of deception in the run-up to the actual attack. The Allies invented a fake army, complete with rubber and plywood props from a movie studio, to convince German spy planes that the troops would land in Calais. The Allies also used elaborate systems of false information, called misinformation, to deflect the Nazis' attention from the real operation. Even on the day of the attack, the Allies were busy parachuting rubber men into Calais and dropping strips of foil to trick the enemy aircraft radar into picking up a landing in Calais. As a result of all this, when the Germans saw the first Allied ships move toward Normandy, they took this to be diversionary, an attempt to distract their attention away from the real landings in Calais. Within a week, the Allies had succeeded in securing a large section of the French coast and could begin pouring in troops and supplies. Although the overall operation was resoundingly successful, thousands of Allied troops were killed in the process. For example, of the 29 amphibious tanks heading for the beach codenamed Omaha, 27 fell victim to German mines and sank with their crews trapped on board. Thousands more were gunned down as they approached the beaches.

> **'The massive operation also involved a complex web of deception in the run-up to the actual attack.'**

January 5
News Travels
The London *Daily Mail* becomes the first transoceanic newspaper.

January 29
Mega-Warship Launched
U.S.S. *Missouri*, the largest warship in the world, is launched.

February 1
D.N.A. Discovered
'Studies on the chemical nature of the substance inducing transformation of pneumococcal types,' a scientific paper written by Oswald Avery, Maclyn McCarty, and Colin MacLeod, is published. In this they explain that genes are made up of D.N.A.

March 10
Female Teachers May Marry
In Britain, the 1944 Education Act lifts the ban on women teachers being married.

1944

GERMAN OCCUPATION OF PARIS ENDS

By mid-August 1944, the French Resistance was closing in on the German occupiers and had begun the battle to liberate Paris from Nazi control. Following a general strike in the city, prompted by the deportation of a further 2,500 French people to Buchenwald concentration camp, the army of the French Resistance called upon the citizens of Paris to mobilize and expel the enemy. Encouraged by rumors that the Allies were close, the Parisians took up arms, constructed barricades, and prepared for a siege. The German occupiers were thrown off-guard and did not have sufficient troops in place. Between August 19 and 24 there was fighting in the streets between the French and Germans, resulting in the death of around 1,000 Resistance members and civilians. On August 25, French troops under General Philippe Leclerc de Hauteclocque entered Paris and delivered an ultimatum to General Dietrich von Choltitz, commander of German occupiers. Leclerc declared: 'I estimate that, from a strictly military point of view, the resistance of German troops in charge of defending Paris cannot be effective anymore. In order to prevent any useless bloodshed, it belongs to you to put an end to all resistance immediately.' Despite Hitler's order not to retreat from Paris before it had been completely destroyed, Choltitz surrendered to the Allies on August 25, 1944. That same day, General Charles de Gaulle, the leader of the Free French who had been living in exile in London since the beginning of the occupation, re-entered his city.

V2 ROCKETS RAIN DOWN ON LONDON

Having failed to destroy Britain from the air and sea, in March 1942 Hitler began to develop plans for long-distance rockets. Thousands of prisoners were set to work building the rockets, and by October 1942 they were ready for mass production. First to be developed was a robot rocket, or pilotless airplane, known as the V1. These weapons, nicknamed 'doodlebugs' and built of plywood and steel, were first launched in June 1944, just before the D-Day landings. However, the long ramps from which they were launched, although hidden in forests, could easily be spotted from the air, making them easy targets for Allied bombs. The Germans therefore switched to mobile ramps and began to fire a steady barrage of V1 rockets at London. Only a small proportion of these hit their target as they were fairly easy to shoot down, so the far more lethal V2 rocket was introduced. This took four minutes to reach its target and carried 2,000 lbs (909 kg) of explosives on board. The V2s could not be detected as the doodlebugs could, so the British counteroffensive tried to make the Germans 'aim' at the wrong place through disinformation. Nonetheless, more than 1,000 V2s were fired on London to devastating effect.

May 30
Monaco Given New Heir
Princess Charlotte of Monaco, with her father's agreement, gives up the throne to her son Rainier on the day before his 21st birthday. She retains the title of Princess of Monaco and goes to live in Paris.

June 1
Colossus II at Work
At Bletchley Park code-breaking facility in England, the Colossus II decryption machine is used for the first time. It is so efficient that the German Navy's Enigma messages can be decoded almost in real time.

July 20
Assassination Attempt on Hitler
Adolf Hitler survives an assassination attempt at the hands of his own officers when a bomb explodes in 'Wolf Lair', his eastern headquarters.

August 4
Anne Frank Found
A tip from an informer leads the Gestapo to the building in Amsterdam where Anne Frank and her family are in hiding.

1944

U.S. ARMY ENTERS ROME

The Allies had first landed in Italy in September 1943. After liberating Naples, they had made their way steadily toward Rome, but they had encountered stiff opposition on the journey north. It took them nearly eight months to reach the capital, but by the time they did so, German manpower had been exhausted by fierce battles in the south, and supplies were low. On June 4, 1944, after dropping propaganda leaflets urging Romans to keep off the streets, a division of the U.S. Army marched into Rome. The Germans were already retreating and had left the place largely intact. Thus Rome became the first capital city of the Axis Powers to be liberated by the Allies. As instructed, the citizens of Rome had stayed inside when the changeover took place, but the following day they poured out of their houses to welcome their liberators with open arms.

> 'Rome became the first capital city of the Axis Powers to be liberated by the Allies.'

Left: Italians take to the streets to celebrate the liberation of Rome.

October 4
Dumbarton Oaks Conference
Allied governments announce plans for a United Nations organization.

November 20
Blackout Ends
London streetlights are back on again as the blackout is lifted.

December 15
Bandleader Missing
Glenn Miller and his plane mysteriously disappear on the way to Paris, giving conspiracy theorists a field day.

December 21
Disney's 'Three Caballeros' Premiered in Mexico City
Commissioned as part of the State Department's 'Good Neighbor Policy', *The Three Caballeros* is Disney's first movie to mix animation and live action.

JAPANESE OCCUPATION OF MANILA IS ENDED

On January 2, 1942, Manila, the capital of the Philippines, had been captured by Japanese forces. American General Douglas MacArthur's decision to withdraw American forces and declare it an 'open city' in the hope that this would keep it safe from Axis bombs had backfired when the Japanese bombed it from the air. During the prolonged Japanese military occupation, the people of Manila had suffered extreme depredation. By the time U.S. forces arrived on January 9, 1945, they were desperate and joined in fighting on the streets. But the Japanese were determined not to lose Manila, and their retreat wrought immense destruction and loss of life. The battle for control of Manila lasted from February 4 to March 3, 1945, and ended in the walled city of Itramuros, where the ruthless fighting in the streets resulted in a horrific number of civilian deaths. Around 100,000 Filipinos are thought to have died during the battle for liberation of the city.

MUSSOLINI EXECUTED

Following the Allied invasion of southern Italy in July 1943 and the subsequent ousting of the Fascist leader Benito Mussolini, the Italians switched sides to join the Allies. However, Mussolini was rescued from captivity by the Germans and made head of the Italian Socialist Republic in Nazi-occupied northern Italy. On April 28, 1945, he was arrested by members of the Italian resistance at Lake Como. The partisans, who were becoming increasingly violent in their underground fight against Nazi occupiers, had spotted him as he attempted to travel to Switzerland. When he realized that they were going to kill him, Mussolini asked to be shot in the chest, but the first two guns failed to fire. Only the third succeeded in killing him, along with his mistress, Clara Petacci. The next day their bodies were hung upside down in a public square in Milan, where they were mutilated by the enraged people.

January 12
Turkey's Channels Open
Turkey opens its straits to Allied shipping, and a month later declares war on Germany.

January 27
Red Army Reaches Auschwitz
Arriving in southern Poland, the Red Army discovers the Nazi concentration camp at Auschwitz, where estimates of the numbers murdered, range from 1 to 3 million.

February 4
Big Three in Conference
The Allied leaders Churchill, Roosevelt, and Stalin meet at Yalta in Ukraine to decide what will happen when the war ends.

February 24
Ahmed Maher Pasha Assassinated
Egypt's Prime Minister Ahmed Maher Pasha is shot dead after reading his country's declaration of war on Germany and Japan.

1945

HITLER COMMITS SUICIDE

By early 1945, it was clear that the Nazis had lost the war. The Russians had entered Berlin, and the German garrison could no longer hold out. Hearing that Mussolini had been executed, Hitler was determined not to suffer the same fate. He retreated to his Führerbunker in central Berlin in January 1945, and there married his mistress, Eva Braun, on April 29. It is believed that on the following day Hitler heard that the Russians had almost reached his bunker, and, after eating lunch, went with his wife into his study – where a shot was heard. When Hitler's valet went in moments later, he found the Führer dead by a single shot through the temple, with the new Frau Hitler also dead by his side, probably from cyanide poisoning. The valet took the bodies outside to burn, but as the Russians had begun to bomb the bunker, he was forced to abandon the hasty cremation. What happened to the bodies thereafter was unknown for a long time, which has caused much speculation as to the truth of Hitler's death. Following the opening of Russian state files, it has now emerged that the charred corpses, along with those of Joseph Goebbels and his family, were buried in a secret unmarked grave. When the whereabouts of the grave became public knowledge in the 1970s, the Russian secret service wanted to avoid the possibility of the site becoming the focus of neo-Nazi attention, so they dug up the bodies, burned them, and scattered the ashes in the Elbe River.

VICTORY IN EUROPE DECLARED AS NAZI GERMANY SURRENDERS

On May 8, 1945, it was announced that Nazi Germany had been defeated, so the Allies declared that date VE-Day to celebrate victory in Europe. Since April 1945, the Allies had been advancing on Germany from the west while the Russians advanced from the east. With

'There was no stopping the spontaneous celebration that took to the streets.'

their army in tatters and their Führer dead, the new leaders of Germany were forced to offer an unconditional surrender, which was signed by German General Alfred Jodl in the presence of American General Dwight D. Eisenhower at his headquarters in France. In London, King George VI and his wife appeared on the balcony of Buckingham Palace, along with Prime Minister Winston Churchill, to salute the cheering multitude, while their daughters, Princesses Elizabeth and Margaret, mingled with the celebrating crowds in the streets. VE-Day had originally been scheduled for May 9, but news of the German surrender was leaked immediately, and there was no stopping the spontaneous celebration that took to the streets, so it was brought forward a day.

Above: Winston Churchill joins the Royal Family on the balcony at Buckingham Palace.

March
Anne Frank Dies
At 15 years old, Anne Frank dies of typhus in the Bergen-Belsen concentration camp in Germany.

April 12
President Roosevelt Dies
Following the death of Franklin D. Roosevelt, Harry S. Truman is sworn in as U.S. president.

July 16
The Trinity Test
The first atomic bomb is detonated near Alamogordo, New Mexico.

July 28
Empire State Building Hit by Bomber
The Empire State building, the world's tallest, is accidentally hit at floors 78–79 by a B-25 bomber.

August 14
'Things Go Better with Coke'
'Coke' was not the intended name for this popular fizzy drink as the company was afraid that the nickname would make it a generic product. But people kept asking for 'Coke', so in 1945 'Coke' was registered as a trademark.

ATOMIC BOMB DEVASTATES HIROSHIMA

On August 6, an American B-29 bomber called *Enola Gay* set off for the city of Hiroshima on Honshu Island in Japan. On arrival, at 8.15 a.m., the plane dropped an atomic bomb codenamed 'Little Boy'. The bomb exploded in the air above Hiroshima, causing mass destruction within moments. An estimated 80,000 people were killed immediately, the majority of them civilians. Within six months, injury and radiation had brought the death toll to 90,000–140,000. The survivors, and their children who were exposed to radiation in the womb, suffered an increased incidence of cancer, leukemia, and certain non-cancer diseases throughout their lives. U.S. President Harry Truman had made the decision to drop the bomb as a means of stopping the war in the Pacific by forcing Japan to surrender. Truman had previously urged the Japanese to surrender several times. He felt that his only remaining option was a display of American military power that would convince the Japanese they had lost. After he had dropped the bomb, the copilot of the *Enola Gay* wrote in his log, 'My God, what have we done?'

Left: Part of a preserved building hit by the A-bomb in Hiroshima, Japan.

JAPAN SURRENDERS

In the immediate aftermath of the Hiroshima bomb, there was no Japanese surrender. The Americans therefore decided to bomb a second city – Kokura. On the appointed day, it was hidden by clouds, so the Americans bombed their second choice, Nagasaki, instead. Codenamed 'Fat Man', the bomb was dropped on August 9, 1945. Estimates for immediate civilian deaths range from 40,000 to 75,000. On August 15, Japan surrendered to the Allied Powers. In doing so, Emperor Hirohito imposed one condition – that the monarchy should not be abolished. The Americans agreed to this condition, and Hirohito announced Japan's surrender in a radio address to the nation, acknowledging the new deadly era of atomic warfare embarked on by the Americans: 'The enemy now possesses a new and terrible weapon with the power to destroy many innocent lives and do incalculable damage. Should we continue to fight, not only would it result in an ultimate collapse and obliteration of the Japanese nation, but it would also lead to the total extinction of human civilization.' Days later, U.S. forces occupied Japan.

September 8
Japanese Prime Minister Attempts Suicide
Hideki Tojo, Japan's prime minister during most of the Second World War, attempts suicide before facing a war crimes tribunal.

October
United Nations Established
The United Nations, designed to maintain world peace, is established in New York.

October 21
French Women's Suffrage
Women in France are allowed to vote for the first time.

October
Penicillin Wins Prize
The Nobel Prize for medicine is awarded to Alexander Fleming, Howard Florey, and Ernst Chain for discovering penicillin.

1946

UNITED NATIONS MEETS FOR FIRST TIME

The first session of the United Nations General Assembly was convened on January 10, 1946 at Central Hall in Westminster, London, with representatives from 51 nations in attendance. The Inter-Allied Declaration, signed in London on June 12, 1941, had put the first building blocks in place for the creation of the United Nations by pledging to 'work together, with other free peoples, both in war and in peace'. On January 1, 1942, while the Second World War raged around them, representatives from 26 countries had met in Washington, D.C. to sign the 'Declaration by United Nations', a title suggested by President F.D. Roosevelt. At various conferences that followed during 1944 and 1945, the great powers of the United States, the United Kingdom, the U.S.S.R., and China worked out the structure and organization of the United Nations. On October 24, 1945, the United Nations officially came into existence with the signing of its charter. The elected president of the first session was the Belgian Paul-Henri Spaak, a socialist politician.

> **'The first session of the United Nations General Assembly was convened on January 10, 1946.'**

Above: The United Nations building, New York.

January 10
Project Diana a Success
In Project Diana, the U.S. Army Signal Corps aims radar waves at the Moon, which reflect off and bounce back to Earth. This proves that communication is possible between Earth and space, and marks the birth of the U.S. space program.

February 14
Meet ENIAC!
The Electrical Numerical Integrator and Calculator (ENIAC) is the first general-purpose computer. It fills an entire room and weighs around 30 tons.

March 5
Iron Curtain Speech
In a speech at Fulton, Missouri, Winston Churchill talks about the 'Iron Curtain', warning that the West is now threatened by the Soviet Union.

April 10
Japanese Women Vote
Women in Japan vote for the first time in parliamentary elections.

JUDGMENT AT NUREMBERG

From November 14, 1945 to October 1, 1946, 22 prominent Nazi leaders stood trial as war criminals in Nuremberg, Germany – chosen as a location because its Palace of Justice had been left unscathed by the war and housed a prison on site. It was also considered to be the birthplace of the Nazi Party and therefore a fitting place to dissolve that party once and for all. Those accused of major war crimes were tried by the International Military Tribunal, made up of American, British, Soviet, and French judges and prosecutors. Twelve of the 22 men were sentenced to death, including Hermann Goering, Alfred Rosenberg, and Joachim von Ribbentrop, and were subsequently hanged on October 16, 1946. Goering, however, committed suicide the night before he was due to be executed. The rest of the men were incarcerated in Spandau Prison, Berlin. Aside from bringing individuals to justice, the Nuremberg Trials helped shape future human rights policies in a significant way by defining codes of acceptable behavior and practice in war. Many of those prosecuted expressed repentance at what they had done, some even going so far as to welcome the trials as necessary. For example, Albert Speer, Hitler's personal architect and minister of wartime production, stated that, 'There is a shared responsibility for such horrible crimes, even in an authoritarian state.'

April 20
League of Nations Dies
At the end of the war, 43 states are still members of the League of Nations, but it exists in name only. At the last assembly all 43 vote that, as of April 20, it will cease to exist.

May 7
Start of Great Things
With no machinery and little scientific equipment, engineer Masaru Ibuka and physicist Akio Morita found Tokyo Telecommunications Engineering Corporation, a company set up to repair and build electrical equipment. Now named Sony, it is a global success.

June 2
Women Win Vote in Italy
Italian women are granted the right to vote in elections.

June 4
Juan Perón Elected President
Juan Perón is elected president of Argentina. He and his wife Eva (Evita) are very popular with the Argentinian people.

1946

NATIONAL HEALTH SERVICE FOR U.K.

Prior to the National Health Service Act of 1946, anyone who received medical treatment in the U.K. had to pay for it. Although it had been common practice for doctors to charge wealthy patients more and use the extra profit to subsidize poorer patients, medical care was generally paid for by private health insurance, leaving the poor to resort to charity where they could. British Prime Minister David Lloyd George had been instrumental in setting up a National Insurance scheme in 1911, which required every working person to pay a monetary contribution that was then added to by employers and the government. This National Insurance provided payouts for medical treatment, as well as unemployment and retirement, forming the backbone of the National Health Service. However, the scheme was not applied nationwide, nor was it evenly distributed across various trades and professions. After the Second World War, Clement Attlee's Labour government, acting on the recommendations of the 1942 Beveridge Report entitled 'Social Insurance', formed a National Health Service that was funded by general taxation, offering free medical treatment to all.

Left: British Minister of Health Aneurin Bevan who founded the National Health Service.

CIVIL WAR IN GREECE

The German occupation of Greece lasted from 1942 to 1944. During this time, the hole created by the absence of the exiled Greek government left room for various resistance groups to gain supporters. The most powerful of these groups was the Communist-led National Liberation Front. Though there were clashes between resistance groups during the occupation, after Greece was liberated in 1944 the groups united against the British-backed Greek government. The National Liberation Front had the backing of Communist states, including Albania, Yugoslavia, Bulgaria, and the U.S.S.R., and formed a united Democratic Army of Greece to oust the Western-backed government. In December 1944, after the Nazis had left, King George II returned to Athens, but elections to reinstate the patriotic party loyal to the king were boycotted by resistance groups. There followed a period of civil war during which the British government helped the Greek government defeat E.L.A.S., the military arm of the National Liberation Front. The Greek Communist Party (K.K.A.) then took over the work of resistance, but the collapse of relations between the U.S.S.R. and Yugoslavia meant they did not have the Communist backing they had been relying on, and by 1948, they too had been defeated.

July 1
U.S. Sends Care Parcels
Parcels of food and supplies are sent to Europe from the U.S.

July 5
Bikini Finds Fame
The bikini, popularized by French car designer Louis Réard, hits the headlines when French dancer Micheline Bernardini models it in Paris.

October 23
Dodgers Sign Jackie Robinson
Jackie Robinson becomes the first African American to sign a contract with a major baseball club, the Dodgers.

December 11
Help for the Children
After the Second World War, the United Nations International Children's Emergency Fund (UNICEF) organization is set up to help children living in countries devastated by war.

INDIA WINS INDEPENDENCE

On August 15, 1947, India finally gained independence from British rule. Although this marked the end of a long struggle for freedom, India's problems were not over. The antagonism had not been exclusively between Indians and their British rulers: it also existed between the Hindus and Muslims within India. In an attempt to resolve the disagreements between Muslims and Hindus at the point of handover, the Asian subcontinent was divided up into Hindu-dominated India and a newly formed Muslim state called Pakistan. This division was to heighten religious tensions between the Muslims and Hindus. At the time of Partition, when lines were drawn between India and Pakistan, much of the tension was focused around the Punjab region, which was divided in two. Thousands of people were dislocated – finding themselves Hindus in Pakistan or Muslims in India – and there was mass migration. Violent unrest over the new arrangements led to severe rioting in the streets, resulting in around 50,000 deaths. After the British departure, Rajendra Prasad became the first President of India, with Jawaharlal Nehru taking office as his Prime Minister. Pakistan became a new member of the United Nations. The union formed from the combination of the Hindu states assumed the name India, which automatically gave it the U.N. seat previously held by British India.

WHAT ARE WE BRITISH DOING HERE?

BRITISH troops stationed in Greece are standing by compelled to witness cruelties and atrocities which are taking place around them.

The atrocities are committed by the all-powerful Greek police and by Greek soldiers in police and army barracks where some of our men are stationed.

Although our men have protested against these inhumanities, they have not been able to stop them. They have carried on, sickened at heart, with their job of training Greek soldiers, but have protested to their officers.

Ex-Corporal Tells of Beatings

Here is the statement of a man who has been demobilised from Greece.

The "Daily Mirror" has checked the facts and is fully satisfied that they are a fair and even moderate statement about a terrible situation.

Ex-Corporal Stephen Harry Starr, aged thirty-two, was demobilised in August last, with a character, "Exemplary," trustworthy and thoroughly reliable," from the Loyal Regiment (North Lancashire). He writes:

"I was attached to Tyklisia, Thessaly, last June as a member of Section 'E,' British Liaison Unit of the British Military Mission in Athens.

"On the way back from collecting stores we saw a crowd and Greek soldiers dressed in British battle-dress uniforms mounted on horses.

"They were carrying human heads of bandits, or, rather, Communists, killed in a clash between the Greek Army and the guerrillas.

"I pulled up my lorry, and Sergeant Alfred Kings, our unit's chief clerk, took pictures. On this particular morning there were nine heads on view—eight men and one woman.

"Gestapo Methods"

"We were not Communists, but we knew that it was God help you if it was known you held Communist sympathies. You may be shot, beaten up or deported to one of the barren isles off the coast of Greece.

"I served with the British Military Mission to Greece for just over two years and I have yet to read an account of the Greek situation which gives a true, unbiased account of life in Greece today.

"The police are all-powerful and the methods are those of the Gestapo at their worst.

"Then there were the inhuman beatings. One of these incidents nearly led to armed warfare between our fellows and the Greek troops.

"It was at Tirnavos, near Larissa. I was

Heads are cheap

one of twenty-five British Tommies and five officers stationed in the Greek Army barracks there, which we shared with Greek troops under instruction.

"They began to beat up men and women in this barracks one day while motor-cycle engines were revved up to drown their screams.

"About thirty women were beaten up on this occasion. One of them was a cripple girl, hobbling on crutches. At least one other woman was pregnant.

"They took the cripple girl's sticks away from her and lashed her repeatedly across the face and stomach. All of the women were injured when they had finished with them, and were in a state of collapse.

"Then they were left in a compound under a boiling sun. They received no medical attention until we complained to our British officers, who brought the C.O. to see them.

"We knew most of the women by sight because they came from local villages and we talked to them every day as we sat in the village square drinking wine.

"Our boys were terribly angry with the Greek troops, who were armed with tommy-guns.

"Some of the boys said: 'Let's take our tommy-guns and do them.'

But the Q.M.S. Sergeant Scott, ordered us not to

Continued on Back Page

The head of a young Greek is paraded through a village street by an armed man on horseback. Corporal Starr says he saw nine such heads in the parade at which these pictures were taken—eight were men's and one a woman's.

I N Greece today, according to the latest available figures, there are between 5,000 and 6,000 British troops.

Commanding them is Major-General E. R. Down, who succeeded Lieutenant-General Kenneth Crawford in March this year.

British troops of liberation returned to Greece in October, 1944.

A British Military Mission went there in 1945 and, under Major-General S. B. Rawlins, organised and armed a small army of three corps.

A delegation of British M.P.s of all parties who had visited Greece said in a report published more than ten months ago:

"Subject to considerations of strategy and high policy, British troops should be withdrawn at an early date."

Referring to the fighting between the opposing factions, the M.P.s said:

"Though it is claimed that the object of some of the Right Wing bands is to prevent the spread of Communism, the fact is they never engage the Communist bands in battle, but devote themselves to terrorising the villages."

India takes over a State

T HE Government of India has taken over administration of the State of Junagadh "at the request of the Junagadh Prime Minister," the Indian Government announced last night.

A battalion of Indian troops with medium tanks has entered Junagadh city, the capital.

Pakistan was told of the move by telegram from Pandit Nehru, Indian Premier.

Pakistan's Premier, Liaquat Ali Khan, said last night, "If India is determined to force war on us, we will not show the white flag."

The Nawab of Junagadh is a Moslem, but 90 per cent. of his 800,000 subjects are Hindus. The State —which is entirely surrounded by Indian Union territory—acceded to Pakistan last month.

Ex-Corporal S. H. Starr

Advertiser's Announcement

Look your best in **Windsmoor**

1947

PRINCESS ELIZABETH MARRIES PHILIP MOUNTBATTEN

Millions will hear the Princess say "I will"

"Daily Mirror" Radio Correspondent

WHEN Princess Elizabeth says "i will" as the High Altar of Westminster Abbey this morning she will be heard by hundreds of millions of people

Four B.B.C. microphones have been installed in the Sanctuary, and they will pick up the voices of the Princess groom and Archbishop of Canterbury.

Fifty engineers will be on duty, and Wynford Vaughan Thomas will give the ceremony. The American networks will share another microphone.

Along the processional route and outside the Abbey commentators will describe the scenes in about twenty languages: their voices will be carried to practically every radio station in the world.

The B.B.C. Home Service will open

its broadcast of the wedding at 11 a.m. with Frank Gillard describing the scenes as the Queen leaves Buckingham Palace. The broadcast will continue until the bridal coach returns to the Palace at about 1 p.m.

As the procession move to the Abbey there will be commentaries from Audrey Russell near the Admiralty Arch, Peter Scott on the roof of St. Margaret's, Westminster, and Richard Dimbleby outside the West Door of the Abbey.

Television cameras will cover the processions, and a special camera will film the bridal procession from the Altar after the ceremony.

Both sound mikes and television cameras outside Buckingham Palace will record the appearances of the Royal Family on the balcony during the afternoon and the departure of the bride and groom for their honeymoon.

For the benefit of people at work this morning recording of the wedding will be broadcast in the Light Programme at 8.15 p.m.

The television films will also be sent out from Alexandra Palace at 8.30 p.m.

LT. PHILIP—17 YEARS AGO

This photograph of Prince Philip, wearing Greek national costume, was taken in 1930, when he was nine. It was the treasured possession of Miss Emily Roose, of Plymouth, nurse-governess to the Greek Royal household for twenty-five years, and was signed for her—" Philip, 1930," in schoolboyish writing.

PHILIP IS NOW THE DUKE OF EDINBURGH

THE KING last night gave Lieutenant Philip Mountbatten the titles of Duke of Edinburgh, Earl of Merioneth and Baron Greenwich.

Announcement of the titles, made from Buckingham Palace last night, says the King has also authorised him to use the prefix "His Royal Highness."

The titles were conferred during a private ceremony at the Palace, when he was also made a Knight of the Garter.

It had been anticipated that the Dukedom of Edinburgh would be revived for Lieutenant Philip ever since Princess Elizabeth's speech in Edinburgh last July, when she received the freedom of the city.

Three titles are normally borne by a duke. The second is usually taken as a courtesy title by the duke's first-born son.

The third title, Baron Greenwich of Greenwich, brings London, the heart of the Empire and its first capital city, into the titles of the consort of the Heiress to the Throne.

It is also a tribute to Lieutenant Mountbatten's naval service, for Greenwich has been called the "cradle of the British Navy."

The title Duke of Edinburgh was last revived by Queen Victoria for her second son, Alfred, who died in 1900.

In 1862, Alfred was elected King of Greece, but refused the Crown for political reasons.

The new Duke was present at yesterday's wedding rehearsal.

He watched Princess Elizabeth on her father's arm walk up the aisle, followed by the eight bridesmaids and two page-boys.

The Irish State Coach, in which Princess Elizabeth and the King today drive to the Abbey, will be heated with special hot-water bottles 3ft. long.

Made of aluminium, they will be filled with boiling water and placed under the seat and floorboards.

The famous Glass Coach in which the bride and bridegroom return to the Palace will be similarly heated.

An anti-dim substance will be used to prevent the windows steaming over, which would disappoint the vast throngs straining to catch a glimpse of the Royal couple and their Majesties.

Yesterday at Buckingham

Continued on Back Page

21 M.P.s will consider King's offer

A SELECT Committee of twenty-one M.P.s is to be appointed to consider the King's offer to use some of his savings to give Princess Elizabeth an additional income and to give her husband an income.

Sir Stafford Cripps said in the Commons yesterday: "I am sure this House will deeply appreciate His Majesty's recognition of our present economic troubles and the generous and characteristic offer he has made to assist."

Royal Wedding

The "Daily Mirror" regrets inability to supply extra copies tomorrow. Newsprint is rationed and the "Daily Mirror" disposes of its full supply every day. A vast public is already disappointed daily, thousands more will be added to this number tomorrow when pictures of this historic event will appear. We are sorry WE HAVE NOT GOT THE PAPER.

The Princess's Gown

ABOVE is the Royal wedding gown—white satin sparkling with pearls and crystals, embroidered with stars and garlands of roses and wheat.

Its low 'sweetheart' neckline is trimmed with pearls. Orange blossom and stars form a deep band round the hem.

The full swirling skirt—11½ yards of satin went to make the frock alone—falls into a slight train. The sleeves are narrow, tight-fitting, ending in embroidery at the wrist.

From the Princess's shoulders will fall a 15ft. fan-shaped train of transparent ivory silk tulle. This, too, is encrusted with

pearls and crystals and embroidered with satin stars.

The veil of white tulle will be caught by a tiara of diamonds and pearls.

The thousands of pearls sewn on to the wedding gown are not real—they were made by a special process in a North London factory.

The Hartnell needlewomen who sewed them on had every half hour to stop every half hour to wash their hands, to make sure the material was not soiled.

Following the Princess will be eight all-white bridesmaids in frocks of ivory silk tulle—full-skirted and the bodices softly gathered, the shoulders swathed in pearl-spotted tulle, bordered with white satin flowers.

The two pages who carry the Princess's train will wear Royal Stuart tartan kilts.

WEDDING WEATHER: RAIN, BUT NO FOG

London's Royal wedding weather, says the Air Ministry, will be dull and misty with occasional rain and drizzle. Thick fog is NOT likely.

Going-away dresses PAGE 2. Wedding details PAGE 5

Whiter teeth fresher that's the COLGA...

Cleans your breath while it cleans your teeth!

COLGATE RIBBON DENTAL...

On November 20, 1947, a royal wedding took place between Princess Elizabeth and Lieutenant Philip Mountbatten at Westminster Abbey, London. The couple had announced their engagement in July of that year. Princess Elizabeth and Philip, Prince of Greece and Denmark, had first been introduced to each other in 1939 at the house of the Captain of the Royal Naval College in Dartmouth. They met several times thereafter, as well as keeping up a correspondence. Prince Philip, who was given the title 'Duke of Edinburgh' prior to the wedding, was at the time a naval officer, and he resumed his career after the marriage. His first posting took him to Malta, where his wife joined him when she could. There was some controversy surrounding the union, caused by Philip's Greek Orthodoxy and the fact that his sisters had married German noblemen with Nazi links, but in general the marriage was seen as offering a new future after the deprivations of the Second World War.

Left: The Duke of Edinburgh and other members of the royal family gather for Remembrance Day.

March 1
International Monetary Fund is Founded

An organization is established to set up the rules for commercial and financial relations among the world's major industrial states.

June 24
UFO Spotted

Pilot Kenneth Arnold sees a series of unidentified flying objects near Washington's Mt. Rainier. It is the first widely reported UFO sighting in the United States and – due to Arnold's description of what he saw – leads the press to coin the term 'flying saucer'.

June 25
Anne Frank's Diary Published

The diary of Anne Frank is published after Miep Gies, one of her family's helpers, finds the papers and keeps them safe.

July 8
Was It a UFO?

A 'flying disc' is allegedly discovered in Roswell, New Mexico, U.S.A. There are later suggestions that it was a weather balloon, but some believe that this is a cover-up of the recovery of an alien spacecraft.

U.S. GIVES EUROPE FINANCIAL AID

In the aftermath of the Second World War, the economies of Western Europe were in ruins. In Britain, war debts, a slump in production, and depleted resources that forced the country to rely on expensive imports had all weakened the economy. In addition to this, moves by Prime Minister Clement Attlee to set up a welfare state did not strengthen the situation. On July 15, 1947, in accordance with the Anglo-American Loan Agreement of 1946, Britain declared that the pound sterling could be converted into any currency, but the government was forced to revoke that declaration when a sudden rush on dollar-conversions drained British dollar reserves. Without dollars, the British were unable to import much needed, though expensive, goods. The crisis prompted a British delegation to go to Washington, D.C. to plea for dollar aid to boost their reserves, armed with the threat of total European collapse if Britain was not helped out. Of all the Allied Powers, only the U.S. economy had remained healthy after the war, so it fell to the Americans to rescue Europe from financial meltdown. The Marshall Plan, formulated by U.S. Secretary of State George Marshall, was one resulting European Economic Recovery Program: its aim was to provide grants and loans to Britain and other European countries. However, the plan was not driven purely by generosity. Financially, the U.S. hoped to open European markets to its own excess goods, and politically, the U.S. hoped to prevent socialism taking hold in Europe by making governments financially dependent on the U.S. However, British Foreign Minister Ernest Bevin was all in favor of 'dollar aid' via the Marshall Plan and took it upon himself to organize conferences promoting economic cooperation and free trade across Europe.

> **'Of all the Allied Powers, only the U.S. economy had remained healthy after the war, so it fell to the Americans to rescue Europe from financial meltdown.'**

July 17
Indian Passenger Ship Capsizes
The 406-ton Indian passenger ship *Ramdas* capsizes off the coast of Mumbai. Over 600 passengers perish.

August 7
'Kon-Tiki' Smashed
Norwegian scientist Thor Heyerdahl's raft, the *Kon-Tiki*, smashes into the reef of the Tuamotu Islands after a 4,300-mile (6,900-km) journey across the Pacific, proving that prehistoric peoples could have traveled there from South America.

October 14
First Supersonic Flight
American pilot Chuck Yeager becomes the first man to fly faster than the speed of sound in the Bell X-1, flying at 670 mph (1,072 kph).

December 22
First Practical Transistor Demonstrated
Bell Laboratories in the U.S. develop a device that can control an electric current and amplify it.

1948

GANDHI ASSASSINATED
BY HINDU EXTREMISTS

On January 30, 1948, Mohandas Gandhi was murdered by a group of Hindu extremists led by Nathuram Godse. Gandhi, who was 78, was shot three times in the chest at close range by Godse as he was walking to the prayer grounds near his home in Delhi. It was the sixth assassination attempt on the man who had fought tirelessly to gain Indian independence from British rule, and who only months earlier had achieved his aim. The murderers justified the assassination on the grounds that Gandhi favored Muslims and that he had destroyed India by allowing its division into two countries, Pakistan and India. In fact, Gandhi had always promoted respect for all religions, a stance that could not fail to make him unpopular with extremists on all sides. Nathuram Godse, along with another conspirator, was hanged for his part in the murder, while others in the group were imprisoned. Millions of Indians mourned Gandhi's assassination.

'It was the sixth assassination attempt on the man who had fought tirelessly to gain Indian independence from British rule, and haad only months earlier achieved his aim.'

January 12
Supermarket Opens in U.K.
The first British supermarket opens in London.

February 21
First Instant Camera
In New York City, Edwin Land demonstrates the first 'instant camera', the Polaroid Land Camera, to a meeting of the Optical Society of America.

March 27
Aswan Dam Started
The foundation stone is laid of the giant Aswan Dam across the River Nile in Egypt.

April 7
First W.H.O. Assembly
The World Health Organization is founded in Geneva.

APARTHEID INTRODUCED IN SOUTH AFRICA

After 14 years in opposition with his National Party, Daniel Francois Malan (known as D.F. Malan) defeated Jan Smuts on May 28, 1948 to become the new prime minister of South Africa. Malan had originally broken away from the National Party when it merged with Smuts' South African Party because he believed it had lost its purity of vision. This vision, founded on a belief in white supremacy, involved the complete segregation of blacks and whites in South Africa by means of the policy that came to be known as apartheid (meaning 'separateness' in Afrikaans). The ideology behind Malan's National Party was the semireligious idea that Afrikaans-speaking whites were the chosen people, whose destiny it was to rule their fatherland of South Africa. Centered on the Dutch Reformed Church, this ideology grew up around anti-British feeling following the Boer Wars (1880–81 and 1899–1902) and gained strength during prolonged periods of economic and social unrest. With links to Nazism, Afrikaans Nationalism feared black domination and set about disabling the black majority by preventing their economic and political growth. The era of apartheid institutionalized racial discrimination in South Africa until close to the end of the 20th century.

SOVIETS BLOCKADE WEST BERLIN

With Germany defeated, the Western Allies and the U.S.S.R. set about dividing up different areas between themselves. Britain, France, the U.S., and the U.S.S.R. were each assigned their zones, but at the time, the Soviets already held Berlin and the Western Allies occupied various areas outside their agreed boundaries. The Soviets were determined to hold the East of Germany, including the east of Berlin. The Americans were determined that the West of Germany should not fall prey to Communism. When the Soviets eventually retreated from West Berlin, they left it a ruin of its former self, but the Americans stepped in and revived it, while the East continued under Communism. As a result, the two halves of Berlin became vastly different regions. As a reaction to this glaring contrast between East and West, on April 1, 1948, Stalin ordered a blockade on Western supply routes in an attempt to starve the Western Allies out of Berlin. His plan did not work, however, as the Allies began instead to airlift food and supplies into West Berlin, and it continued to thrive. Stalin was forced to abandon his plan in May 1949.

May 4
Hamlet Hits Screens
Laurence Olivier's film version of *Hamlet* makes its world premiere in London.

June 3
Telescope Completed
The Palomar Observatory's Hale telescope, the largest in the world at the time, is completed. The telescope is named in memory of astronomer George Ellery Hale, who had died ten years earlier.

June 21
L.P.s Introduced
Columbia Records holds a press conference to announce the introduction of L.P.s, long playing records replacing previous records which could hold only one song.

August 23
Council of Churches
World Council of Churches is founded in Amsterdam.

1948

BRUSSELS PACT SIGNED

BRITAIN & 4 POWERS SIGN 50-YR. PACT: U.S. CONSCRIPTION CALL

Best yet outlook of food from the Empire

BRITAIN will get more food from the Empire this year than even in pre-war days, Mr. John Strachey, Food Minister, said yesterday.

There will be more eggs, butter and, eventually, more meat from Australia and New Zealand.

Recovery of the Empire and of Europe from drought and war damage has lessened Britain's dependence on the United States and other dollar areas.

We have been able to cut dollar food purchases by one half.

Since the war we have had to buy about half our food from dollar countries and have been getting only half as much food from Europe as before the war.

'In Nick of Time'

This year we shall get nearly half our food from the Empire and Europe instead of only one-third.

From the dollar area—Canada, the U.S.A. and Argentina—we shall get one-quarter.

We're buying roughly three - quarters of our wheat, three-quarters of our cheese and a big share of our bacon, most of our meat from the Canadians.

During the past nine months the Government had completed trade treaties, under which we shall get more food, with Denmark, Poland, Holland, Italy, Hungary, Portugal, France, Spain, Iceland and Eire.

"All this," said Mr. Strachey, "indicates that the non-dollar world is beginning to recover—in the nick of time for us.

"But on no account must this lead to the suggestion that we do not need to grow every ton of food which it is economically possible to grow at home."

Brenda Dorothy Marsh, 25, girl student, gaoled for twelve months at Winchester Assizes yesterday, for trying to blackmail a college lecturer for £300. Story on Page 3.

NO LABOUR 'REVOLT' FROM BAN ON EXTREMISTS

"Daily Mirror" Political Correspondent

THERE will be no "revolt" in the Labour Party over the Government decision to weed out Communists and Fascists from Government posts where they might learn vital secrets.

At yesterday's meeting of the Parliamentary Labour Party, attended by both the Prime Minister and Mr. Herbert Morrison, a number of M.P.s expressed regret that such a step should be found necessary and declared themselves against it in principle.

There was, however, no indication that there was any great opposition and Mr. Attlee's reply appeared to satisfy most of those at the meeting.

EXTRA DUBLIN BOATS FOR EASTER

Holyhead-Kingstown (Eire) boats will run a daylight service as an Easter extra, both ways, from March 24 to April 3 (not Sunday).

TWO major developments in the defence of democracy, personal freedom and political liberty in the West took place yesterday:

1.—Britain, France, Belgium, the Netherlands and Luxemburg signed a fifty-year treaty of economic and military co-operation.

2.—President Truman called on the U.S. Congress to re-impose conscription and to speed Marshall aid to Europe "to curb the growing menace" of Russian expansion.

The five-nation pact, signed in Brussels, provides that if an armed attack in Europe should be made on any one of them the others will give all possible military and other aid.

A permanent council is to be set up which can be immediately called at the request of any of the five countries to deal with "any situation constituting a threat to peace in any area."

It can also be called should there be any danger to economic stability.

Mr. Truman told Congress: "I am here to report to you on the critical nature of the situation in Europe and to recommend action for your consideration."

Then he listed "the most urgent steps towards securing peace and preventing war" as Marshall aid, universal military training and conscription.

"Must be Strong"

These, he said, were the measures "best calculated to give support to the free and democratic nations of Europe, and to improve the solid foundation of our own nation's strength.

"Until the free nations of Europe have regained their strength, and so long as Communism threatens the very existence of democracy, the U.S. must remain strong enough to support those countries of Europe which are threatened with Communist control and police State rule".

He declared that the responsibility for the critical situation was chiefly that of one nation which has "not only refused to co-operate in the establishment of a just and honourable peace but, even worse, has actively sought to prevent it."

His quiet attempt to find a way out of the impasse between doctors and Parliament was called "disguising appeasement" and "scandalous surrender."

His motion was lost.

But Not This ...

The doctors' general in the fight is Dr. H. Guy Dain, chairman of the Council.

He urged the doctors to restrict their amendments and to concentrate on the main battle which he calls a battle for freedom.

He repeated that the B.M.A. is most anxious to have a health service—but not this health service.

He got the loudest cheer of the day when he declared that the doctors will not serve

These are his words:

"I should be failing in my duty to the profession and to the public if I did ..."

TO AUSTRALIA FREE—OFFER TO SERVICES

The free passages to Australia scheme will apply to all ex-Service men and women released from the Forces on or before September 30, 1948, the Ministry of Labour and National Service announced last night.

Doctors shout down a plea for statesmanship

"DAILY MIRROR" REPORTER

ALL day yesterday 400 doctor delegates of the British Medical Association roundly refused, in motion after motion, to have anything to do with the National Health Act, due to begin on July 5.

The atmosphere was martial. One speaker after another declared that the time for words was past. Now was the moment for action.

Throughout the day only one voice—the refined Scots voice of Dr. G. Ireland, of the Lothians—called for concessions and peacemaking.

Dr. Ireland warned his colleagues that continued conflict, with no attempt to make new offers, would lead to a public reaction against the doctors.

"I don't ask for weakness," he said, "I want statesmanship."

He tried to persuade the meeting to pass a resolution giving representatives power to make concessions on condition that a whole-time salaried service is not introduced.

He spoke in vain.

New Palace strike 'if troops'

FORTY-TWO electricians, with twenty-one mates and fitters, working in Buckingham Palace, paused a resolution yesterday that unless troops stoking the Palace boilers are withdrawn they will strike in sympathy with the boilermen already out.

The meeting was held inside the Palace grounds and followed a demonstration march by 750 strikers. The marchers were a man in an invalid chair, Edward Kirkpatrick, lifeman, who was paralysed at Dunkirk.

The strikers claim an increase in their £4 17s. wage rates.

Advertiser's Announcement

"HIS MASTER'S VOICE" Push-Button Radio

Above is MODEL 1119 a 5-valve A.C. mains receiver with push-button control for 5 wavebands and 4 stations. Incomparable tone quality. Distinguished walnut finish cabinet. 27 gns. (plus £9 · 4 · 4 tax.)

Also in a similar cabinet MODEL 1407 4-valve, superhet battery receiver with push-button control. Equal in every way—performance, tone, appearance—to a mains set. Complete with batteries. 25 gns. (plus £8 · 10 · 8 tax.)

See the range of "His Master's Voice" Radio, Radiograms and Television in Stand 4a, Labour Home Exhibition.

THE GRAMOPHONE CO., LTD. HAYES, MIDDLESEX

TRANSPORT MEN END STRIKE

Cardiff tram and busmen are going back after a twelve-day strike, but they reject the offered 7s. 6d. a week, as an inadequate rise.

Manchester bus also rejected the 7s. 6d. offer. Liverpool was 100 buses short yesterday when 200 busmen struck.

Baronet's daughter falls to her death from train

"Daily Mirror" Reporter

SOCIETY folk, titled and rich, journeyed from London to the country last week-end for a house party.

One of the gayest and most attractive was Mrs. Valerie Josephine Lea, 34, daughter of a baronet and wife of an industrialist.

She was laughing when she left the house on Monday morning, with a peer and her host, to catch a train back to London.

In the train the little party talked and watched the scenery.

Then, as the train sped through Hampshire, between Liss and Liphook, the carriage door flew open and Mrs. Lea fell to her death.

Someone pulled the communication cord. The train drew sent for help.

But when they got Mrs. Lea to Midhurst Hospital she was dead.

Her mother, Lady Domville, said last night:

"I know what happened, but I may not tell you.

"My daughter had been to a house party for the week-end. She was gay

Mrs. Valerie Lea

'LIGHTS OUT' STRIKE

Strike by thirty-four lamp-room attendants yesterday brought five pits of the Monckton (Yorks) collieries to a standstill and made 2,800 men idle.

SWISS VOUCHERS PLAN DROPPED

The system called last year for British visitors to Switzerland, in which part of the travel allowance was drawn in vouchers which could be used to pay hotel, food and travel bills only, has been dropped.

From the monthly quotas of Swiss francs allowed from May to October this year travellers will be allowed a sum based on the length of their visit, and will draw the money in cash, said the Treasury last night.

Mrs. Valerie Lea

On March 17, 1948, the United Kingdom, Belgium, France, Luxemburg, and the Netherlands signed the Brussels Pact, which was largely a security measure to help combat the perceived threat of Communism. The group elected to contribute to a military formation headed by British Field-Marshal Bernard Law Montgomery (known as 'Monty'). The pact formed an early version of what would eventually include America and become N.A.T.O. (the North Atlantic Treaty Organization).

Above: The flag of N.A.T.O.

October 5
Devastating Earthquake
An earthquake in Turkmenistan, U.S.S.R., kills 110,000 people.

December 10
Universal Declaration of Human Rights Adopted
The United Nations General Assembly adopts a Universal Declaration of Human Rights that should be accepted all over the world.

Fast Oven
The microwave oven is invented by American Percy LeBaron Spencer.

Struck Oil
The world's largest oil field, Al-Ghawar, is discovered in Saudi Arabia.

GERMAN DEMOCRATIC REPUBLIC ESTABLISHED

In the years following the Second World War, the wealth gap between the Soviet-held and the Western-held regions of Germany continued to widen. In the Soviet-controlled areas, many Germans had been expelled. Stalin had created a new political party called the Socialist Unity Party. In pursuit of Communist ideals, property and industry were nationalized, a move that brought with it social and economic deprivation. On October 7, 1949, East Germany officially declared itself the German Democratic Republic, a separate socialist state, with Wilhelm Pieck as its president. In anticipation of a decisive break from the Soviets, Britain, France, and America had already united their zones into one Federal Republic of Germany in May 1949, with the city of Bonn as its capital. As a result, a division was created that would cause first the Berlin Wall and then the metaphorical Iron Curtain to be erected. For the next forty years, Germany was to exist as two separate states.

'A division was created that would cause first the Berlin Wall and then the metaphorical Iron Curtain to be erected.'

January 4
Raging Storms Hit Nebraska
A blizzard lasting for almost three days hits western, central, and northern Nebraska in the U.S. High winds drive heavy snow on top of earlier falls. Then the last two weeks of January bring sub-zero temperatures.

January 19
Poe Toaster First Appears
On Edgar Allen Poe's birthday, a dark figure appears at his grave and raises a toast to him. A toaster returns every year on Poe's birthday and has not yet been identified.

February 1
Clothes Rationing Ends
The rationing of clothes enforced during the war, ends in Britain.

March 1
Boxing Champ Retires
Joe Louis retires as heavyweight boxing champion. He was world champion for 11 years and 10 months.

1949

ISRAEL'S WAR OF INDEPENDENCE ENDS

Since declaring itself an independent state free from British control on May 14, 1948, Israel had faced a series of armed conflicts with surrounding Arab countries who refused to recognize the State of Israel. The United Nations Partition Plan of November 29, 1947 had agreed to the division of Palestine into two separate states – one Arab and one Jewish – with Jerusalem a multi-racial, multi-ethnic city administered by the U.N. to avoid conflict. Following the declaration of independence, Egypt, Syria, Lebanon, Jordan, and Iraq invaded Israel, launching the War of Independence. At least 726,000 Palestinians become refugees during the conflict. The war continued, with various ceasefires, until the 1949 Armistice Agreements. On February 24, 1949, Israel and Egypt signed an armistice agreement. This was followed by agreements with Lebanon (March 23), Jordan (April 3), and Syria (July 20). The armistice lines stayed in place as Israel's new borders until 1967, with the Gaza Strip and the West Bank being occupied by Egypt and Jordan respectively.

CANDY RATIONING ENDS IN U.K.

In April 1949, the British government announced the end of sweet rationing and allowed each household 5 oz (140 g) of sweets a week. It was also decided that each household should have an extra 7 lbs (3 kg) of sugar. Children and adults alike flocked to sweet shops to celebrate by indulging in their favorite confectionary. Sweets and chocolate were first rationed in 1942, along with many other food items, because of the shortage of supplies. Many, particularly women, took up smoking when sugar became scarce, so the tobacco industry expected a drop in sales once sugar became more widely available. It was soon discovered that the abolition of sweet ration-ing had been a rash move. The demand for sweets far exceeded the supply of sugar, so the ration had to be put back in place after only four months. It was not lifted again until 1953.

March 2
Flight Around the World
In Fort Worth, Texas, Captain James Gallagher lands the *Lucky Lady II*, a B-50 bomber, after making the first nonstop, round-the-world flight, in 94 hours 1 minute.

April 4
North Atlantic Treaty Signed
In Washington, D.C., 12 countries create the NATO defense alliance, agreeing that an attack on one of them will be considered an attack on them all.

April 18
From Eire to Ireland
Eire leaves the British Commonwealth and becomes the Republic of Ireland.

BRITAIN GAINS FIRST SELF-SERVICE SHOPS

More news of things that make life easier

'SERVE YOURSELF' SHOPS: STATE BACKS A BIG TRY-OUT

BRITAIN is to have more "Serve yourself" grocery shops, through which the busy housewife can stroll, choose ready-wrapped food, put it in a wheeled basket provided by the firm, and pay on the way out.

The Ministries of Food and Works, as an experiment, are to allow 100 big firms to spend £3,000 each on conversion to this no-queue, staff-cutting lay-out.

He wouldn't miss match to collect £49,000

Cheaper furniture and paint forecast

Milk off the ration

Railway lunch boxes soon

I'VE GONE AND DONE IT NOW, SAYS ADA, BUT I'M STILL THE SAME GIRL

ADA FISHBURN, 24, the British factory worker from Spennymoor, Durham, who exchanged jobs for a few weeks with an American girl, will soon return home—Americanised from top to toe.

Cinemas can show more U.S. films

MEAT BLACKMAIL GOES ON

HILTONE makes you a Natural Blonde by lightening the natural colour of your hair. Hiltoned hair will harmonize with your skin tones. Your hair will delight you with its sheen . . . its natural glinting lights. For home users 5/10 from Chemists & Hairdressers.

HILTONE BLEACH

COUNTY PERFUMERY CO. LTD., STANMORE, MIDDX.

In March 1949, the British government announced that it would license 100 companies to try out self-service shops, which had already been trialed successfully in America. The move marked the birth of the modern supermarket. Instead of queuing to be served, customers would be able to select pre-wrapped items themselves, put them in a basket or trolley, and take their purchases to a checkout near the exit. It was hoped that the altered layout would reduce staffing requirements, thus lowering costs, and make shopping more efficient for everyone.

June 24
Cowboys Hit TV
Hopalong Cassidy becomes the first network television cowboy series, airing on N.B.C. A radio version of *Hopalong Cassidy* is broadcast by the Mutual Broadcasting System in January 1950.

July 27
First Jet-Powered Airliner
The de Havilland Comet, the world's first jet-powered airliner, makes its maiden flight.

December 15
Deadly Typhoon
A typhoon strikes a fishing fleet off the coast of Korea, killing thousands of fishermen.

December 28
No UFOs
After an official inquiry, the U.S. Air Force reports that 'flying saucers' do not exist.

1950

NORTH KOREAN TROOPS ENTER SOUTH KOREA

On June 25, 1950, several units of the Communist North Korean People's Army crossed the north–south divide and invaded the Republic of Korea in the south. The attack came without warning, and the Republic of Korea was unprepared for war; their minimal troops were forced to retreat toward their capital, Seoul. Two days later, after North Korea had failed to abide by a United Nations Security Council resolution to withdraw, American President Truman took the decision to involve the United States in the war. He offered significant military support to assist the Republic of Korea in fighting back against the Communist onslaught, and by August, the United States Congress approved a budget of $12 billion to be spent on military involvement in Korea.

January 21
Israel Has Capital City
The Israeli Knesset passes a resolution making Jerusalem the capital of the new state.

January 26
Indian Republic is Formed
Rajendra Prasad is sworn in as the first president of the Republic of India.

February 12
Einstein Warns the World
Physicist Albert Einstein warns that nuclear war could end in mutual destruction.

March 8
Soviets Develop Bomb
The Soviet Union announces that it has developed a nuclear bomb.

U.S. WARNS SOVIET UNION TO STAY OUT OF YUGOSLAVIA

For some time, U.S. foreign policy toward Central Europe was uncertain. Although the anti-Communist stance of the U.S. was clear, its relationship with Communist Yugoslavia under Marshall Josip Broz Tito, who had shown a great deal of independence from the Soviet Union, was an ambivalent one. However, in January 1950, George Allen, the new U.S. ambassador to Yugoslavia, issued a clear warning to the Soviet Union when he announced that America would not stand by idly if the Soviets attacked Yugoslavia. Stopping in London on his way to the Yugoslav capital, Belgrade, Allen told a press conference that U.S. foreign policy had always been to resist aggression, wherever it came from and whomever it was directed against.

PLANE CRASHES IN WALES

On March 12, 1950, an airliner carrying 78 passengers and five crewmembers crashed in a field in Llandow, South Wales. The plane was returning from Dublin, Ireland, where the passengers had all been supporting their country at an international Rugby Union match between Wales and Ireland. Only three people on the plane survived. The survivors had all positioned themselves at the tail end of the plane before the crash. The dead included nine players from Welsh rugby clubs. According to eyewitnesses, the airliner was flying too low as it approached the runway in Llandow, and when the pilot tried to correct its position, the nose lifted too high, bringing the plane into a vertical position before the engine stalled and the plane plummeted to earth. An investigation into the crash eventually ruled accidental death, although the possibility of pilot error was investigated. There was speculation that unbalanced luggage had altered the plane's center of gravity, and Fairflight, the company that owned the plane, was ordered to pay a fine and damages. The tragedy was the worst air disaster of its time.

April 27
Apartheid Laws in South Africa
South Africa passes the Group Areas Act, formally segregating people by race.

May 13
Formula 1 Begins
The first Formula 1 race is held at Silverstone race track, England.

August 15
Earthquake Shakes India
An earthquake in Assam, India, causes flooding that leaves 5 million homeless.

October 2
Peanuts First Published
Charles M. Schultz's comic strip *Peanuts* appears in seven U.S. newspapers.

1950

U.N. SUPPORTS SOUTH KOREA

On June 27, 1950, the United Nations Security Council passed a resolution urging all of its 52 member states to give military support to South Korea following the North's invasion. In the early days of the Korean War, U.N. member states stalled. Britain and Australia, for example, both held back and claimed that they would not be committing troops. As a result, U.S. and South Korean troops suffered heavy losses initially, and were pushed south toward Japan. Eventually, however, swayed by the prospect of friendship with the U.S., and in the face of further pleas from the U.N., other countries began to commit troops to the cause. The Korean War was to last three years and involve more than 20 countries, resulting in around 2 million civilian deaths in addition to the military losses. U.N. and South Korean forces together suffered around 500,000 casualties; North Korea and China's losses were in the region of 1,500,000 million.

SACRED STONE STOLEN BY SCOTTISH NATIONALISTS

Below: Westminster Abbey

In the early hours of Christmas Day 1950, the Coronation Stone was stolen from beneath the Coronation Chair behind the High Altar at Westminster Abbey in London. During the robbery, the Coronation Chair, which had seen the coronation of 27 British monarchs, was also damaged. The stone, variously known as the 'Stone of Scone' and the 'Stone of Destiny', had long been a point of contention between the English and the Scots. In the 13th century, when Edward I of England first defeated the Scots and annexed Scotland, he took the sacred stone, regarded by Scots as a talisman, from the castle of Stone, the ancient crowning place of Scottish kings. As soon as police were alerted to the missing stone, they sealed the border with Scotland. Despite this unprecedented measure, the stone did cross the border into Scotland, where it found. Once the stone was returned to Westminster Abbey, the whole episode was viewed as a prank, although when the thieves were apprehended, they insisted that it had been a political act. In the end, they were never prosecuted because it was too difficult to prove that the British Crown actually 'owned' the stone.

November 1
Attempt on Truman's Life
Puerto Rican nationalists attempt to kill U.S. President Harry Truman.

December 11
Muslim Riots in Singapore
Eighteen people are killed in riots in Singapore as Muslim protestors demonstrate against the British colonial government. The unrest lasts for two days.

December 12
America's First Female Rabbi
Paula Ackerman is the first woman to perform rabbinical duties in the U.S.A.

December 28
Britain's First National Park
The Peak District in England is designated Britain's first national park.

BRITAIN CELEBRATES NATIONWIDE FESTIVAL

The Festival of Britain, an event first conceived during the difficult post-war years when Prime Minister Clement Attlee presided over 'austerity Britain', was intended to complement the newly formed welfare state. Although officially a celebration of past and current achievements, the festival was also the left-wing government's declaration that Britain would move into a future of social equality. As a celebration of Britain's history and culture, it was intended to boost morale after the war, but as a political manifesto, it was also meant to shape a new British identity based on equality. The nationwide exhibition covered industry, science, and the arts, as well as everyday life, showcasing the best in design. The Royal Festival Hall, which still stands on London's South Bank, was the only building erected during the festival and intended as a permanent structure.

'As a popular celebration of Britain's history and culture, it was intended to boost morale after the trauma of the war.'

Right: The South Bank, London, which today is a thriving center for the arts.

January 9
U.N. Opens Headquarters
The United Nations' new headquarters opens in New York.

February 6
85 Die in Train Crash
A passenger train derails in New Jersey, killing 85 people..

March 29
Spies Receive Death Sentence
In the U.S., Ethel and Julius Rosenberg are sentenced to death for spying.

April 18
Treaty of Paris is Signed
Six European nations sign the Treaty of Paris to form the European Coal and Steel Community.

53

1951

BURGESS AND MACLEAN SPY SCANDAL

Guy Burgess and Donald Maclean were members of a Soviet spy ring in Britain known as the Cambridge Five (although they were also commonly referred to as the Cambridge Four, since the suspected fifth man was not formally identified for some time). All members of the ring went to Cambridge University, and had at some point belonged to a secret debating society known as the Apostles, although they were recruited at different times and not while at Cambridge. During the Second World War and for some time afterwards, various members of the group passed sensitive information to the U.S.S.R. As committed Communists, they worked their way up through the British Civil Service and the British Secret Service, all the while passing information to the K.G.B. By 1951, British intelligence had long known that there was a mole within the British Embassy in Washington, D.C., and they commissioned Kim Philby to investigate Donald Maclean, not knowing that Philby was himself a member of the Cambridge Five. Philby instructed Guy Burgess, who worked with Maclean in the embassy, to warn Maclean that he was a chief suspect. On hearing this information, Burgess and Maclean both suddenly and publicly defected to the U.S.S.R. It had never been part of the plan that Burgess would defect, too, and this action cast immediate suspicion on Kim Philby, with whom he was known to be close. Although Philby called a press conference to declare his innocence, he also defected to the U.S.S.R. in 1961 as suspicion about him increased.

WEST GIVES MORE FREEDOM TO FEDERAL REPUBLIC OF GERMANY

Toward the end of the 1940s, the British, French, and American zones of West Germany had begun to merge politically and economically in preparation for the handover of power back to the Germans. The Allies had formed an economic council that united their zones and paved the way for reunification of the separate parts, as well as setting measures in place for self-government. By 1949, a constitution had been established for a new self-governing Federal Republic of Germany, and following elections, that government was formed in August 1949 with its provisional capital in Bonn. The former capital of Berlin was still a separately administered zone, divided into four zones, three of which were controlled by the Allied powers. It was surrounded by Soviet-occupied territory. In 1951, Britain, France, and the U.S. gave up their control of West Germany's foreign affairs, and the Republic began to re-establish links with its European neighbors in its own right. West Germany quickly joined the European Coal and Steel Community, an alliance between France, Italy, Belgium, Luxembourg, and the Netherlands. When the outbreak of the Korean War in 1950 prompted the U.N. to call for German rearmament to guard against Communist invasion, it was proposed that rearmament take place under the umbrella of a European Defense Community, an expansion of the European Coal and Steel Community. However, France pulled out, fearing a loss of autonomy, and a wider Western European Union was established instead, with regulatory powers over the armies of its member states. Although the Western Allies still occupied parts of Berlin and British troops remained in Germany, by the mid-1950s, the Federal Republic of Germany was a sovereign state in charge of its own military.

May 3
Royal Festival Hall Opens
The London concert hall is opened by King George VI, marking the start of the Festival of Britain.

July 20
Jordan's King Assassinated
King Abdullah I of Jordan is killed while at Friday prayers in Jerusalem.

August 12
The Catcher in the Rye Published
J.D. Salinger's novel is published and becomes a bestseller.

September 8
Peace Treaty Signed with Japan
Forty-eight nations sign a treaty with Japan to formally end the Pacific War.

1951

CHURCHILL WINS GENERAL ELECTION

On October 26, 1951, the Conservative Party won the general election in Britain by a small margin, bringing Winston Churchill, the leader of the party, into the office of Prime Minister for a second time. At 76, he was the second-oldest prime minister in history to take office, second only to the Victorian politician William Gladstone, who was 83 when he formed his final government. Churchill succeeded Labor Prime Minister Clement Attlee. The Conservatives had campaigned on the promise of a 'strong and free' Britain and warded off Labour's depiction of Churchill as a warmonger. At the time, Britain was facing a rapid increase in the cost of living, a severe housing shortage, and an indebted economy burdened by the costs of rearming after the Second World War. In his victory speech, Churchill stressed the need for solidarity and an end to party rivalry so that everyone could pull together to work out the best way to restore the nation.

'At 76, he was the second-oldest prime minister in history to take office.'

8 24

Election race drama

TORIES IN —OVERALL LEAD MAY BE 17

But most votes go to Labour Party

THE Conservatives will form the next Government, with an overall lead expected to be under twenty. This was the result of the Election as it emerged last nigh: after a day of drama in which the issue—stalemate or a sizeable majority—was always in doubt.

The Tories at one stage chalked up a lead over Labour of forty-two seats, only to see it whittled down to as low as twenty towards the finish.

If the results still to come go as expected, the final state of the parties will be: Conservatives 321, Labour 296, Liberals 6, Others 2—overall majority 17.

The first step in the formation of the new Tory Government came soon after 5 p.m. Mr. Churchill went to Buckingham Palace to see the King.

Mr. Attlee had by then handed in his resignation as Prime Minister. A silent crowd of about a hundred watched him leave Downing-street.

Here is the time-table of yesterday's struggle:

Dawn: Labour leads by 30.
12.53 p.m.: Level—205 seats each.
12.58 p.m.: Tories two up.
2.8 p.m.: Tories lead by 42.
3.9 p.m.: 29 up.
3.50 p.m.: Tories in, Labour out.

Tory H.Q. are by no means satisfied with the size of the majority. They fear it will mean continuous strain on Tory M.P.s who must be ready for every Labour challenge.

The result means that the country has split fifty-fifty in the poll. The Conservatives are in with a small majority of the seats, but Labour will have a majority of the votes.

It retains its solid grip on the industrial centres of Britain.

Mr. Morgan Phillips, Labour Party Secretary, said Labour's vote in this election would be a record—it was far above the 1950 total.

The Election, in fact, has failed to give a clear-cut mandate to the Conservatives to carry through any sweeping reversal of the policies of the last six years.

The Opposition will feel able to look forward to the next Election with confidence.

There has been no "swing to the right." There has been less than the normal loss of seats any Government expects when it asks for a fresh vote of confidence.

For the Conservatives it is a victory without jubilation. They face tremendous problems with a majority below their expectations.

The first eighty results declared yesterday showed no change in any constituency.

At 12.53 p.m. the parties were level, each with 205 seats. Five minutes later the Conservatives snatched the lead.

Liberal Party headquarters in London last night said: "We do not disguise the fact that we are disappointed at the small number of Liberal Members returned.

"There is, however, clear evidence that a hard core of Liberalism will continue in this country. The party juggernaut has again defeated us. Our beachhead

Continued on Back Page

have all much in common'

who wore a sprig of white heather in his buttonhole, receives a kiss
his wife. After his election at Woodford, Essex, he said: "We have
eat deal in common. Now, perhaps, there may be a lull in our party
ill enable us to understand more what is good in our opponents and
not to be so very clever at all their shortcomings."

EGAN 'OUT' AFTER 22 YEARS

GEST election casu-
ty among Parliamen-
personalities was at
esey, where Lady
Lloyd George, who
d the seat for twen-
ears, lost to Labour
ee-cornered contest.
a "switch" in the
fortunes for her
Major Gwilym
eorge, who was
ring the last Par-
as returned this
iberal and Con-
for Newcastle

of the personal
Mr. Churchill,
let Bonham-
e-president of
ral Party.
Bonham
Carter.

Continued on Back Page

A kiss for Mr. Attlee

Mrs. Attlee kisses her husband, tired after his arduous election campaign, but pleased with his personal success in the polls at West Walthamstow, London. The Attlee family spent part of the day at Transport House, Labour Party H.Q., studying the election results.

The new House —and the old

With 7 results to come	Today	Old House
Tory and Allied Parties	318	298
		Including Speaker's Seat
Labour -	294	315
Liberal -	5	9
Others - -	1	3
	Irish Nat.	One Ind. Two Irish Nats.

GAINS AND LOSSES

	Gains	Losses
Labour - - - -	3	22
Tory - - - - - -	23	1
Liberal - - - -	1	4

The withdrawal of 371 Liberal candidates who contested seats in 1950 threatened the Tory majority in 98 constituencies and the Labour majority in 72. In the results from these constituencies the Tories held all 98 seats and gained 17 from Labour. Labour held 55 and gained none from Tories.

HOW THE VOTES WENT

	AFTER 613 RESULTS	TOTAL VOTE IN 1950
LAB.	13,865,019	13,295,736
TORY	13,614,730	12,526,686
LIB.	... 707,635	2,621,489
COMM.	 21,640	91,815
OTHERS	... 143,792	233,751
	Total vote so far 28,352,816 1951 electorate 34,915,112	Total vote 28,769,477 out of a 34,269,764 electorate

Four results to be declared today are:
ARGYLL (1950: Con. maj., 10,044);
INVERNESS (1950: Con. maj., 4,829);
WESTERN ISLES (1950: Lab. maj., 1,437);
ORKNEY and SHETLAND (1950: Lib. maj., 2,956).

The 625th and final result, from BARNSLEY, where a candidate died, will not be known till after a by-election on November 8. In 1950 Labour held the seat with 31,209 majority.

OTHER WOMEN'S LIVES

She delights in dancing!

hard work doesn't catch her on the wrong foot!

Mrs. Joan Boss, charming London housewife, just dances the work away! She cooks, shops and sews for family of four; makes the house sparkle upstairs and down like well polished silver. She trims the garden, exercises the Alsatian, teaches dancing classes and composes music! After each crowded day she needs her beaker of soothing Bourn-vita *every night*. It helps her enjoy the sound, dreamless sleep that makes tomorrow a lovely day.

sleep sweeter—Bourn-vita

Made by Cadburys

Right: When he died in 1965, Winston Churchill was given a full state funeral.

October 16
Pakistan Prime Minister Killed
Prime Minister Liaquat Ali Khan is assassinated in Rawalpindi.

November 1
War Games
The U.S. military holds exercises to prepare for nuclear war in the Nevada Desert.

November 11
Perón Reelected
Juan Perón is reelected president of Argentina.

December 20
Nuclear Power Plant Opens
The world's first nuclear power plant, an experimental site in Idaho, opens.

December 24
Libya Gains Independence
Libya, in North Africa, wins independence from Italy.

1952

ELIZABETH BECOMES BRITAIN'S NEW QUEEN

Princess Elizabeth and Prince Philip were in Kenya at the start of a tour of the British Commonwealth when, on February 6, 1952, they were sent news of her father King George VI's sudden death. The news meant that, at the age of 25, Princess Elizabeth had become Queen Elizabeth II. She immediately flew back to Britain and was met by Prime Minister Winston Churchill. There followed a 16-week period of official mourning, after which it was deemed acceptable to celebrate the accession of the new monarch. In her address to the nation, Queen Elizabeth declared: 'I shall always work, as my father did throughout his reign, to uphold constitutional government and to advance the happiness and prosperity of my peoples, spread as they are all the world over.' The coronation did not take place until the following year, but the Queen embarked on her official duties immediately, including the annual State Opening of Parliament and a weekly meeting with the Prime Minister.

She also undertook a series of regional tours, taking her to every part of Britain, as well as a wide-ranging tour of the Commonwealth, which took her to countries never before visited by a British monarch.

Left: Queen Elizabeth II at the State Opening of Parliament.

February 6
First Open Heart Surgery a Success
A mechanical heart is used during surgery for the first time in the United States. The operation is a success.

March 22
Hundreds Die in Tornados
Tornados in the Mississippi River Valley leave 208 people dead.

March 27
Letter Bomb in Munich
A letter bomb addressed to West German Chancellor Konrad Adenauer, explodes at Munich police station.

April 9
Revolution in Bolivia
The government of Hugo Ballivián falls in Bolivia. The new revolutionary government promises widespread reforms to help the poor.

DIARY OF ANNE FRANK PUBLISHED IN ENGLISH

On April 30, 1952, the diary of Anne Frank was first published in Britain under the title *The Diary of a Young Girl*. Originally published in Dutch by her father in 1947, it recounts the experiences of a Jewish family hiding from the Gestapo in Nazi-occupied Amsterdam, from the point of view of 13-year-old Anne. The Franks had moved from Nazi Germany to the Netherlands in 1933. They were forced into hiding in July 1942 when the Nazis occupied the Netherlands.

The Franks occupied a small apartment with another family, and in Anne's diary she details the difficulties of their shared life, as well as the joys that the world around her continues to reveal, despite living in fear. The apartment was raided in August 1944, and the families were sent to Auschwitz and Bergen-Belsen concentration camps. Anne died at Bergen-Belsen aged 15, together with her sister. Her mother died in Auschwitz-Birkenau. Her father, Otto Frank, survived, and when he returned to Amsterdam, he discovered Anne's diary among salvaged family papers. The commentary of the aspiring writer is by turns petty and sublime: she expresses her daily irritations and criticisms, the feelings of awakening sexuality typical of a girl her age, as well as comments that reveal a wisdom beyond her years. On a particular day weeks before her capture, she wrote: 'I hear the approaching thunder that, one day, will destroy us ... and yet when I look up into the sky, I somehow feel that everything will change for the better ... that peace and tranquility will return once more.'

KENYANS REBEL AGAINST BRITISH RULE

In November 1952, a revolutionary movement dedicated to the violent overthrow of colonial rule in Kenya began to attack European settlers in a bid for independence. Resentment of the British was felt most keenly by the Kikuyu in the Highlands who, by the 1950s, had become badly treated, poorly paid tenant farmers on their own land. After peaceful attempts to win reform failed, the independence fight became concentrated on the Kikuyu Central Association, which took responsibility for the uprising and began to raise funds and weapons. Rebels began to prepare for military action and pressured the moderate Kenya African Union into supporting the cause of independence. On October 20, 1952, the Colonial Office in London declared a state of emergency in Kenya. The war was to last eight years, with atrocities committed on both sides, but with a huge imbalance in casualties: 32 Europeans were killed, while the Kenyan death toll was in excess of 20,000. The rebels were referred to as Mau Mau in the British press, a term of unknown origin. Although Britain won the war in military terms, they eventually made the political and social concessions originally demanded by the Kenyans, and Kenya won its independence in 1963.

May 3
Plane Lands at North Pole
Two U.S. airmen land a plane on the geographical North Pole.

May 18
Woman Sails Atlantic Solo
Ann Davison leaves Plymouth, England, to sail the Atlantic solo. She arrives in Dominica in December.

July 13
East Germany Forms an Army
East Germany announces that it will form a National People's Army.

July 19
Olympic Games Begin
The 15th Olympiad begins in Helsinki, Finland.

1952

BRITAIN TESTS ITS FIRST NUCLEAR BOMB

THIS BANG HAS CHANGED THE WORLD

Hit-and-run gunman shot her twice

By BILL GREIG

TODAY Britain is GREAT BRITAIN again.

The orange-coloured flash which marked the explosion over the Monte Bello Islands after Britain's first atomic bomb, did more than signal the unleashing of a new and terrifying weapon of war.

It changed the world. It signalled the undisputed return of Britain to her historic position as one of the great world Powers.

Today she stands alongside America and Russia in possessing not only the secret of the atomic weapon, but also the power to produce it.

It may be that in knowledge she is ahead of both.

Today Britain is again the greatest European Power. She can defend herself, she can defend others.

Now Western Europe knows that without Britain she cannot survive.

Britain's A-bomb also lessens Western Europe's need to rely on America's strength.

Equals Now

To the Commonwealth it means that the Mother Country is now more able to deter the enemies of her sister nations in any part of the world.

'SHE THOUGHT HIS PISTOL WAS A TOY . . .'

The world asks: Was it H-bomb?

PICTURED above is the deadly radio-active cloud that rose over the Monte Bello Islands, off North-West Australia, yesterday, after scientists had exploded Britain's first atomic bomb.

Three facts set scientists all over the world guessing. The facts were:

Nothing gets her goat!

sleep sweeter **Bourn-vita**
Made by Cadburys

In the years immediately following the end of the Second World War, the British Labour government, under Prime Minister Clement Attlee, had secretly begun to develop atomic weapons. Although a committee met regularly on this development, its existence was not known about for many years. The aim was to ensure that Britain could match the U.S.A. and the U.S.S.R. The team assembled to build an atomic bomb was led by the British physicist William G. Penney, who had been instrumental in the development of the American bomb. The first plutonium production reactor was built in Windscale (now called Sellafield) in the North of England, in October 1950, but it did not go into operation until February 25, 1952, producing its first plutonium metal five weeks later. The small size and high population density of Britain meant that it was impossible to find a suitable site to test such

> 'The explosion left a crater in the seabed 20 ft (6 m) deep and 1,000 ft (326 m) across that is still there today.'

weapons. So instead the team set about sourcing a site in other Commonwealth countries, eventually settling on the Montebello Islands in Australia. On September 15, 1952, the first British nuclear device, code-named 'Hurricane', left Windscale for Australia. It was a plutonium-implosion bomb, similar to the type dropped on Nagasaki, and although most of the plutonium had been manufactured at Windscale, some of it came from Canada. On October 3, 1952, 'Hurricane' was placed inside the shell of the 1,450-ton frigate HMS *Plym*, which was anchored in 40 ft (12 m) of water 1,300 ft (400 m) from the shore of Trimouille Island. The explosion left a crater in the seabed 20 ft (6 m) deep and 1,000 ft (326 m) across that is still there today.

November 4
Eisenhower Wins U.S. Election
Republican Dwight D. Eisenhower is elected president of the United States.

November 25
The Moustrap Opens
The Agatha Christie play *The Mousetrap* opens in London. It is still playing today, more than 20,000 performances later.

December 5
London Chokes on Smog
The Great Smog, a cold fog filled with coal fumes, covers London for five days. Thousands die.

STALIN DIES

On March 5, 1953, Soviet dictator Joseph Stalin was declared dead, apparently of a brain hemorrhage, at his country home outside Moscow. The official announcement of his death was made by his closest political allies, including Lavrentiy Beria, Nikita Kruschchev, and Georgi Malenkov, and came after days of uncertainty following the announcement that he was seriously ill. His body was laid out in the Hall of Columns near the Red Square, Moscow, and millions of Russians crammed the streets to see it. Although Stalin had ruled ruthlessly and inflicted terrible deprivation on his people, many were hypnotized into such reverence for the leader they called 'Father' or 'God' that they wept openly on seeing his body. The fervor surrounding his death was so intense that hundreds of people were crushed to death in the crowds gathering to see the body. There was widespread speculation as to who would succeed him as leader, as well as speculation as to whether he had really died of natural causes.

'The fervor surrounding his death was so intense that hundreds of people were crushed to death in the crowds gathering to see the body.'

Right: St. Basil's Cathedral on Red Square, Moscow, Russia.

January 31
North Sea Floods
A tidal surge floods large parts of the Netherlands, killing 2,000 people.

February 28
D.N.A. Discovered
Scientists James Watson and Francis Crick announce that they have discovered the D.N.A. molecule.

March 26
New Polio Vaccine
Jonas Salk develops a vaccine for polio, which is made available two years later after testing for safety.

May 29
Mt. Everest Conquered
Edmund Hillary and Tensing Norgay reach the summit of Mount Everest.

1953

ELIZABETH II CROWNED

CORONATION SOUVENIR
HAPPY
This was the happiest picture of all —AND

Right: Buckingham Palace, where the Queen appeared after her coronation.

On June 2, 1953, more than a year after the death of her father King George VI, Queen Elizabeth II was crowned at a ceremony in Westminster Abbey in London. Her coronation was witnessed by more than 8,000 guests who filled the Abbey, including heads of state from all over the Commonwealth. The Archbishop of Canterbury, Dr. Geoffrey Fisher, presided over the ceremony, which involved the Queen's acceptance of the four symbols of authority: the orb, the scepter, the rod of mercy, and the royal ring of sapphires and rubies. The Archbishop placed the St. Edward's Crown on her head, and a shout of 'God Save the Queen!' was heard, followed by gun salutes. In a radio broadcast the Queen declared to the nation: 'Throughout all my life and with all my heart I shall strive to be worthy of your trust.' The streets between Buckingham Palace and Westminster Abbey were lined with crowds of well-wishers, 3 million strong, hoping to catch a glimpse of the golden state coach. The B.B.C. broadcast the ceremony live on radio and television across the world. It was the first coronation to be televised, and there had been debate as to the properness of televising such a solemn event, but the sales of television sets had rocketed in the months leading up to the coronation, and everyone crowded around the black-and-white 14-inch (35-cm) screens to see the event. It had been the Queen's own decision to televise the coronation, so that as many people as possible around the world could participate in the momentous occasion. The crowds in London, some of whom had camped out overnight to ensure a good position, were rewarded when the Queen appeared on the balcony of Buckingham Palace. In the evening, there was a display of fireworks in London and street parties spread across the country.

> 'The Archbishop placed the St. Edward's Crown on her head, and a shout of "God Save the Queen!" was heard, followed by gun salutes.'

June 7
Italian Election
The Christian Democrats win a majority in the Italian general election.

June 17
Berlin Uprising
The Soviet Union sends troops into East Berlin to put down an uprising of workers.

July 4
Miners Strike
There are riots in Poland as coal miners strike.

July 26
Castro Attacks Cuban Barracks
Fidel Castro leads a failed attack on Moncada Barracks in Santiago de Cuba.

ROSENBERGS EXECUTED

Julius and Ethel Rosenberg, both from Jewish immigrant families in New York, had met when they were just 18 and 21 at the Young Communists' League. Julius Rosenberg later qualified as an electrical engineer and worked in the Army Signal Corps. As a member of the Communist Party U.S.A., and one with access to military material, Rosenberg was recruited by the K.G.B. and began to provide design information about U.S. defense systems. Julius also recruited his wife's brother, David Greenglass, who worked at the Los Alamos National Laboratory on the development of the hydrogen bomb. Although the U.S. and U.S.S.R. had briefly been allies during the Second World War, there was great hostility and distrust between the two nations. The U.S. was particularly concerned that the Soviets might get hold of information about U.S. atomic weapons. Suspicious of how quickly the Soviets had managed to develop their own atomic bomb, the U.S. government soon tracked down insiders who they believed had passed information to the Soviets, and David Greenglass was questioned. He confessed to having passed drawings of the implosion atomic bomb to

'Rosenberg was recruited by the KGB and began to provide design information about U.S. defense systems.'

his brother-in-law, Julius Rosenberg, via his sister Ethel. Greenglass later retracted his accusation, claiming he had acted to save his wife and children and had never realized that the death penalty would be involved. The Rosenbergs were both arrested, and although Ethel's personal involvement was difficult to pin down, she was charged with conspiracy to commit espionage. Their trial was widely and unsympathetically publicized. Julius and Ethel Rosenberg were convicted of espionage on March 29, 1951 and sentenced to death – the first and last American citizens to receive such treatment during the entire Cold War period. Judge Irving Kaufman, the man who sentenced the Rosenbergs, accused them of being responsible for the deaths in the Korean War. He said, 'By your betrayal, you undoubtedly have altered the course of history to the disadvantage of our country.' Though many prominent figures, including the Pope, appealed for the couple to be spared, the Rosenbergs were executed by electric chair on June 19, 1953. Their two sons were adopted by teacher and songwriter Abel Meeropol. The Rosenbergs' execution is now widely viewed as a miscarriage of justice prompted by a heightened level of fear and hysteria during the Cold War.

August 8
Soviets Get the Bomb
The Soviet Union announces that it has developed a hydrogen bomb.

August 18
Sex Report
The Kinsey Report is published in the U.S. It is the most extensive report on sexual habits ever written.

November 9
Cambodia Wins Independence from France
Cambodia becomes an independent constitutional monarchy.

December 23
Beria Executed
Former head of Stalin's secret police, Lavrentiy Beria, is executed for treason in Moscow.

1954

FRENCH FORCED OUT OF VIETNAM

France had first begun to colonize Indochina in the late 1800s, setting up protectorates in Vietnam, Laos, and Cambodia. The Democratic Republic of Vietnam, led by Ho Chi Minh, was created after the Second World War. With British assistance, Viet Minh forces expelled the Japanese forces that had infiltrated Vietnam after France surrendered to Nazi Germany during the war. However, from 1946 to 1953, there were various outbreaks of violence between the French colonists and the Communist Viet Minh. By 1954, the French were desperate to win a decisive victory against the Viet Minh. General Navarre, in charge of the French troops, decided to provoke an all-out battle in order to give the French the best chance of securing a major victory. Convinced that if he blocked the Viet Minh's route to Laos he would force them to attack, he set up a French fortress in Dien

'The French, trapped, cut off from supplies and coming under increasing mortar fire, appealed for American assistance.'

Bien Phu. However, Navarre had wrongly assumed that the Viet Minh, under General Giap, would stage a frontal attack. Instead, they surrounded French forces in Dien Bien Phu and began digging trenches. They then moved inward, digging more trenches, while simultaneously bringing in massive reinforcements. By the time they had encircled the French, the Viet Minh outnumbered them five to one. The French, trapped, cut off from supplies, and coming under increasing mortar fire, appealed for American assistance. But President Eisenhower stalled, waiting to see what British Prime Minister Churchill would do, while Churchill was keen to await the outcome of the Geneva peace talks. Eventually, after suffering massive losses, the French were forced to withdraw from Vietnam. Between November 1953 and May 1954, the French had lost 7,000 lives and a further 11,000 soldiers had been taken prisoner. The French defeat led to the Geneva Accords, which divided Vietnam into the Communist North and the pro-West South.

March 1
Bomb Tested
The U.S. tests a hydrogen bomb in the South Pacific that is 1,000 times more powerful than the Hiroshima bomb.

May 6
First Four-Minute Mile
British athlete Roger Bannister runs a mile in under four minutes.

May 17
Court Rules Against Segregation
The U.S. supreme court rules that racially segregated schools are unconstitutional.

1954

NASSER TAKES CONTROL OF EGYPT

Following the 1952 nationalist revolution in Egypt, the Egyptian monarchy was overthrow by an army faction known as the 'Free Officers', with Colonel Gamal Abdul Nasser at its head. Setting themselves up as the Revolutionary Command Council (R.C.C.), they nominated a president and a prime minister, abolished civil titles, and ordered all political groups to rid their parties of corruption. The Egyptian monarchy had long been seen as under British control, and it was the common aim of the Free Officers to free Egypt from British interference. The revolution prompted King Farouk to abdicate in favor of his son and flee the country, but even though the monarchy remained in name, its days were numbered. Muhammed Naguib, a respected army officer and hero of the 1948 Arab–Israeli War, was nominated as President and Ali Mahir as Prime Minister – but it was Nasser who pulled the strings. He set about creating an independent republic and righting the imbalance of wealth and power in the country. The R.C.C. dealt harshly with opposition to its regime and eventually banned all political parties in 1953. In the same year, Egypt was declared a republic and the monarchy was officially abolished. A struggle followed between President Naguib and Nasser for control of the government – a struggle eventually won by Nasser. Nasser's chief aim was to evacuate the British from the base that they held at the Suez Canal. However, the British would only consider entering negotiations if the Egyptians signed the Baghdad Pact, a defense agreement designed to ward off a Soviet invasion. But Nasser, who was more wary of Western imperialism than Soviet Communism, would not agree to this. Instead, he managed to negotiate a British evacuation, with certain conditions attached, that allowed the British to return to their Suez Canal base if Egypt or Turkey were attacked. The Anglo-British agreement did not earn Nasser much popularity among his people, and there was an attempt on his life by the Muslim Brotherhood, but his nationalist reforms in Egypt steadily increased his popularity and consolidated his position.

Left: Sunset in the Egyptian capital, Cairo.

June 17
Coup in Guatemala
The reformist government of Jacobo Arbenz is overthrown in a C.I.A.-backed coup.

July 4
Rationing Ends in U.K.
The last form of food rationing in the U.K., meat rationing, ends.

August 24
President Vargas Kills Himself
Facing charges of conspiracy to murder, the president of Brazil, Getulio Vargas, kills himself.

July 7
Elvis Debut
Elvis Presley performs on the radio for the first time, singing 'That's All Right.'

63

1954

MCCARTHY KICKED OUT OF SENATE

SENATOR JOE IS KICKED OUT

COMMERCIAL TV

Prince Littler's challenge

A DEMAND that the Independent Television Authority give reasons for refusing commercial TV programme time to one of the leading entertainment groups was made last night.

The demand came in a statement by the chairman of the Incorporated Television Programme Company, Ltd., the group headed by Prince Littler as chairman and Val Parnell as managing director.

This company controls most of the top variety and dramatic talent in Britain.

Mr. Littler, in his statement issued last night, says it is admitted by the Authority that his company can make a great contribution to independent television and, therefore, they feel there must be some other reason for leaving the group out of the list of programme contractors selected.

The full statement declares:

"The exclusion of this company from the list of programme contractors so far named appears to be completely inconsistent with every reason given by the Independent Television Authority for their choice of programme contractors.

'Ludicrous'

"Apart from a ludicrous suggestion that a company with our resources should confine its activities to sub-contracting, the Authority have advanced no valid reason for our omission either to us or in any of its published statements, but on the contrary have informed us of the deep impression which our application made on them and their consciousness of the great contribution we could make to independent television.

"SINCE

1—We are non-political;

2—We have the financial resources;

3—We are completely representative in the entertainment field and capable of producing 'the balanced programmes' upon which the Independent Television Authority have lain such stress;

4—We have offered to co-operate with all other programme contractors and to make our programmes available to them;

5—We have offered to combine with varying newspaper interests.

"We can only conclude that other considerations have influenced the Authority in excluding our company from placing its wide entertainment facilities before the public and we therefore think that in fairness to us and the viewing public these considerations should be disclosed by the Independent Television Authority.

Discussion

"It was our intention to discuss this statement with the Independent Television Authority before issuing same but, as we have been unable to obtain an appointment during the last forty-eight hours, we feel its issue can be no longer held up now that the final allocations have been announced."

● *Sir Robert Fraser, Director-General of the Independent Television Authority, said last night: "I am sure that the I.T.A. will consider this statement at its next meeting."*

What the "Mirror" Says. See Page 2.

Democrat victory in Senate strips him of his power

From RALPH CHAMPION, New York, Thursday

SENATOR Joe McCarthy, most-feared man in America because of his notorious witch-hunts, has been kicked out of power by the voters.

The last election result to be announced gave the Democrats control of the Senate.

This means Republican McCarthy will be sacked from his job as chairman of two Senate committees investigating people accused of subversive activities.

For in the New Year the Democrats will have the right to nominate all chairmen of Senate committees now presided over by the Republicans.

And the cry "Joe must go" will no longer be just a political slogan. It will be a Congressional ORDER.

Shattered Ambition

So, the family man of America has shattered the dreams and ambitions of the man who coined a new and hated word in the English language, "McCarthyism."

Though McCarthy remains a Senator, the Democrats' election victory will strip him of the semi-police powers which he used to force reluctant witnesses to undergo gruelling cross-examination.

And some of those grillings by red-baiter Joe led even President Eisenhower to protest.

But now Joe will have no more power than any other Senator with a bee in his bonnet.

His job as chairman of the investigating committees will be taken over by one of his most avowed enemies — Senator John McClellan of Arkansas.

McClellan, who was a Democrat minority member of the committees, has always bee one of McCarthy's bitterest critics.

It was a hairsbreadth Democrat victory in Oregon that finally crushed the power-dreams of Senator Joe.

This win gave the Democrats a 48-47 majority in the Senate, with one Independent pledged to vote for them. They already had won a majority in Congress.

Recount Possible

The result at Oregon was so close—the final majority, not yet announced, may be only 2,000—that a recount may be ordered.

Recounts have already been ordered in New Jersey and Ohio, and these may still change control of the Senate.

But all the experts concede that the Democrats have won.

But the saddest political figure of all is Senator McCarthy, the man who gambled his future on a nation's hysteria — and found, after all, that the ordinary decent family voters were against him.

● President Eisenhower is no happier than Senator Joe. In future he will be unable to take any major step without first consulting his opponents, the Democrats.

Witch-hunter McCarthy

She fell in love at 14

FOURTEEN-YEAR-OLD Beryl Smith (above) is the girl whose love affair with a German schoolboy ended in his death from an overdose of sleeping-tablets.

Yesterday, as told on Page 3, Beryl, who lives at Rothwell, Yorks, talked about her romance with Egbert Gretzschel, 15.

"We were hoping to be married," she said.

And of their letters Beryl said: "Instead of putting kisses, we wrote our thoughts. . . . He said he couldn't sleep for thinking of England and me."

Egbert tried to get back. But at Dover he found that he could not land. And Egbert was found dead in his steamer cabin.

Joseph McCarthy was a self-made man who worked his way up from uneducated farm boy to Republican senator. His first election to office was as a Republican circuit court judge, and it was achieved by means of a campaign that hinted at the senility and financial corruption of his Democrat opponent. After the war, when he ran for the Senate office as a Republican candidate, he tarnished the name of his Republican rival Robert La Follette by deriding his lack of military service (when in fact he had been too old to join) and falsely accusing him of war profiteering. In the Senate, McCarthy made a name for himself as a harsh dealer, in one instance suggesting that striking miners should be enlisted in the army and then shot for insubordination. He was not popular, and some of his past deceptions began to surface. When it came time for his re-election in 1950, McCarthy searched for a way to keep hold of his position of power and decided to launch a brutal attack on American Communists within the government. He teamed up with the journalist Jack Anderson and feared F.B.I. boss J. Edgar Hoover, and together they created a list of Communist subversives within the Democrat ranks. McCarthy devoted all his energy to exposing politicians who were so-called 'loyalty risks'. In this climate of Red hysteria, Republican Dwight D. Eisenhower was elected President in 1952. McCarthy continued to pursue his campaign, now targeting writers, artists, actors, and academics and prompting many to leave the country for Europe in disgust. Gradually, more and more journalists and broadcasters gained the confidence to speak out, and McCarthy's reputation was steadily eroded. One newspaper article said: 'In this long, degrading travesty of the democratic process, McCarthy has shown himself to be evil and unmatched in malice.' He was finally fired from the Senate in 1954. McCarthy died three years later from cirrhosis of the liver caused by severe alcoholism.

'McCarthy searched for a way to keep hold of his position, launching a brutal attack on American Communists.'

October 18
First Transistor Radio
Texas Instruments makes the first transistor radio in the U.S.

October 31
Algeria Revolts
The Algerian National Liberation Front begins armed campaign against French rule.

November 14
Nasser Made President
Prime Minister Gamal Abdel Nasser is made President of Egypt.

December 2
McCarthy Condemned
The U.S. Senate votes 67–22 to condemn Senator Joseph McCarthy.

December 24
Laos Wins Independence
Laos becomes a constitutional monarchy independent from France.

PRINCESS CHOOSES ROYAL POSITION OVER LOVE

Queen Elizabeth II's sister Princess Margaret first met Group Captain Peter Townsend when she was still a teenager. He was equerry to her father King George VI and at the time was married, with two children. Townsend later separated from his wife and became romantically involved with Margaret. The affair was kept out of the press for many years, but at the Queen's coronation, when Princess Margaret was still only 22, she let slip a gesture of familiar affection when she brushed some fluff from his jacket, and the news of their relationship broke at last. Queen Elizabeth, who already knew of their plans to marry, had asked them to wait until after her coronation to announce the news. Marrying a divorcé was still viewed with considerable disapproval, especially in light of the Church's stance that Christian marriage could never be dissolved. According to the British constitution, however, Princess Margaret needed only the permission of her sister to marry up until the age of 25. Once she was older than 25, she needed the permission of Parliament. Group Captain Townsend was still working in the royal household at the time, and soon after the coronation he was sent to Brussels to work for the British Embassy. He was away for two years, and in that time Princess Margaret turned 25. She was already well aware that Parliament would not consent to the marriage, so if she wanted to go ahead with it, her only choice was to renounce her title, including any financial income that went with it, as well as her succession to the throne. She chose instead to renounce Group Captain Townsend, and, on October 31, 1955, issued a statement through the press that she would not marry him. She said: 'I have reached this decision entirely alone, and in doing so I have been strengthened by the unfailing support and devotion of Group Captain Townsend.' Princess Margaret later married the photographer Antony Armstrong-Jones in 1960.

MARGARET DECIDES: DUTY BEFORE LOVE

PRINCESS MARGARET, in this dramatic announcement from Clarence House last night, told the world that she had renounced the love of Peter Townsend:

"I would like it to be known that I have decided not to marry Group Captain Peter Townsend. I have been aware that, subject to my renouncing my rights of succession, it might have been possible for me to contract a civil marriage. But, mindful of the Church's teaching that Christian marriage is indissoluble, and conscious of my duty to the Commonwealth, I have resolved to put these considerations before any others. I have reached this decision entirely alone, and in doing so I have been strengthened by the unfailing support and devotion of Group Captain Townsend. I am deeply grateful for the concern of all those who have constantly prayed for my happiness. (Signed) Margaret."

Townsend leaves—alone SEE BACK PAGE

Left: Princess Margaret meets The Beatles in November 1963.

January 25
Atomic Clock
Scientists at Columbia University develop an atomic clock that is accurate to within one second every 300 years.

February 28
Israelis Enter Gaza
Israeli troops enter Egyptian-controlled Gaza in pursuit of attackers. Tensions between Israel and Egypt rise.

March 20
Rock'n'Roll Movie
American teenagers dance in the aisles to the music of Bill Haley in the film *Blackboard Jungle.*

April 5
Churchill Resigns
Eighty-year-old Winston Churchill resigns as Prime Minister of the U.K.

April 18
Einstein Dies
Physicist Albert Einstein dies in Princeton, New Jersey, at the age of 76.

1955

CIVIL UNREST IN CYPRUS ESCALATES

By the 1950s, around 80% of the residents of Cyprus were Greek. The Greek government claimed a right of ownership over the island, and Greek Cypriots longed for *enosis* – or union with Greece. But Turkish Cypriots made up about 18% of the population, and looked to Turkey as their homeland. Turkey had been the legal owner of the island until 1923, when it was colonized by Britain. In 1951, an organization of Greek Cypriots seeking *enosis* formed a military wing known as E.O.K.A. ('National Organization of Cypriot Fighters' in the Greek language). The decision to take arms was prompted by the refusal of the British to consider loosening their hold on Cyprus. In 1955, British troops were posted to Cyprus after being evacuated from Egypt. Anti-British riots broke out, and on April 1, 1955, E.O.K.A. launched a campaign of violence against British rule in a series of planned attacks on police and military institutions. After a few months of attacks and counterattacks, a tripartite conference was convened in August 1955 in London, with representatives from the Greek, Turkish, and British governments. All sides were dissatisfied by the conference, which achieved nothing concrete. Shortly afterwards, Cyprus was offered a limited form of self-government. The offer was rejected, and E.O.K.A. continued its campaign of violence, using explosives and weapons smuggled in from Greece. Talks between British Governor Harding and Cypriot representative Archbishop Makarios were unsuccessful, and Makarios was eventually exiled. However, the level of violence on Cyprus only increased. It was not until 1960 that an agreement was reached. Rather than union with Greece, Cyprus was granted full independence.

MALENKOV FORCED OUT IN U.S.S.R.

Following the death of Joseph Stalin in 1953, Georgy Malenkov was the sole leader of the U.S.S.R. for six months, until Nikita Khrushchev was made First Secretary, creating a power share. It was a time of increasing treachery within the U.S.S.R., making it impossible to judge whether associates were allies or enemies. During the two years of Malenkov's premiership, from 1953 to 1955, he tried to move the U.S.S.R. toward the production of consumer goods, rather than relying solely on heavy industry. He also spoke out against the nuclear armament program. However, he soon fell out of favor, just as he had watched others fall. His previous association with Lavrentiy Beria, who had been executed as a traitor in 1953, tarnished his reputation, and Khrushchev seemed to offer more rapid reform. Malenkov was fired from the government in February 1955. He would try once more to seize power from Khrushchev in 1961, a move that got him thrown out of the Communist Party and exiled from the U.S.S.R.

May 9
West Germany Joins N.A.T.O.
The newly formed Federal Republic of Germany joins N.A.T.O.

May 14
Warsaw Pact Signed
The Soviet Union and Communist regimes in Eastern Europe sign a defense treaty as a response to N.A.T.O.

July 13
Ellis Hanged
Ruth Ellis is hanged for the murder of her lover, the last woman to be executed in the U.K.

August 20
Riots in North Africa
Hundreds are killed in anti-French riots in Morocco and Algeria.

August 27
New Book of Records
The *Guinness Book of World Records* is published for the first time.

ACT PASSED TO END KILLER SMOG

The winter of 1952 to 1953 was a particularly cold one in the U.K. As a result, more coal than usual was burned in household fires, and more people used their cars. The combined effect of increased soot, tar, and exhaust fumes created thick smog that hung in the air over London for four days. It became known as the Great Smog. The smog was so thick that it infiltrated buildings – cinemas and theaters were forced to close – and made transportation almost impossible. Substances in the smoke combined with sulfur dioxide to form a lethal acid rain, and hospitals were swamped with the sick. In the course of a few months, death rates multiplied by almost ten: most victims were the vulnerable, both young and old, and most fatalities involved respiratory problems. In all, thousands of deaths were attributed to the smog. In the following year, the smog reappeared – though less critically – and hospitals went on red alert. The increasing gravity of the situation forced the government to seriously address the issue of air pollution, and officials from the Ministry of Housing worked on new proposals throughout 1955. The result of this work was the Clean Air Act of 1956.

'In the course of a few months, death rates multiplied by almost ten.'

KILLER SMOG
London gasps again
HOSPITALS READY FOR VICTIMS

David saved his mother's life

DAILY MIRROR REPORTER

IT'S that killer smog again— the worst this winter.

IKE WANTS CHINA TRUCE

A DRAMATIC move by President Eisenhower is reported in World News Spotlight on the Back Page.

September 19
Perón Ousted
Argentinian President Juan Perón is overthrown in a military coup.

September 30
James Dean Dies
Actor James Dean dies when his car crashes at high speed in California.

November 12
End for Ellis Island
The immigration center on Ellis Island in New York Harbor closes.

December 1
Parks Makes a Stand
African American Rosa Parks is arrested in Alabama for refusing to give up her seat on a bus.

December 14
United Nations Expands
Sixteen nations join the U.N., the biggest single expansion since it was formed.

1956

BOYCOTT ON BUSES ENDS SEGREGATION

Right: Rosa Parks

Although the American Civil War had brought about the abolition of slavery in America, a massive divide remained between North and South in terms of their policies toward African Americans. In the South, a strict enforcement of black and white segregation remained in place despite a federal ruling banning segregation in public education. A movement to desegregate, or integrate, buses in Montgomery, Alabama was instigated in 1949 by a black academic, Jo Ann Robinson, after she was abused by a bus driver for refusing to move to the back of a bus. Over the next few years, there were a few well-publicized incidents involving blacks who refused to give up their bus seats to whites. The most famous was the case of the seamstress Rosa Parks, who was arrested for her refusal to give up her seat. In 1954, Jo Ann Robinson wrote to the Mayor of Montgomery, warning him of the planned boycott. When, on December 1, 1955, Rosa Parks was arrested, the bus boycott was launched. The boycott had the backing of a group of ministers, including Martin Luther King Jr., who formed the Montgomery Improvement Association (M.I.A.) to manage the boycott. It took a great deal of organization, since most black people relied on the bus service to get them to work, and the white city officials did everything in their power to make it difficult, including prosecuting the black cab services that had begun to charge a 10-cent fare (the same as the bus fare). There were several acts of violence, including the bombing of Martin Luther King's home, but still the boycott continued, and various attempts at negotiating an end came to nothing. Next, it was decided that the ringleaders should be arrested using an old law prohibiting boycotts, and Dr. King was the first defendant to be tried, receiving a $1,000 fine and 386 days in jail. The original aim of the movement had been to make the segregation policy fairer, but now complete desegregation on the buses was the goal. The M.I.A. took the issue to the federal court, and segregation on public buses was ruled to be unconstitutional. On December 21, 1956, with the federal ruling that buses could no longer be segregated, the boycott ended. The Civil Rights movement had won its first major victory.

February 25
Stalin Denounced
Soviet leader Nikita Khrushchev attacks the cult of personality surrounding Stalin.

March 23
Pakistan Celebrates
A national holiday is held in Pakistan to celebrate its becoming an Islamic Republic.

April 19
Princess Grace
Actress Grace Kelly marries Prince Rainier III of Monaco to become Princess Grace.

April 22
Morocco Joins the U.N.
Newly independent Morocco joins the United Nations.

May 8
Groundbreaking Play Opens
John Osborne's *Look Back in Anger* marks a new era of political theatre in the U.K.

SUEZ CRISIS DEEPENS

On October 29, 1956, Britain, France, and Israel launched an attack on Egypt following Egypt's decision, three months earlier, to nationalize the Suez Canal. The British had taken control of the canal when they occupied Egypt in 1882. In the 1950s, the canal played a vital role in the passage of oil from the Middle East to Europe, and Britain presided over a massive garrison of some 80,000 military personnel at their Suez Canal base. In July 1952, the military coup of the Free Officers movement in Egypt ousted the British-backed monarchy, eventually leading to the staged evacuation of the British from their Suez base in October 1954. The new Egyptian republic under General Nasser was angered by Britain's role in the creation of Israel and had begun a policy of refusing access through the canal to ships bound to or from Israel. The United States had previously offered to fund the building of the Aswan Dam. But in July 1956, their offer was withdrawn after Nasser officially recognized the People's Republic of China. Nasser responded by ordering the immediate nationalization of the Suez Canal. The nationalization dealt a severe blow to Britain, in both economic and military terms. In August 1956, crisis talks were held in London between the British, French, and Americans. The French and British agreed to work together, and three months after the nationalization, they enlisted Israeli support in a bid to regain control of the Suez Canal. The plan was that Israel would invade Egypt, and Britain and France would intervene and insist on the need for Anglo-French protection of such an important area. Although the military operation was successful, U.S. President Eisenhower was concerned that the Soviet Union would become involved, and U.S. opposition eventually forced the British and French to abandon their hard-won position. The U.N. General Council demanded that Britain and France withdraw from Egypt immediately, which they did. British Prime Minister Anthony Eden announced a ceasefire on November 6, 1956, without consulting France or Israel, and then resigned as Prime Minister, having lost political authority over his handling of the crisis. U.N. peacekeepers were stationed in the region to restore stability, marking the first use of U.N. personnel in this way.

May 24
First Eurovision Song Contest
Lys Assia wins the inaugural Eurovision Song Contest for Switzerland.

June 10
Revolt in Argentina
A Peronist revolt in Argentina is crushed. Twenty-six revolt leaders are executed.

June 28
U.K. Votes to End Hanging
The House of Commons votes to end capital punishment but is overruled by the House of Lords.

August 11
Artist Killed in Car Crash
American artist Jackson Pollock dies aged 44 after crashing his car.

September 21
Dictator Assassinated
Anastasio Somoza, the dictator of Nicaragua, is shot dead.

1956

NEW DRUG TO FIGHT POLIO USED IN BRITAIN

Polio, the common term for *anterior poliomyelitis*, is a viral disease of the nervous system that can cause complete paralysis and death. Until the 1950s, there were outbreaks of polio every summer, affecting between 15,000 to 30,000 each year. In 1949, Professor John Enders made the Nobel Prize-winning discovery that the polio virus could be grown in large quantities, and for the first time, the possibility of a vaccine became real. However, turning a living virus into a 'killed' vaccine requires an additional substance to destroy the sickness-producing effect without preventing the production of antibodies. In 1952, Jonas Salk, head of the Virus Research Laboratory at the University of Pittsburgh, used formaldehyde to 'inactivate' the viral matter so that it would cause antibody production without causing the disease. In April 1954, the first polio immunization campaign was launched in the U.S., focusing on schoolchildren. That same year, hundreds of people contracted polio from Salk's vaccine, and many died. Apparently, the virus had not been completely inactivated. However, the vaccine was redeveloped, despite intense controversy, and in the summer of 1955, over 4 million doses were administered in the United States. By 1956, the vaccine was being used in the U.K., and by 1959, it was available in nearly 100 other countries. In 1958, a new form of the vaccine, developed by American physician Albert Sabin, would become available in oral form. This was a live virus, but it was a rare type that had been isolated specifically because it did not penetrate the central nervous system.

NEW WATER SPEED RECORD

Englishman Donald Campbell was as obsessed with speed as his father Malcolm Campbell had been. Sir Malcolm Campbell had set 13 speed records on land and water, and his son Donald began his own attempts in his father's boat *Bluebird K4*. However, Donald soon realized that he would need a new craft to set new records, and so the *Bluebird K7* was built for him. The boat was made entirely of metal and had a jet engine. It was a time of exciting technological advances, and the British nation was thrilled. In 1955, Donald Campbell reached 202 mph (324 kph) on Coniston Water in the Lake District of England, breaking the world water-speed record. In 1956, he reached 225 mph (362 kph).

Above: Donald Campbell in Bluebird.

October 24
Soviets Invade Hungary
The Red Army crosses into Hungary to put down an anti-Soviet revolution.

November 6
Ike Wins Second Term
President Dwight D. Eisenhower wins the U.S. presidential elections.

December 2
Castro Enters Cuba
Fidel Castro lands in Cuba to start a guerrilla war against the Batista regime.

December 5
Britain's First Female Judge
Defense barrister Rose Heilbron is appointed the U.K.'s first female judge.

1957

STRAY DOG BECOMES FIRST CREATURE IN SPACE

On October 4, 1957, the U.S.S.R. launched a satellite called *Sputnik 1* into space. The satellite was a 183-lb (83-kg) metal sphere, outstripping anything the Americans had been preparing to launch, and it became the first artificial satellite to successfully orbit the earth. The day after the launch, it was reported in the Russian newspaper *Pravda*: 'As the result of a large, dedicated effort by scientific-research institutes, the world's first artificial satellite of the Earth has been created. On October 4, 1957 in the U.S.S.R. the first successful satellite launch has been achieved. According to preliminary data, the rocket launcher carried the satellite to the necessary orbital speed of about 8,000 meters per second. At the present time the satellite is moving in an elliptical trajectory around the Earth, and its flight can be observed in the rays of the eastern and western Sun with the help of simple optical instruments.' Although the Americans were beaten in the space race, they did not hold back congratulating the Russians for this major achievement. Only a month later, the Russians launched a second artificial satellite, *Sputnik 2*, weighing 250 lbs (114 kg); this time with a living passenger on board in the form of a stray dog named Laika. At the time, there was a good deal of controversy over the cruelty inflicted on Laika, and though the Soviets acknowledged that she would not return alive, they claimed that she would die painlessly during the journey. At the time, it was reported that Laika had survived for several days in orbit, but it was revealed in 2002 that she died of overheating and panic not long after takeoff. But she had by then served her purpose in proving that a living being could survive takeoff, and opened up the possibility of humans undertaking space travel.

> **'Sputnik 1 became the first artificial satellite to successfully orbit the earth.'**

Above: Laika installed in the tiny cabin of Sputnik 2.

January 10
Britain Has New Prime Minister
Harold Macmillan becomes the Prime Minister of the U.K. following Anthony Eden's resignation.

March 6
Ghana Wins Independence
Ghana is the first African country to win independence from Britain.

March 25
E.E.C. Formed
Six European nations sign the Treaty of Rome to establish the European Economic Community.

April 12
Poem Seized for Obscenity
U.S. customs seize a copy of Allen Ginsberg's poem *Howl* for obscenity.

71

1957

FIGHT TO DESEGREGATE SOUTH CONTINUES

The Civil Rights Act of 1957, which had been squeezed through the U.S. Congress after Senator Lyndon B. Johnson watered it down, outlined measures for desegregation, including permitting black students into previously white-only schools. The Governor of Arkansas, Orval Faubus, was determined to oppose the federal law of desegregating schools. In September 1957, on the day that Little Rock High School was due to accept its first African-American students, Governor Faubus stationed 270 National Guards at the school, ostensibly to prevent any outbreak of violence. In truth, the Guards were there to prevent the nine black students from entering the school. The students stayed away for the first day of term, but on the second day, they were accompanied to school by two white ministers and two black ministers. The National Guards barred their entry, and white students and adults alike hurled verbal abuse. The whole episode was televised, drawing attention to the ugly reality of segregation in the South. A state governor had been seen the world over disobeying federal law, and President Eisenhower was forced to act. When the nine students made a second attempt to enter the school some weeks later, the President sent 1,000 paratroopers to keep order. Although the nine students eventually made it through the school year, it was a year filled with hatred, abuse, and resentment. In the school year of 1958 to 1959, Faubus closed all schools rather than allow blacks into white schools. The first attempts to end segregation had failed.

QUEEN VISITS NEW YORK

More than 1 million New Yorkers turned out to welcome Queen Elizabeth II at the end of her five-day American tour to promote the U.N. in October 1957. Overhead planes performed victory rolls to the sound of a 21-gun salute.

April 24
Sky at Night Begins
Patrick Moore presents the first episode in the long-running astronomy show *The Sky at Night* on the B.B.C.

May 2
McCarthy Dies
Senator Joe McCarthy dies of cirrhosis of the liver brought on by years of alcoholism.

May 15
Matthews Retires
Footballer Stanley Matthews plays his last game for England in a 23-year-long international career.

June 27
Hurricane Destroys Town
The town of Cameron, Louisiana, is flattened by Hurricane Audrey, killing 400 people.

July 25
Tunisia Becomes Republic
Habib Bourguiba is elected President of Tunisia and abolishes the monarchy.

IKE'S PROUD SPACE ROCKET BOAST

In the ongoing space race between the U.S. and the U.S.S.R., President Eisenhower was proud to announce in November 1957 that the Americans could bring a rocket *back* from space; a feat that he was sure the Russians had not yet achieved. As proof, at a press conference he held up the very cone-shaped rocket head that he said had been to space and back. The cone was intended to hold an H-bomb warhead in the experimental X-17 rocket, and Eisenhower's announcement signaled to the American people that they were ahead of the Soviets in the space race. To drive the point home, Eisenhower told the nation: 'Although the Soviets are obviously ahead of us in satellite development, the overall military strength of the free world today is greater than that of the Communist countries.' He added, 'We are well ahead of the Soviets in the nuclear field, both in quantity and in quality, and we intend to stay ahead.'

> **'President Eisenhower was proud to announce in November 1957 that the Americans could bring a rocket back from space; a feat that he was sure the Russians had not yet achieved.'**

Left: A Jupiter-A rocket launched by the Army Ballistic Missile Agency in 1957.

August 28
Senator's Epic Speech
U.S. Senator Strom Thurmond makes a 24-hour-long speech in a failed attempt to block a civil rights bill.

November 1
Mackinac Bridge Opened
The Mackinac Bridge in Michigan opens to traffic, and becomes the world's longest suspension bridge.

November 25
Ike Suffers Stroke
U.S. President Eisenhower suffers a stroke that leaves his speech impaired.

December 4
Train Crashes in London
Ninety-two people die when a train crashes in Lewisham in London.

December 6
U.S. Rocket Blows Up
The rocket blows up on the launch pad in the U.S.'s first attempt to launch a satellite into space.

1958

FRANCE VOTES FOR NEW REPUBLIC

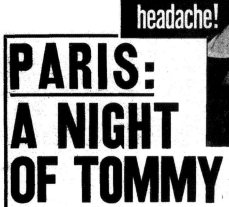

Above: Charles de Gaulle

French statesman Charles de Gaulle was a military man who had distinguished himself in both world wars, and led the Resistance group, the Free French, after France fell to the Nazis. As president and military commander of the Free French, he had successfully led them to liberate Paris from the Nazis in August 1944. After the liberation of France, de Gaulle became the provisional president of the new France, but over the following years he was both in and out of power. By May 1958, France was on the brink of civil war over the issue of Algeria's independence. De Gaulle was called back to office to deal with the crisis, and he drafted the constitution of a Fifth Republic of France. The new constitution granted more power to the president and was designed to put an end to a series of weak governments. De Gaulle himself became the first president of the new republic on January 8, 1959.

February 1
New Arab State
Egypt and Syria unite to form the United Arab Republic. Nasser is nominated as president.

February 23
Fangio Kidnapped
Argentinian racing driver Juan Manuel Fangio is kidnapped by Cuban rebels. He is released the next day.

February 25
C.N.D. Launched
In Britain, the Campaign for Nuclear Disarmament is launched by philosopher Bertrand Russell.

March 27
New Soviet Premiere
Nikita Khrushchev becomes the new leader of the Soviet Union.

May 13
Protesters Storm Offices
French Algerians, fearing a French withdrawal from Algeria, seize government offices in Algiers.

SOCCER AIR TRAGEDY

On February 6, 1958, a plane carrying Manchester United Football team and their entourage back from a European Cup match in Belgrade crashed while taking off from Munich Airport. Seven Manchester United players died in the accident, depriving the country of some of its most promising football talent. The team was known as the 'Busby Babes' after their manager Matt Busby and the nation mourned the loss of such youthful promise. Their star striker, Bobby Charlton, was one of the survivors. In total, 21 people died in the crash, including sports journalists and team managers. The British European Airways plane had stopped to refuel in Munich, Germany, where there was a heavy snowstorm. Twice the pilot tried to take off, and on his third attempt, he overshot the runway, crashing into a house, and the plane burst into flames. The runway had been swamped in slush, leaving the plane unable to take off. The pilot was later cleared of any blame.

Above: A clock at Manchester United's ground, Old Trafford, showing the time of the crash.

PROTESTORS MARCH AGAINST THE BOMB

In 1950s Britain, mainstream protest against the development of nuclear weapons came under the wing of the Campaign for Nuclear Disarmament (C.N.D.). However, a more radical group also existed. This group was known as the Direct Action Committee Against Nuclear War (D.A.C.), and its aim was to halt nuclear armament via marches, vigils, industrial action, and civil disobedience. D.A.C. leaders were prepared to go to jail for their actions and had systems in place to enable protest to continue while their leaders were jailed. The D.A.C. was headed by Harold Steele, and their first major action was a march on the Atomic Weapons Research Establishment at Aldermaston in 1958. From that point on, the C.N.D. took over and made the march from Aldermaston to London an annual event over the Easter weekend.

'DAC leaders were prepared to go to jail for their actions.'

June 16
Nagy Hanged
The anti-Soviet former Prime Minister of Hungary, Imre Nagy, is hanged for treason.

June 29
Brazil Win World Cup
Brazil beat Sweden 5–2 in the final to win their first World Cup.

July 29
N.A.S.A. Created
The National Aeronautics and Space Administration is formed to further the U.S.'s space program.

September 1
Cod War
A conflict over fishing rights breaks out between Iceland and the U.K. It is popularly known as the Cod War.

October 21
Women in Lords
Female peers are allowed to sit in the British second chamber, the House of Lords.

1958

KING KILLED IN IRAQI COUP

On July 14, 1958, an army group of Arab nationalists calling themselves the Free Officers seized power in Iraq, assassinating 23-year-old King Faisal II, as well as members of his family and the Prime Minister of the Iraqi-Jordan Alliance. British control in Iraq via the King had long been a source of violent resentment for many Iraqis. Although this control had officially come to an end in 1932, the Iraqi government upheld British interests to the last, especially with regards to oil. Under the monarchy, all resistance had been ruthlessly stamped out, with any form of protest or demonstration banned, as well as opposition political parties. The people took to the streets to celebrate the overthrow of the monarchy, and the British Embassy was ransacked and set alight. Major-General Abdul Karim el Qasim, the leader of the coup, declared himself Prime Minister and Commander-in-Chief of the new Iraqi regime, which would be a 'people's republic' closely allied to its Arab neighbors. He immediately set about making a defense pact with the United Arab Republic (U.A.R.), a recently formed alliance of Egypt and Syria. Western powers were concerned not only about their own oil interests in the region but about the stability of the Baghdad Pact, the defense pact between Turkey, Persia, and Pakistan that was aimed at protecting the Middle East from the threat of Soviet Communism. Following emergency meetings, British and U.S. troops were sent to Jordan and Lebanon to guard against possible copycat Arab nationalist revolts.

'British control in Iraq via the King had long been a source of violent resentment for many Iraqis.'

Right: King Faisal II.

October 28
New Pope Elected
Angelo Giuseppe Roncalli is elected the new Pope. He takes the name Pope John XXIII.

November 10
First Bossa Nova Record
Joao Gilberto makes the first Bossa Nova record in Rio de Janeiro.

November 30
French Elections
Supporters of Charles de Gaulle win a parliamentary majority in France.

December 5
Britain's First Motorway
The Preston Bypass, the first stretch of motorway in Britain, is opened.

NIXON SPEAKS ON SOVIET TELEVISION

SO CHILLY AS JOVIAL MR. K DROPS IN ON IKE

● Silent crowd drama

On July 24, 1959, during Richard Nixon's 11-day tour of the U.S.S.R., the American Vice-President and Soviet leader Nikita Khrushchev engaged in a heated public debate about the relative merits of capitalism and Communism. While walking together around an American trade fair in Moscow, they stopped at a mock-up of an American kitchen boasting all the latest gadgets, including a refrigerator, toaster, and juicer. Khrushchev waved it off dismissively, claiming that although the Americans thought to impress the Soviets with their technological advancement, the Soviets themselves already had all these gadgets in their own kitchens. Nixon replied: 'We do not claim to astonish the Soviet people. We hope to show our right to choose. We do not wish to have decisions made at the top by government officials who say that all homes should be built in the same way.' From there, the argument escalated, with Khrushchev threatening Nixon over foreign military bases and Nixon declaring that the Americans would not be dictated to. Khrushchev then boasted that the Soviets built better rockets, a claim that Nixon tried to counter by implying that the U.S. could equal them. Eventually, the two men laughed off their argument and apologized, but what made this exchange into international news was that it was filmed on the first video tape recorder. Unexpectedly, Khrushchev allowed Nixon to make a televised address to the Soviet people, and Nixon used the occasion to once again denounce Communism, warning of dire consequences if it was forcibly spread beyond Soviet borders. Nixon's popularity on returning home was considerably increased.

Right: An American cooker from the 1950s.

1959

BATISTA FLEES CUBA

On January 1, 1959, the Cuban dictator Fulgencio Batista fled his country in the face of a revolutionary coup led by Fidel Castro. While declaring that government forces had been victorious in the Battle of Santa Clara against Castro's guerrilla forces, Batista simultaneously evacuated his family, his cabinet, and his military aides to the Dominican Republic, Florida, and New Orleans on various planes. He left behind a military junta to rule in his absence, but it was swiftly toppled by rebel forces. A former soldier, General Batista had twice held absolute power in Cuba, first from 1933 to 1942 and then again from 1952. His regime had enjoyed the support of the United States for a number of years, but his loss of popularity forced the U.S. to consider alternatives. Faced with the prospect of Castro's 'leftist' revolutionary group, the U.S. continued to support Batista, albeit halfheartedly. However, Batista's own people had become increasingly disillusioned with his government. On the other hand, Fidel Castro offered hope and change with his fiery nationalistic talk and personal charisma. On January 7, 1959, he and his followers – including his brother Raúl Castro and Ernesto 'Che' Guevara – entered Havana in triumph. Cubans everywhere celebrated the departure of Batista and welcomed Castro with open arms. The U.S. was increasingly concerned about the safety of their interests in Cuba. It was not long before the new leader Castro nationalized American properties and made strong ties with Communist Russia. The U.S. reacted by cutting all ties with Cuba and bringing a trade and travel embargo into force.

May 28
Monkeys in Space
Two rhesus monkeys on board a U.S. spaceship return to Earth alive.

July 17
Early Human Skull Found
A skull of an early hominid, named *Australopithecus*, is discovered in Tanzania.

July 27
Holliday Dies
U.S. singer Billie Holliday dies of liver failure aged 44.

August 21
Hawaii Becomes U.S. State
Hawaii is made the 50th state of the United States.

September 15
Khrushchev in America
Soviet premier Nikita Khrushchev begins a 13-day visit to the U.S.A.

SOVIET ROCKET LANDS ON THE MOON

On September 12, 1959, the U.S.S.R. launched a second rocket aimed at the Moon, and this time the target was reached. The first attempt, launched on January 2, 1958, had successfully launched, but it missed the Moon and continued out into space. It was necessary for the Moon rocket, *Luna 2*, to reach a speed of 7 mps (11 kps) in order for it to counter the pull of Earth's gravitational force and break away from the Earth. *Luna 2* reached the Moon, 236,875 miles (382,056 km) away, 36 hours after its launch – 1 minute and 24 seconds later than estimated. On board were various scientific instruments intended for measuring the magnetic fields of the Earth and Moon, among other things. The instruments were sealed in a container to prevent any contamination of the Moon. The container also held the Communist 'sickle and star' flag, although the U.S.S.R. denied that it would be making any territorial claims on the Moon. The successful landing took place just days before Soviet leader Nikita Khrushchev was due to visit Washington, D.C. The timing was extremely opportune given the competitive nature of the space race between the U.S. and the U.S.S.R.

Right: The Soviet 'sickle and star' flag.

September 26
Typhoon Hits Japan
Over 5,000 people are killed when Typhoon Vera hits the Japanese island of Honshu.

October 21
New York Museum Opens
The Guggenheim Museum in New York opens its doors to the public.

December 1
Antarctic Agreement
Twelve countries, including the United States and the Soviet Union, sign a pact to preserve Antarctica.

December 2
Dam Collapses
The Malpasset Dam in southern France collapses, flooding the town of Frejus and killing over 400 people.

December 9
Ike in India
U.S. President Eisenhower visits India and addresses the country's parliaments.

1960

J.F.K. WINS U.S. PRESIDENTIAL ELECTION

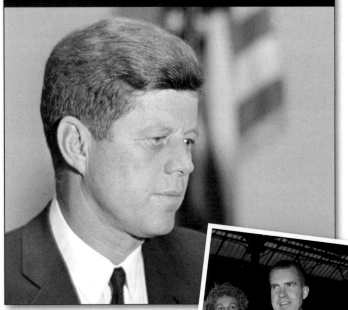

GIANT U.S. RUSH TO VOTE

'In his inauguration speech, he made the famous declaration: "Ask not what your country can do for you – ask what you can do for your country"'

Above: Richard and Pat Nixon.

On November 8, 1960, at the age of 43, John F. Kennedy made history by becoming the youngest ever and first Roman Catholic President of the United States. In a presidential campaign that featured televised public debates for the first time, Kennedy narrowly defeated the Republican candidate, Richard Nixon, winning over the nation with confidence and charisma that perfectly suited the medium of television. One of the major issues that divided the two candidates was American foreign policy, particularly the Cold War with the Soviet Union. Nixon claimed that the Republican administration had successfully contained the spread of Soviet power over the previous eight years and that the young Kennedy lacked the necessary experience to handle such dangerous matters. Kennedy, on the other hand, claimed that the Republicans, under 'Ike' Eisenhower, had allowed the U.S.A. to fall behind in the arms race, to the point where it was in danger of being outstripped by Soviet technological advances. He also accused the Republicans of needlessly losing Cuba to the Soviets through a lack of proactive intervention. Kennedy won the election, but foreign policy failures dogged his administration. In his first two years in office, the Cold War grew colder: the Bay of Pigs invasion, when a U.S. force of expatriate Cubans tried to invade Cuba and oust Fidel Castro, ended in defeat and led directly to the Cuban Missile Crisis the following year, and the erection of the Berlin Wall to separate the democratic and Communist halves of Germany. However, Kennedy's brief administration was also characterized by his special brand of idealism. He vigorously supported equal rights and world peace, while also tackling poverty and encouraging cultural and artistic development. In his inauguration speech he made the famous declaration, 'Ask not what your country can do for you – ask what you can do for your country,' and it was this spirit of personal responsibility and sacrifice in a common cause that lived on after his death.

> **'Kennedy's brief administration was also characterized by his special brand of idealism.'**

February 3
Apartheid Under Attack
U.K. Prime Minister Harold Macmillan condemns South Africa's apartheid policy in a speech given in Cape Town.

February 9
Walk of Fame Inaugurated
Actress Joanne Woodward is the first person to be commemorated with a star set into the pavement on Hollywood Boulevard.

March 8
Elvis Leaves the Army
'The King' finishes nearly two years of military service.

April 21
Brazil Inaugurates New Capital City
After four years of construction, the inauguration of Brasilia is celebrated across the country.

PROTESTERS KILLED IN APARTHEID SOUTH AFRICA

The apartheid laws that underpinned the regime of Hendrik Verwoerd, Prime Minister of South Africa, were designed to separate the privileged white citizens from the black masses. One such law required black South Africans to carry passbooks, which, beyond identification details, noted if they had paid taxes or been arrested. These books had to be stamped every month by employers, and if a black man stepped outside his front door without carrying his pass, he could be arrested, imprisoned, and fined. The African National Congress (A.N.C.), the most significant of the anti-apartheid groups, had been campaigning peacefully for many years against the institutionalized oppression of black people. But when, in April 1960, it organized a demonstration against the discriminatory passbook laws, a more militant group, the Pan African Congress (P.A.C.), joined in, calling for mass civil disobedience. The leader of the P.A.C., Robert Mangaliso Sobukwe, pleaded for all black males to

FURY IN SOUTH AFRICA

'In the mayhem that followed ... 69 people were shot dead ... including innocent bystanders and children.'

descend on police stations without their passbooks and demand to be arrested. His aim was to create a mass demonstration against the ruling white oppressors that could be witnessed the world over. In most locations there were some arrests and one or two casualties. However, in Sharpeville, near Johannesburg, the situation erupted into an outbreak of brutality that would never be forgotten. Initially, there were 20 policemen to 20,000 black protestors. Although the crowd was unarmed, there was some stone-throwing, and the police called in reinforcements. As scuffles continued and the crowd advanced on the police station, the police chief panicked and gave the order to load and fire. In the mayhem that followed, the unarmed crowd scattered in terror, and 69 people were shot dead within a couple of minutes, including innocent bystanders and children. The incident prompted international outrage, and for the first time worldwide attention was drawn to the situation that apartheid policies were creating in South Africa.

Above: In 1996, Nelson Mandela, the first president of a democratic South Africa, signed the country's new constitution at Sharpeville, the scene of the 1960 massacre.

May 16
First Laser Tested
U.S. scientist Theodore Maiman builds the first working prototype of a laser using synthetic ruby.

June 16
Psycho Premiere
Alfred Hitchcock's stylish suspense movie thrills audiences around the world despite lukewarm reviews.

June 30
Belgian Congo Crisis
Belgium's grant of independence to the Congo triggers a four-year crisis in a struggle to gain control of the country's mineral resources.

July 20
World's First Woman Prime Minister
Sirimavo Bandaranaike becomes the Prime Minister of Sri Lanka (or Ceylon as it was then known).

1960

U.S. PILOT SHOT DOWN OVER SOVIET AIRSPACE

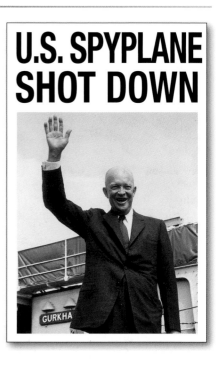

U.S. SPYPLANE SHOT DOWN

On August 19, 1960, American pilot Francis Gary Powers was sentenced to ten years in a Soviet prison after pleading guilty to spying for the C.I.A. Captured after his U-2 plane entered Soviet airspace and was shot down on May 1, Powers admitted to spying for the American government, but the evidence found in the plane's wreckage, including tape recordings of signals from Soviet radar stations, incriminated him anyway. He was also in possession of a poisoned pin with which he was meant to commit suicide under torture. Powers had been recruited by the C.I.A. after leaving the U.S. Air Force, and had been told that his espionage work would involve flying along the Soviet border in an attempt to pick up radio and radar signals. The incident created bad press for the government of President Eisenhower (right), particularly when America was publicly denounced by the Soviet prosecutor for deliberately sabotaging world peace. The prosecutor further claimed that it had been America's deliberate intention to jeopardize the international summit due to be held in Paris. The aim of the summit was to discuss a relaxation of Soviet–U.S. relations and the possibility of arms control, and it was indeed canceled when Soviet leader Nikita Khrushchev pulled out over the Powers incident. Powers himself spent two years in a Soviet jail before being swapped with Soviet spy Colonel Rudolph Abel in a mutual and highly publicized handover.

PRIME MINISTER OF CONGO EXECUTED

EXECUTED

In September 1960, Patrice Lumumba, African anti-colonialist and first prime minister of independent Congo, was deposed from power only two months after being instated. He had long fought for independence from the Belgian rulers, and when it was granted, the first elections were set for May 1960. Lumumba was duly elected, but his fiercely anti-colonialist inauguration speech provoked various authorities present. His first mistake as prime minister was to increase the pay of all government employees, except those in the army. This sparked an immediate army revolt, which quickly erupted into full-blown civil war, with the Katanga province declaring its own independence with Belgian backing. President Kasa-Vubu fired Lumumba from his government, and chaos ensued. The U.S.S.R. intervened on behalf of Lumumba, while the U.S. backed the Belgians and set up its own candidate, Joseph Mobutu, to oppose both Lumumba and Kasa-Vubu. Initially, Lumumba was under U.N. protection, but when he escaped and attempted to set up his own government, he was on his own. He was arrested in December and executed by firing squad on January 17, 1961.

September 5
Cassius Clay Takes Boxing Gold
Cassius Clay (later Muhammad Ali) wins the Light Heavyweight gold medal at the Rome Olympics.

September 10
O.P.E.C. Established
The Organization of the Petroleum Exporting Countries (O.P.E.C.) is formed at a meeting in Baghdad with the aim of securing stable oil prices.

October 1
Nigeria Becomes Independent
Britain grants Nigeria independence, although the Queen remains Head of State until 1963.

October 27
Lady Chatterley's Lover Trial
After a six-day trial, D.H. Lawrence's novel is ruled not obscene, after publisher Penguin mounts a defense to prove that the book has 'redeeming social merit'.

1961

SOVIETS LAUNCH MAN INTO SPACE

FIRST MAN IN SPACE

On April 12, 1961, the Soviet spacecraft *Vostok 1* was launched into space with a man on board: thus did Russian cosmonaut Yuri Gagarin became the first man to go where no man had gone before. After completing one orbit of the Earth, which took 108 minutes, Gargarin ejected himself from the craft and parachuted safely to the ground (although it was claimed at the time that he landed *with* the spacecraft, as required by official rules). The spacecraft was controlled automatically, so Gagarin had no power over its course. This was done to protect him, as it was not yet known how a human being would react to the weightlessness of space. However, he was in possession of an envelope containing a set of codes that would unlock the controls system and enable him to pilot the spacecraft in case of an emergency.

'After completing one orbit of the Earth, which took 108 minutes, Gargarin ejected himself from Vostok 1 and parachuted safely to the ground'

Above: A rocket similar to the type used to blast Gagarin into space, and a stamp issued to celebrate the event.

January 24
Nuclear Bombs Dropped on U.S. Soil
A B52 bomber flying over North Carolina breaks up in mid-air, dropping two nuclear bombs. Safety devices prevent disaster.

January 31
First Chimp in Space
Ham, a male chimp, is the sole passenger on a sub-orbital test flight. Ham survives the flight and landing and lives until 1983.

February 5
War Breaks Out in Angola
The emergence of three independence groups in the Portuguese colony leads to a wave of violence.

February 9
Beatles' First Performance
A lunchtime session at the Cavern Club, Liverpool, sees the debut of new local band The Beatles.

April 11
Bob Dylan's Debut
Dylan plays his first paying gig, supporting John Lee Hooker at a New York club.

1961

CASTRO'S ARMY DEFEATS U.S. INVADERS IN CUBA

The 1959 Cuban Revolutionary War that had toppled dictator Fulgencio Batista and placed Communist revolutionary Fidel Castro in power had drastically altered relations between the U.S. and Cuba. In March 1960, President Eisenhower had approved a C.I.A. plan to train a group of U.S.-based Cuban exiles to invade Cuba. If successful, anti-Castro exile José Miró Cardona would take over the government of Cuba. By the time the invasion came about, John F. Kennedy was President, and he gave the go-ahead even though the secret mission was so widely publicized that Castro himself knew of it. The invasion began on April 15, 1961 with the aerial bombing of Cuban airports. For this, U.S. Second World War planes were painted to look like Cuban Air Force planes. Not only were they unsuccessful, but their poor disguise made American involvement clear for all to see. This caused Kennedy to cancel the second planned air strike. On April 17, some 1,400 Cuban exiles landed at the Bay of Pigs, an area chosen for its obscurity but that proved to be unhelpful territory from which to launch an invasion. The mission was a complete failure: within three days of the landings, 1,189 of the paramilitaries had been captured by Castro's 20,000-strong force, and more than 100 were killed. The incident caused embarrassment for the new President, and Kennedy sacked the C.I.A. director promptly.

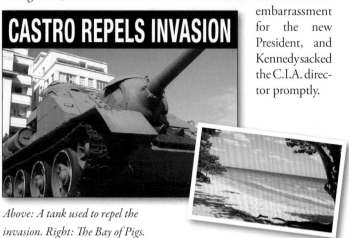

Above: A tank used to repel the invasion. Right: The Bay of Pigs.

BARBED WIRE DIVIDES BERLIN

On August 13, 1961, the people of Berlin awoke to discover that a wall of barbed wire had been constructed along the border between East and West Germany, and no one was allowed to cross it. The barbed wire was soon replaced with a permanent concrete structure 12 ft (4 m) high and over 66 miles (106 km) long. The wall was in complete violation of the post-war agreement that placed Berlin under the control of four powers – Britain, France, the U.S.S.R., and the United States – and it provoked international outrage. However, both Britain and the U.S.A. were reluctant to intervene, despite pleas from West Germany, and in fact saw the wall as a positive signal that the East Germans and Soviets would leave the rest of Berlin alone. Meanwhile, the East German government, with Soviet support, was planning to separate from the rest of Germany. The wall divided families and cut off East Berliners from their jobs in West Berlin. Although the official justification for the wall was that it would protect East Germany from Western aggression and spies, the reality was that it acted as a one-way block to prevent East Germans from fleeing to the West. The Berlin Wall stayed in place for 28 years, during which time around 200 people were killed trying to cross it because border guards had been instructed to shoot potential defectors. It did not come down until the Communist government resigned in 1989.

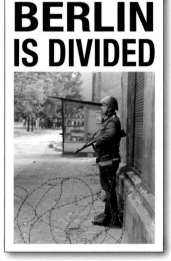

BERLIN IS DIVIDED

'The wall divided families and cut off East Berliners from their jobs in West Berlin.'

May 17
South Africa Leaves Commonwealth
South Africa officially leaves the Commonwealth of Nations.

June 16
Nureyev Defects
After a run of performances in Paris, the brightest young star of Soviet ballet, Rudolf Nureyev, defects to the West.

July 2
Ernest Hemingway Commits Suicide
The American author shoots himself after a bout of depression.

September 10
Crash at Italian Grand Prix
German driver Wolfgang von Trips is killed along with 14 spectators when he crashes at Monza.

October 30
Nuclear Test
The Soviet Union detonates a 58-megaton-yield hydrogen bomb known as Tsar Bomba over Novaya Zemlya.

U.N. SECRETARY GENERAL DIES

On September 18, 1961, a plane carrying the U.N. Secretary General Dag Hammarskjöld between two Congolese provinces exploded and crashed, instantly killing 14 of its 15 passengers. The only survivor, who died of his injuries days later, explained that the plane was about to land in Ndola, where Mr. Hammarskjöld was due to hold face-to-face talks with the leader of the breakaway Katanga province in the Congo. But at the last minute Mr. Hammarskjöld ordered the pilot to divert elsewhere. Soon after, there were three explosions on board, and the plane went down. The Swedish statesman, who had been U.N. Secretary General for the previous eight years, had done much to promote peacekeeping in troubled regions, including China and the Middle East, and was posthumously awarded the Nobel Peace Prize. In the six weeks before his death, Hammarskjöld had visited 21 countries and territories in Africa, and entered troubled waters by providing U.N. military intervention in the Congo after it descended into civil war following independence. The move had angered the Soviets, who thought he was supporting colonial rule in Africa, and they called for his resignation. While tributes for the deceased statesman poured in from foreign leaders all over the world, the Soviets were silent.

U.N. LEADER KILLED IN AIR CRASH

Right: The headquarters of the United Nations in New York.

November 11
Catch-22 Published
Joseph Heller's satirical novel was written in the late 50s but does not appear in print until 1961. The title of the novel has passed into common usage to mean a no-win situation.

December 11
U.S. Troops Arrive in Vietnam
U.S. aircraft carrier *Core* arrives in Saigon with a cargo of over 30 helicopters and 400 servicemen to support the South Vietnamese in their struggle against the Communist North. The event marks the start of America's military build-up in the area.

December 15
Eichmann Sentenced to Death
Adolf Eichmann, who organized the deportation of Jews to the Nazis' extermination camps, is sentenced to death by an Israeli court. He was captured by Israeli agents in Argentina.

85

1962

SATELLITE COMMUNICATIONS ARRIVE

WONDERFUL TELSTAR

Above: The original Telstar.
Right: A modern telecommunications satellite and dish receiver.

In 1960, the company AT&T, which enjoyed a monopoly in terrestrial communications in the U.S. at the time, teamed up with N.A.S.A. to design and create the first satellite communications system. Called Telstar, the system involved having 55 satellites in orbit at the same time, and 25 ground stations spaced across the globe to receive signals. The Telstar spacecraft was designed and built by Bell Telephone Laboratories, and N.A.S.A. provided and operated the launch vehicles.

Although it was not, in fact, the first ever communications satellite, Telstar is the best known, and is generally considered to have launched the era of satellite communications. N.A.S.A.'s chief of communications has explained why so many people mistakenly think Telstar was the first of its kind: 'This impression was a result of the tremendous impact upon the public by the first transmission of live television across the Atlantic Ocean. Telstar 1 was launched on July 10, 1962, and on that same day live television pictures originating in the United States were received in France.' Receiving stations had been set up in the U.S. state of Maine, as well as in France and Britain. The day after its first transmission, President Kennedy made the following statement: 'The successful firing and subsequent operation of the Telstar communications satellite is an outstanding example of the way in which government and business can cooperate in a most important field of human endeavor. There is no more important field at the present time than communications, and we must grasp the advantages presented to us by the communications satellite to use this medium wisely and effectively to ensure greater understanding among the peoples of the world.'

> 'The system involved having 55 satellites in orbit at the same time, and 25 ground stations spaced across the globe to receive signals.'

January 15
Yves Saint-Lauren Launches Own Label
At the age of 25, the Algerian-born French fashion designer founds his own label.

March 1
New York Plane Crash
A Boeing 707 crashes soon after takeoff from New York's Idlewild Airport, plummeting into Jamaica Bay, and causing the death of all 95 passengers and crew on board.

April 8
Bay of Pigs Trial
The largest mass trial in Cuba's history ends with the conviction of over 1,000 Cuban exiles who had attempted to invade the country in 1961.

April 23
Stirling Moss in Coma After Crash
The racing driver is almost killed in a crash at Britain's Goodwood circuit.

U.S. AND SOVIET UNION CLASH OVER CUBA

The Cuban Missile Crisis is so far the closest the world has ever come to nuclear war. In the ongoing arms race between the U.S.S.R. and the U.S.A., the Soviets were behind and desperate to improve their position. Aware that America already possessed missiles powerful enough to wipe out the entire Soviet Union, while Soviet missiles could reach only Europe, the U.S.S.R. decided to create a nuclear base closer to the U.S. from which they would be able to pose a genuine threat. In April 1962, Soviet premier Nikita Khrushchev approached Fidel Castro, his Communist ally in Cuba, with the idea of setting up a Soviet nuclear missile on his island. Castro was delighted with the plan, which would solve his concerns over a second American invasion of Cuba. On October 15, 1962, U.S. spy-planes garnered information that Soviet missile bases were being built in Cuba and that the missiles were already being shipped over. After several days of intense talks, President Kennedy made the information public and openly declared that, if Soviet missiles were not removed from Cuba, the move would be viewed as an offensive on the United States. On October 22, Kennedy set up a naval quarantine around the island. Four days later, Khrushchev, realizing that he could not contend with the combined might of the U.S. Navy's artillery pointing directly at him, responded by letter, stating that the Soviets would remove their missiles if America would promise not to invade Cuba. To the entire watching world, it seemed that nuclear war was on the point of breaking out in earnest. International tension reached a peak on October 27, when an American U-2 spy-plane was shot down over Cuba. In a second letter, Khrushchev also demanded that the Americans deactivate their missile bases in Turkey, but Attorney General Robert Kennedy chose to ignore this and instead agreed to guarantee that the U.S. would not attack Cuba. Tensions finally eased on October 28, when Khrushchev began to remove Soviet missiles from Cuba and dismantle the stations.

'The Cuban Missile Crisis is so far the closest the world has ever come to nuclear war.'

KHRUSHCHEV SENDS MISSILES TO CUBA

Right: A ballistic missile.

May 3
Tokyo Train Disaster
A train crashes north of Tokyo. Over 160 people are killed.

June 22
Plane Crash in Guadeloupe
An Air France Boeing 707 jet crashes at Guadeloupe's Le Raizet airport, killing all 113 passengers and crew on board.

July 20
Hovercraft Service Launched
The world's first hovercraft passenger service opens between Moreton in England and Rhyl in Wales.

July 21
Rolling Stones' Debut Gig
The Rolling Stones make their first ever live appearance, at London's Marquee Club.

1962

MARILYN MONROE DIES OF OVERDOSE

On August 5, 1962, the actress Marilyn Monroe was found dead in the bedroom of her Los Angeles home. She had died from an overdose of sleeping pills, and the coroner ruled it a 'probable suicide'. The world-famous film star was only 36 at the time of her death, and it was rumored that she had been due to remarry her second husband, baseball star Joe DiMaggio. Born Norma Jeane Mortenson to an impoverished mother with mental health problems, Marilyn Monroe spent her childhood between foster homes and orphanages. She then shot to fame after being spotted by a fashion photographer. At the age of 20, Monroe signed a contract with the film studio 20th Century Fox, and starred in several box-office hits, including *The Seven Year Itch*, *Gentlemen Prefer Blondes*, and *Some Like It Hot*. She became a sex icon across the globe, but in her professional life she was considered difficult to work with and had been typecast as a dumb blonde. After three failed marriages, the last to playwright Arthur Miller, Monroe was romantically linked with various public figures, including President Kennedy. Only months before her death, she famously sang the President a breathy version of 'Happy Birthday', her last public performance.

FIRST AMERICAN IN SPACE

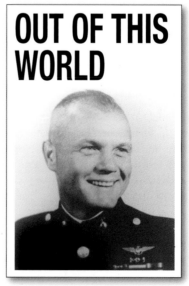

OUT OF THIS WORLD

'After successfully orbiting the Earth, John Glenn became an instant national hero.'

On February 20, 1962, the Americans finally achieved what the Soviets had already achieved less than a year earlier – they sent a man into space to orbit the Earth. American astronaut John Glenn, in the Mercury capsule *Friendship 7*, circled the globe three times in 4 hours and 56 minutes, covering 80,000 miles (130,000 km) and reaching speeds of 17,000 mph (27,000 kph). There were 24 American ships on standby at various points across the globe, each one ready to recover the spacecraft when it landed. Eventually it executed a successful splashdown in the Atlantic Ocean between Bermuda and Puerto Rico, and was picked up by a U.S. destroyer. Glenn had originally been selected as one of seven test pilots for N.A.S.A. in 1959 because he met all the necessary criteria: apart from being one of the best test pilots in the country, he was in excellent physical shape, less than 40 years old, shorter than 5 ft 11 in (182 cm), a qualified jet pilot, and had a degree in engineering. After successfully orbiting the Earth, John Glenn became an instant national hero.

October 5
Beatles Release First Single
'Love Me Do' is the first release from new Liverpool beat combo The Beatles.

October 5
First James Bond Film
The first big-screen appearance of 007 takes place at the London Pavilion, and features Sean Connery as the MI6 agent.

December 21
U.S. Offers Nuclear Bombs to U.K. and France
President Kennedy offers to sell Polaris nuclear missiles to Britain and France. France declines the offer, but Britain accepts.

CIVIL RIGHTS MARCH ON WASHINGTON D.C.

MARCH ON WASHINGTON

Throughout 1963 there was racial unrest in Birmingham, Alabama, and international sympathy for the civil rights movement was heightened by media coverage of the police using attack dogs and fire hoses against protestors, some of them children. Demonstrations frequently turned into riots, and Martin Luther King Jr. was arrested during one such riot for not carrying an identity card, but he continued to advocate civil disobedience against unjust laws. There were further demonstrations throughout the United States, culminating on August 28, 1963 in a march on Washington, D.C., which was attended by six different civil rights organizations. The march attracted around 250,000 supporters and was given wide broadcast coverage. The aim of the march was to achieve meaningful civil rights legislation, an end to racial segregation and public acts of discrimination, increased job opportunities for African Americans, and an end to police brutality. In short, it was for 'jobs and freedom'. President Kennedy supported the march, although originally he had been against it, purely on the grounds that it might stall the progress through Congress of a civil rights bill. On the day, the marchers, a quarter of them white, marched from the Washington Monument to the Lincoln Memorial. It was a calm, nonviolent protest from beginning to end. All of the leading civil rights leaders spoke, and Martin Luther King Jr.'s rousing speech became one of the most famous in history. He began by urging the crowd not to collapse into violence, saying, 'Again and again, we must rise to the majestic heights of meeting physical force with soul force.' He then moved on to his now landmark 'I have a dream' theme, looking forward to an America in which his children would 'not be judged by the color of their skin but by the content of their character'. The phrase has been repeated ever since and has come to represent the heart of Dr. King's teachings.

> **'Martin Luther King Jr.'s rousing speech became one of the most famous in history.'**

Right: The Lincoln Memorial, where Dr. King delivered his 'dream' speech.

January 2
North Vietnamese Down U.S. Choppers
Five U.S. helicopters are shot down during a botched operation over the rice marshes southwest of Saigon.

March 22
Beatles Release First Album
Recorded in a single day, *Please Please Me* is rushed out to capitalize on the success of the single of the same name.

May 18
Riots in Alabama
In the U.S., civil rights protestors are attacked and Martin Luther King is arrested. President Kennedy sends in troops to quell the subsequent riots.

May 25
Organization of African Unity Established
At a meeting in Addis Ababa, Ethiopia, 32 countries form the Organization of African Unity.

1963

MONEY STOLEN FROM BRITISH MAIL TRAIN

THE GREAT TRAIN ROBBERY

On August 8, 1963, a gang of 15 robbers held up the Glasgow-to-London mail train and fled with £2.6 million. The train, which had run without event every night for 125 years, was forced to stop in the early hours of the morning by signals the gang had tampered with. The driver was stunned with a blow, and in a 20-minute operation, the thieves uncoupled the engine and front two carriages, drove them up the line, and transferred 120 sacks of money into a waiting truck. Most of the used banknotes were due to be destroyed, but they had not been marked and were all untraceable. The meticulously planned heist, which was to go down in history as the 'Great Train Robbery', was the master plan of Bruce Reynolds, who evaded capture until 1969. Two others, Ronnie Biggs and Charlie Wilson, escaped abroad, while the remaining 12 were convicted after a large-scale, six-month police operation and given significant jail terms. Ronnie Biggs was discovered in Brazil, but not brought to justice because Brazil has no extradition treaty with England. However, in 2001 he finally returned to the U.K. of his own accord and was sent to prison.

Above: Ronnie Biggs celebrates 25 years since the Great Train Robbery.

FRENCH BLOCK U.K.'S ENTRY INTO E.E.C.

The Second World War had made European countries strongly aware of their relative weakness when acting alone, and post-war reliance on American aid made the need for greater European integration – both economically and politically – all the more pressing. European states realized that to contend with the U.S. and U.S.S.R. superpowers, they would need to form a homogenous unit. In 1946, Winston Churchill recognized the need to 're-create the European family … to provide it with a structure under which it can dwell in peace, in safety, and in freedom'. He foresaw the creation of what he called a united states of Europe. The first stage of this allowed free trade between European states and the pooling of natural resources, with the Treaty of Paris creating the European Coal and Steel Community, consisting of France, Germany, Italy, Belgium, the Netherlands, and Luxembourg. Next, the European Economic Community (E.E.C.) was enshrined in the 1957 Treaty of Rome. Reluctant to give up its sovereignty, Britain kept away from the E.E.C. However, realizing its growing economic strength, British Prime Minister Harold Wilson decided to apply for entry in 1962. In January 1963, French President Charles de Gaulle rejected the application on the grounds that Britain did not have a European mindset and was too attached to its Commonwealth. De Gaulle was known to be anti-British in his stance on Europe, and was particularly wary of American intervention in European affairs, which he felt would be a side-effect of British membership of the E.E.C.

DE GAULLE BLOCKS U.K. FROM EUROPE

June 16
First Woman in Space
Lieutenant Valentina Tereshkova is carried into orbit aboard the Soviet rocket *Vostok 6*.

June 26
Kennedy Visits Berlin
President Kennedy offers U.S. support for the residents of West Germany.

August 5
Nuclear Test Ban Treaty
The U.S., U.K., and Soviet Union sign a treaty banning the testing of nuclear weapons in the atmosphere, under water, or in space.

August 18
Civil Rights Landmark
James Meredith becomes the first black person to graduate from the University of Mississippi, U.S.A, with a degree in political science.

U.S. PRESIDENT SHOT DEAD

On November 22, 1963, the world was stunned by the assassination of U.S. President John F. Kennedy. He was 46 and had been in office for only three years when a gunman fired on the presidential car as it traveled from the airport to downtown Dallas, Texas. The Governor of Texas, John Connally, who was riding alongside him, was also seriously wounded. Although the two men's wives were also in the presidential car, they were unhurt. Bullets had struck President Kennedy's head and throat, and he died 35 minutes later in hospital. The shots were believed to have been fired from a School Book Depository building, and the rifle found at the scene was thought to be the assassin's weapon. One hour after the shooting, a policeman approached Lee Harvey Oswald, whom he believed matched the description of an employee reported missing from the School Book Depository in Dallas. The policeman was shot dead by Oswald, who was arrested immediately. Oswald was himself shot dead by a nightclub owner, Jack Ruby, two days later, before he was able to be tried for the assassination. After his arrest, Oswald denied shooting the President and claimed he had been made a scapegoat. John F. Kennedy had represented vibrant hope and progress to a new generation of Americans, so his death struck terrible grief in the nation. Vice-President Lyndon B. Johnson was sworn into office as President the same day. According to a recent opinion poll, 70% of Americans believe there was a wider assassination plot behind the shooting, which has been covered up. There is still no agreement as to who was responsible, with speculation ranging from Fidel Castro to Lyndon Johnson, via the F.B.I. and the C.I.A.

KENNEDY ASSASSINATED

Right: The School Book Depository.

Right: J.F.K.'s simple grave with its eternal flame in Arlington Cemetery.

August 30
Cold War 'Hotline' Established
Following the Cuban missile crisis of 1962, the U.S. and Soviets set up a new communication system between them, for use in emergencies.

November 1
World's Largest Telescope Opened
The Arecibo Observatory is the world's largest radio telescope, with a reflector of nearly 1,000 ft (330 m).

November 18
Push Button Telephone Launched
Pennsylvania, U.S.A., sees the introduction of the world's first touch-tone telephone service, featuring telephones with push buttons instead of a dial.

91

1964

CAPITAL OF ALASKA REDUCED TO RUBBLE

MASSIVE EARTHQUAKE

Although March 27, 1964 seemed like any other Good Friday to Alaskans preparing for the holiday weekend, it was to become the day the fault line under the mountains surrounding Prince William Sound finally gave in to the years of pressure from shifting tectonic plates, giving rise to the worst earthquake Alaska had ever experienced. Earthquakes were a part of life in Alaska, but the people of Anchorage, the capital of the state, soon realized that this one was in a different league: the ground rolled in waves, cracks 30 ft (9 m) wide opened and closed, houses collapsed, lampposts toppled, and trees were torn from the ground. Within the space of five minutes, the capital lay in ruins. But Anchorage was not the only Alaskan city to be devastated by this earthquake. In the city of Valdez, the ground rose in waves 3 ft (1 m) high, and the area was hit by tsunamis throughout the night. In the city of Seward a chunk of the waterfront slipped into the ocean, and an oil tank farm caught fire. Other towns lost parts of their waterfront, and in Kodiak, tsunamis destroyed half of the fishing fleet and carried off two fish canneries. In addition, the U.S. states of Oregon, California, and Hawaii, and as far afield as Japan, were also struck by tsunamis resulting from the earthquake, while seismic waves were felt in Seattle, Washington state, as well as Texas and Florida. With a magnitude of 9.2 on the Richter scale, the earthquake was the second most powerful in recorded history, claiming 128 lives, most of them caused by the resulting tsunamis. Fortunately, the death toll was relatively low compared to other major earthquakes around the world, largely because Alaska is so sparsely populated.

> **'Earthquakes were a part of life in Alaska, but the people of Anchorage soon realized that this one was in a different league'**

Right: The placid appearance of modern-day Anchorage belies the upheavals of the past.

January 11
Health Risks of Smoking Highlighted
A report by the U.S. Surgeon General identifies a causal link between smoking and cancer (as well as other diseases).

February 6
Plans for Channel Tunnel Announced
The British and French governments announce a plan to build a tunnel between the two countries. However, it is not until 1984 that a company is selected to build the tunnel.

February 7
Beatlemania Hits America
The Fab Four's arrival in the U.S. is marked by a crowd of several thousand screaming fans.

February 25
Muhammad Ali Is Heavyweight Champion
Cassius Clay beats heavyweight champion Sonny Liston in seven rounds. Shortly afterwards he changes his name to Muhammad Ali.

NELSON MANDELA CONVICTED OF SABOTAGE

When the African National Congress (A.N.C.) was banned in South Africa following the Sharpeville Massacre, its leaders felt they had no alternative but to resort to illegal and sometimes violent means to achieve their goals. Their aim was an end to the oppression of the black population in South Africa, which meant an end to the state that had been built on the system of apartheid. The underground A.N.C. now began to plan for an armed struggle. When Nelson Mandela, a lawyer and leading figure in the A.N.C., was arrested on charges of sabotage, he pleaded guilty. Mandela famously told the court: 'I do not deny that I planned sabotage. I did not plan it in a spirit of recklessness nor because I have any love of violence. I planned it as a result of a calm and sober assessment of the political situation that had arisen after many years of tyranny, exploitation, and oppression of my people by the whites.' Mandela was arrested in Rivonia, Johannesburg, along with seven other A.N.C. members. On June 12, 1964, all eight men were found guilty and sentenced to life imprisonment. In sentencing them, Judge Quartus de Wet said he was not convinced that they were acting to alleviate the suffering of black Africans, but instead detected personal ambition for power in their actions. Mandela had already been tried for high treason in 1956, but after a four-year trial, he had not been convicted. Despite international disapproval and a world petition given to the United Nations, Nelson Mandela remained in prison for 27 years.

MANDELA IMPRISONED

Right: Mandela's prison on Robben Island.

'Despite international disapproval and a world petition given to the United Nations, Nelson Mandela remained in prison for 27 years.'

March 15
Richard Burton Marries Liz Taylor
The two actors met on the set of Cleopatra. Burton is Taylor's fifth husband, and she is his second wife.

April 4
Beatles Claim Top Five Chart Positions
With Beatlemania in full swing, the band occupy all five of the top slots in the U.S.A.'s Top 40.

April 17
Ford Mustang Launched
The Ford Motor Company introduces this iconic car at the New York World's Fair.

April 25
Little Mermaid Statue Decapitated
The famous statue sits in Copenhagen Harbor as a tribute to the ballet of the same name.

1965

U.S. INVOLVEMENT IN VIETNAM INCREASED

Following independence from France, Vietnam had been divided into the Communist North and French-backed South. The North wanted Vietnam united under Communist rule, and in 1959, with the support of the southern National Liberation Front, or Viet Cong, attacked the South. When Lyndon B. Johnson (right) took his oath as U.S. President, he declared: 'We can never again stand aside, prideful in isolation. Terrific dangers and troubles that we once called "foreign" now constantly live among us.' Perceived as chief among these dangers was Communism. Days later, Johnson was told by his advisors that America's limited involvement to date in the Vietnam War was doing no good and that America would either have to withdraw altogether or significantly escalate its military commitment. When Viet Cong guerrillas attacked an American base in February, President Johnson responded by approving the bombing of a North Vietnamese army camp. Thereafter, without any official announcement, the U.S. began to commit greater numbers of troops to the cause of the South Vietnamese. Operation Rolling Thunder was launched on March 2, 1965, with 100 American fighter-bombers heading for targets in North Vietnam. The campaign was meant to take just eight weeks, but ended up lasting three years. The first U.S. combat troops to arrive in Vietnam were marines, 3,500 of them, and they landed at China Beach to defend an American air base. Even when a further two marine battalions were sent to Vietnam on April 1, 1965, President Johnson still did not inform the American people that the United States was involved in offensive operations. During this time, North Vietnam rejected several attempts by Johnson to negotiate a peace settlement, with the result that America committed more and more troops to crushing the Communist North.

MORE TROOPS FOR VIETNAM

Left: Entrance to the Viet Cong tunnels at Chu Chi. These warrens were vital to guerrilla warfare.

January 30
Churchill Buried
Former British Prime Minister Winston Churchill is given a full state funeral in London.

February 6
Soccer Legend's Last Game
Stanley Matthews plays his final match in England's First Division, as he turns out for Stoke City at the ripe old age of 50.

March 7
Bloody Sunday
Civil rights protestors are attacked by State Troopers in Selma, Alabama, on a day that becomes known as Bloody Sunday.

April 23
Pennine Way Opened
The walking trail in the North of England is completed.

April 28
U.S. Troops Enter Dominican Republic
President Johnson sends the U.S. army into the Dominican Republic in defense of the country's military government after an uprising by supporters of former President Juan Bosch.

MALCOLM X SHOT DEAD AS WIFE LOOKS ON

The man who began life as Malcolm Little and, after a youth of crime, converted in prison to the Nation of Islam, was assassinated in New York City on February 21, 1965 by members of the group he had once championed. Renamed Malcolm X by the Nation of Islam leader Elijah Muhammad, he was released from prison in 1952, and subsequently devoted his life to the cause of black rights. However, he was opposed to the civil rights movement headed by Martin Luther King Jr., rejecting integration and endorsing the Nation of Islam view that all whites were evil. His oratory impressed many people, but by 1963 his bluntness was beginning to alienate him from the Nation of Islam. When he described the assassination of President Kennedy as 'chickens coming home to roost', adding that it made him glad rather than sad, Elijah Muhammad banned him from public speaking for 90 days. On March 8, 1964, Malcolm X broke from the Nation of Islam and

announced his intention of forming the Organization of Afro-American Unity. His popularity increased, but the Nation of Islam began making death threats against him. On February 14, 1965, his house was burned to the ground, but his family survived. Seven days later, while addressing an audience in Manhattan's Audubon Ballroom, Malcolm X was shot by three men, the first with a sawn-off shotgun, the others with pistols. In all, he was shot 16 times. Three members of the Nation of Islam were arrested and imprisoned for his murder.

FIRST EVER SPACEWALK

Right: An Australian stamp marking the first U.S. spacewalk.

Ever since the U.S.S.R. had won the race to send the first man into space, the Americans had wanted their own 'first'. N.A.S.A.'s *Gemini 4* program aimed to deliver this, its goal being that an American would be the first to walk in space. By early 1965, astronauts were in training, and Ed White looked set to be the first man to exit a spacecraft and engage in extra-vehicular activity. Once again, though, the Soviets got there first, and on March 18, 1965, Aleski Leonov became the first man to walk in space. When *Gemini 4* launched in June 1965, Ed White got his walk, but with more advanced technology. He carried a handheld gas jet, which he could use to 'fire' himself back to the spaceship if he came loose from his tether. White walked in space for around half an hour, and the pictures appeared in newspapers across the globe. On his return, he was awarded the N.A.S.A. Space Flight Medal, and posthumously received the Congressional Space Medal of Honor.

April 28
Australian Troops Sent to Vietnam
Australian Prime Minister Robert Menzies announces his intention to increase his country's involvement in the Vietnam War. The first Australian combat troops arrive a month later.

May 29
Hundreds Die in Mining Disaster
Nearly 300 workers are killed in an accident at a coal mine in Dhanbad, India.

July 25
Dylan Goes Electric
Folk singer Bob Dylan causes uproar among folk music fans by playing an electric guitar at the Newport Folk Festival in Newport, Rhode Island.

August 9
A New Island State
Singapore leaves the Federation of Malaysia to become an independent nation. Lee Kuan Yew is the new country's first prime minister.

1965

MASSIVE POWER CUT IN NORTH AMERICA

On November 9, 1965, there was a serious disruption to the power supply in the northeastern provinces of America and Canada. The major incident occurred when a maintenance worker set a protective relay to trip at too low a value. As a result, an area covering 80,000 sq miles (207,000 sq km), including Ontario in Canada, and Connecticut, Massachusetts, New Hampshire, Rhode Island, Vermont, New York, and New Jersey in the United States, was plunged into darkness and did not regain power for 12 hours. The power cut affected 25 million people, and only those areas with independent old-fashioned generators were able to maintain any power. Sparks from the affected power stations were widely reported as 'fireballs' in the sky, and these in turn became inflated into sightings of U.F.O.s (Unidentified Flying Objects). The official explanation of the 'fireballs' was made known the following day.

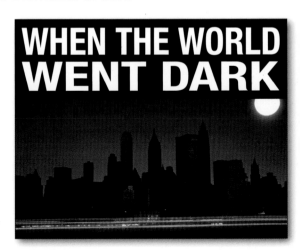

RHODESIA BREAKS TIES WITH BRITAIN

On November 11, 1965, Ian Smith, Prime Minister of Rhodesia (now Zimbabwe), made a Unilateral Declaration of Independence from Britain. The move was deemed illegal by the British, and economic sanctions were immediately imposed. Britain's aim had been to help Rhodesia toward black-majority rule. But although blacks outnumbered whites in Rhodesia by 16 to one, Smith had declared that they would never rule the country. To this end, he suppressed black political parties and detained their leaders. British Prime Minister Harold Wilson made it clear that Britain would support Rhodesia's independence only if Smith's regime allowed for majority rule. Meanwhile, the declaration of independence isolated the country economically and increased violence between blacks and whites. Although Smith declared Rhodesia a republic in 1969, it was still not internationally recognized. Eventually, he was forced to hand over power to the elected black leader Robert Mugabe in 1980.

Below: Robert Mugabe, who became leader when Ian Smith stepped down.

October 3
Che Leaves Cuba
Cuban President Fidel Castro announces that Che Guevara has resigned from the Cuban government and left the country.

November 8
Britain Abolishes the Death Penalty
The Murder Act 1965 is given Royal Assent, thus formally ending the death penalty in the U.K.

November 24
Mobutu Seizes Power in Congo
Lieutenant-Colonel Mobutu Sese Seko overthrows President Joseph Kasavubu to take power in Congo.

June 26
Soviet Scientist Denounced
Agronomist Trofim Lysenko, whose false ideas regarding heredity have guided official Soviet agricultural policy for two decades, is officially denounced.

BRADY AND HINDLEY JAILED FOR LIFE

On May 6, 1966, 28-year-old Ian Brady and his lover Myra Hindley were jailed for life for the murders of three children. The pair was convicted of torturing and murdering Edward Evans (17), Lesley-Ann Downey (10), and John Kilbride (12) in what became known as the 'Moors Murders'. In each case the children had been lured to the couple's Manchester home, subjected to sexual abuse and torture, and then brutally murdered. Their remains were buried on remote moorland in Lancashire and Yorkshire. Brady and Hindley were arrested for the murders after Hindley's brother-in-law, David Smith, witnessed the murder of Edward Evans as an intended 'initiation ceremony' into the killings. Smith, terrified by what he saw, later called the police. Brady confessed to the crimes, and he and Hindley were each given three life sentences. The pair also murdered two other children, Pauline Reade and Keith Bennett. When they were taken back to the moors in the 1980s to identify the burial sites, the remains of Pauline Reade were uncovered, but Keith Bennett's body has never been found. Hindley died in prison at the age of 60, even though she had completed her 30-year sentence. Brady remains in a psychiatric hospital, where he has been on hunger strike for several years.

'The children were sexually abused and tortured, and then brutally murdered.'

Left: Ian Brady (third from left) leads police officers back to Saddleworth Moor, searching for the remains of the victims whose bodies were not found in the initial investigation.

January 1
Coup in Central Africa
Jean-Bédel Bokassa takes power in a military coup in the Central African Republic.

January 19
Indira for India
Indira Ghandi is elected Prime Minister of India. She is the daughter of Jawaharlal Nehru, who was independent India's first Prime Minister.

March 1
Soviet Space Probe Reaches Venus
Soviet space probe Venera 3 crashes into Venus. It is the first spacecraft to land on another planet.

March 4
'More Popular than Jesus'
In an interview with the London newspaper the Eveneing Standard, John Lennon claims that The Beatles are now more popular than Jesus.

1966

LONE GUNMAN BRINGS TERROR TO CAMPUS

On August 1, 1966, Charles Whitman, a student at the University of Texas in Austin, shattered a peaceful summer's day on campus. Whitman killed 14 people and wounded 32 others during a shooting rampage on and around campus after murdering his wife and his mother in their homes. Whitman seemed destined for the American Dream – he was good-looking, came from a prominent and wealthy family, and did well in school and sports. However, under the seemingly idyllic facade, Whitman's family was troubled, mainly due to physical and emotional abuse from his father. In a bid to please his father, as well as remove himself from his father's abusive behavior, Whitman joined the U.S. Marines in 1959. He won several performance medals, exceled at rapid fire shooting, and earned a scholarship to study engineering in Austin. But Whitman immediately floundered in his studies and he took up gambling. Although his marriage to Kathy Leissner in 1962 steadied him for a while, his life continued to unravel and he acknowledged, via journal entries, that he was on the verge of doing something terrible. Although he was seeing a psychiatrist and taking medication, Whitman's self-control snapped on July 31. After killing his wife and mother, he climbed to the observation deck of the white granite tower of the University of Texas administration building and started shooting. After he held police at bay for a while, assault teams got close enough to gun him down.

> 'His life continued to unravel and he acknowledged, via journal entries, that he was on the verge of doing something terrible.'

UNIVERSITY KILLINGS

March 20
World Cup Stolen
The World Cup trophy, popularly known as the Jules Rimet trophy, is stolen from an exhibition in London. It is found in a hedge a week later by a dog named Pickles.

March 31
Labour Win
Harold Wilson's Labour government wins the general election in the U.K.

April 21
Ethiopian Emperor Visits Jamaica
The emperor of Ethiopia, Haile Selassie, visits Jamaica. He meets with leaders of the Rastafarian movement, who revere him as an incarnation of God.

May 26
Guyana Becomes Independent
The South American state wins independence from the United Kingdom.

SCHOOL CRUSHED BY COAL SLURRY IN SOUTH WALES

MINING DISASTER

On the morning of Friday, October 21, 1966, Tip No. 7, a heap of colliery waste that lay 500 ft (153 m) high above the village of Aberfan in Wales, began to slide. Below it were the Panglas Schools, which were just about to break for half-term. There was low cloud on that day, so no one could see the heap of waste beginning to slide, but they could hear it. The coal slurry had been liquefied by springs beneath the heap, and it flowed as fast as molten lava. No one had time to get out of the way before the liquid waste destroyed a farm, killing its inhabitants, and engulfed Panglas Junior School, killing 109 children and five teachers. A subsequent inquiry found the National Coal Board (N.C.B.) negligent and entirely responsible for the disaster. The tip should never have been placed on top of known springs, had already slid twice in the past, and had never been inspected, though it was known to be a hazard. The N.C.B. tried to deny responsibility, and avoided paying compensation to the bereaved families until some years later. Scandalously, the chairman of the N.C.B., Lord Robens, staged a false resignation, and he himself wrote his M.P.'s letter of refusal to accept the resignation. The Aberfan disaster was one of the worst ever cases of negligence and cover-up, the shameful facts of which only emerged 30 years later when related documents became public.

Left: Aerial view of Aberfan after the disaster.
Right: Memorials to the children killed in the deluged school.

September 6
'Architect of Apartheid' Killed
The Prime Minister of South Africa, Hendrik Frensch Verwoerd, the primary architect of the country's policy of apartheid, is stabbed to death during a parliamentary session.

September 30
Speer Released
Architect and former Nazi government minister Albert Speer is released from Spandau Prison after serving a 20-year sentence.

November 30
Barbados Wins Independence
The Caribbean island wins its independence from Britain.

December 31
Art Theft in London
Thieves steal millions of pounds' worth of artwork from Dulwich Picture Gallery.

1967

OIL TANKER SPILLS ITS LOAD

On March 18, 1967, the supertanker *Torrey Canyon*, carrying 120,000 tons of oil, struck a rock between the Isles of Scilly and Land's End in Cornwall, England. Instantly, its 31 million gallons (141 million litres) of oil began to leak out into the sea between England and France, destroying the majority of the marine life along the coasts of both countries and contaminating miles of beaches. Because such a major environmental disaster had never occurred before and had not been anticipated, there were no emergency plans in place, and some knee-jerk reactions, such as spraying the slick with gallons of chemical dispersants, caused even greater harm. It was estimated that these chemicals had killed more marine life than the oil itself. The crew was lifted to safety by helicopter, and the tanker was bombed for two days in an attempt to sink it and burn up the rest of its oil. The *Torrey Canyon* eventually sank 12 days later, but the effects were felt for years afterwards. An inquiry in Liberia, where the ship was registered, found that the captain was to blame for the disaster, as he had taken a short cut in order to reach his destination in Wales earlier.

> **'The tanker was bombed for two days in an attempt to sink it and burn up the rest of its oil.'**

SHATTERED TANKER BREAKS UP IN GALE

Above: Burning off the oil and cleaning up the beaches.

DYING MAN GETS NEW HEART

WORLD'S FIRST HEART TRANSPLANT

The world's first human heart transplant was performed by Professor Christiaan Barnard (left) in South Africa on December 3, 1967. The patient was Mr. Louis Washkansky, whose heart was about to fail, and the donor was a young woman who had been killed in a car accident. Professor Barnard had devoted his professional life to the development of heart surgery, and had the opportunity to work in Minneapolis, Minnesota, with Professor Owen Wagensteen, a pioneer of experimental surgery. When the heart-lung machine was perfected in the United States, Professor Barnard was given one as a gift to take back to his native South Africa. He returned to Groote Shuur Hospital in the Western Cape in 1958 and assembled a cardiac team ready to perform a cardiac bypass operation. He also practiced performing kidney transplants until eventually, in 1967, he felt that his team was ready to perform the first heart transplant. The operation took nine hours and was deemed to be successful. However, Mr. Washkansky died 18 days later from pneumonia, though his new heart was apparently still beating strongly to the end.

January 14
Human Be-In
The 'Human Be-In' is held in Golden Gate Park, San Francisco, a prelude to the Summer of Love.

March 7
Union Leader Sent to Jail
Jimmy Hoffa, president of the Teamsters union in the U.S., begins an eight-year sentence for attempting to bribe a jury.

April 21
Coup in Greece
The military seize power in Greece. Ex-Prime Minister Andreas Papandreou is imprisoned.

April 24
Cosmonaut Dies
Vladimir Komarov is the first Soviet cosmonaut to die when the parachute of his space capsule fails during re-entry into the Earth's atmosphere.

ISRAEL AND ARAB STATES FIGHT SIX DAY WAR

WAR IN THE MIDDLE EAST

The combined Anglo-French-Israeli invasion of Egypt during the crisis over the Suez Canal in 1956 had left many lasting effects on the region. Although Egypt succeeded in recapturing the canal, the U.N. ordered the invaders to leave and installed a peacekeeping force to maintain order. While Israel withdrew its troops from the Sinai Peninsula, and Egypt agreed to reopen the canal to Israeli shipping, Israel declared the borders agreed in the 1949 armistice no longer valid, and the Arab states still refused to recognize the existence of Israel, so major issues remained unresolved. When, in 1965, a dispute arose between Israel, Jordan, and Syria over access to water, the Israel Defense Forces (I.D.F.) carried out a series of air strikes designed to stop water diversions set up in Syria. In November 1966, when a border mine exploded and killed Israeli soldiers, Israel attacked a Jordanian region of the West Bank, which Israel claimed harbored Palestinian terrorists. King Hussein of Jordan, who had good relations with the U.S. and was generally a peaceable influence in the region, was forced to retaliate, and mobilized his army on November 20, 1966. A further dispute between Israel and Syria over land being farmed by Arabs in the demilitarized zones prompted an exchange of fire. In 1966, Egypt and Syria signed a mutual defense pact, agreeing to help each other if attacked. Over the ensuing months, Syrian-Israeli disputes continued, escalating into almost constant bombing and shelling on both sides, but without a formal declaration of war. In May 1967, the commander of Egypt's Army informed the peacekeeping United Nations Emergency Force (U.N.E.F.) that Egypt was prepared to go to war with Israel as soon as Israel attacked any Arab state, and he asked U.N. troops to withdraw for their own safety. The commander of U.N.E.F. tried to negotiate, but in the end was forced to withdraw, and Egypt began to remilitarize the Sinai Peninsula. While U.N. troops were preparing to depart, hostilities broke out in earnest on June 5, 1967, when Israel initiated an air strike on Egyptian airfields. Jordan and Syria promptly joined forces with Egypt, and over the next six days Iraq, Saudi Arabia, Sudan, Algeria, Morocco, and Tunisia also sent troops. By June 10, though, Israel had captured the Gaza Strip, the Sinai Peninsula, the West Bank, and the Golan Heights, and the Arab states were forced to sign a ceasefire.

> **'Disputes continued, escalating into almost constant bombing and shelling on both sides.'**

Right: The Sinai Peninsula, where Egypt mustered its troops for the Six Day War against Israel.

April 27
Expo 67 Opens
A World's Fair in Montreal, Quebec, is opened by Canadian Prime Minister Lester Pearson.

May 2
U.K. Applies to Join E.E.C.
Prime Minister Harold Wilson announces his intention to apply for membership of the E.E.C.

June 28
Israel Annexes East Jerusalem
Israel takes control of the whole of the city of Jerusalem.

July 1
Color T.V. Reaches the U.K.
The first ever color broadcast is made from the Wimbledon tennis championship.

1967

BIAFRANS DECLARE INDEPENDENCE

On May 30, 1967, the people of Biafra in Nigeria proclaimed their independence only a few years after Nigeria itself had gained independence from Britain. Occupying the eastern region of Nigeria, the people were mainly Igbo and had fled massacre by another tribe. The people of Biafra numbered some 30 million, but their numbers were no advantage when faced with food blockades. General Yakubu Gowon (below), leader of Federal Nigeria, immediately cut off all supply lines to the breakaway state. Coming under international pressure, the Nigerian military government eventually allowed the Red Cross to deliver medical aid, but it is estimated that millions of Biafrans died of starvation. British involvement on behalf of the starving Biafrans was tainted by the fact that the British government was selling arms to Nigeria. For three years the Biafrans held out in appalling conditions, but they were eventually beaten by federal troops and their republic ceased to exist in January 1970.

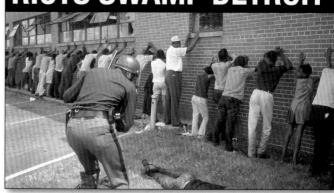

Left: Colonel Ojukwu, leader of the Biafran separatists.

RIOTS IN THE U.S.A.

In the 1960s, the U.S. city of Detroit, in Michigan, had serious economic and social problems. The roots of these lay in the 1940s and 1950s, when white inhabitants, who resented the influx of black migrants, built physical barriers between neighborhoods and tried to bar black residents from social housing. Urban regeneration projects in the 1950s, which involved building new freeways from city to suburbs, invariably resulted in the complete destruction of predominantly black neighborhoods. Lack of housing became a major problem and caused forced integration, which increased hostility between blacks and whites. By the 1960s, several predominantly white neighborhoods had become predominantly black. Added to this, the Detroit police, who were notoriously racist and brutal, made frequent raids on bars in black neighborhoods. One such raid, on the night of July 23, 1967, intended to round up a few drunks from an after-hours drinking establishment. Instead police found a bar full of people celebrating the return of two men from the Vietnam War. The police called in reinforcements and arrested all 82 of those present, but rioting and vandalism broke out. Over the next five days the situation grew worse and spread across the city. By the time the police and military regained control, 43 people were dead, 1,189 injured, and 7,000 had been arrested.

August 5
The Piper at the Gates of Dawn Released
British band Pink Floyd release their debut album.

September 3
Swedish Drivers Cross the Road
At 5 a.m. local time, all the traffic in Sweden switches from left-hand drive to right-hand drive to fall in line with the rest of Scandinavia.

November 8
Local Radio Station Launched in the U.K.
B.B.C. Radio Leicester, the B.B.C.'s first local radio station, goes on air. Within a few years, the B.B.C. dominates local radio.

November 30
Pakistan People's Party Founded
Zulfiqar Ali Bhutto is the first chairman of the new political party.

MARTIN LUTHER KING SHOT DEAD

On the evening of April 4, 1968, Martin Luther King Jr., the inspirational leader of the civil rights movement in America, was shot dead on the balcony of his motel in Memphis, Tennessee. Dr. King was a deeply religious man, a gifted preacher who advocated peaceful protest and fought with bravery and dignity for equal rights and social integration for African Americans. The F.B.I. arrested a white man named James Earl Ray for the fatal shooting. However, many, including King's own family, believed Ray to be innocent, and the involvement of the F.B.I. itself was strongly suspected. Ray was sentenced to 99 years and died in prison, despite claiming that he had been part of a larger conspiracy. Dr. King had gone to Memphis in March 1968 to support a strike among black sanitation workers over unfair treatment, but, to his dismay, the protest march turned violent. Not wanting the movement to be tainted by violence, he returned in April to counsel the people against violence, before leading another peaceful march. Dr. King knew on April 3, when he addressed the audience in Memphis, that his life was in danger. There had been a bomb threat the day before, and he had recently been stabbed, but he said in his speech: 'Like anybody, I would like to live a long life; longevity has its place. But I'm not concerned about that now. I just want to do God's will. And he's allowed me to go to the mountaintop. And I've looked over, and I've seen the Promised Land. I may not get there with you. But I want you to know tonight that we as a people will get to the Promised Land. And so I'm happy tonight; I'm not worried about anything; I'm not fearing any man. Mine eyes have seen the glory of the coming of the Lord.' After his assassination, rioting broke out in cities across America.

'Dr. King knew on April 3, when he addressed the audience in Memphis, that his life was in danger.'

MARTIN LUTHER KING ASSASSINATED

Right: Coretta Scott King, widow of the assassinated civil rights leader, became a campaigner herself after his death.

Above: The great man's son, Martin Luther King III, campaigns widely against poverty.

January 30
Viet Cong Offensive
The Viet Cong launches a series of attacks across South Vietnam in an attempt to spark an uprising against the Saigon government.

March 16
Mai Lai Massacre
U.S. troops kill hundreds of unarmed civilians in Vietnam. The massacre is revealed a year later to worldwide condemnation.

March 16
Kennedy Enters Race
Senator Robert F. Kennedy enters the race for the Democratic Party presidential nomination.

March 22
French Students Occupy University
Eight students occupy offices in the University of Nanterre, the first in a series of protests across France.

March 31
Johnson Steps Down
Lyndon Johnson announces that he will not seek re-election as U.S. president.

1968

'CURSE OF THE KENNEDYS' STRIKES AGAIN

On June 5, 1968, Robert Kennedy, a younger brother of John F. Kennedy, was fatally shot in the head while delivering a victory speech in the ballroom of a Los Angeles hotel. At the time, U.S. Senator Robert Kennedy was the favorite for the Democrat presidential candidacy in the forthcoming election, and he had just won the California primaries. The gunman was a 24-year-old Palestinian man named Sirhan Bishara Sirhan, and it was assumed that Senator Kennedy's well-known support for Israel was behind the assassination. Robert Kennedy died the following day in the hospital, after emergency brain surgery failed to save him. Sirhan Sirhan was sentenced to life in prison, but, as ever, theories emerged about more complex conspiracies behind the shooting – the second Kennedy assassination in a decade.

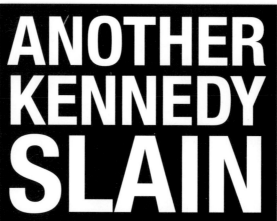

ANOTHER KENNEDY SLAIN

'The gunman was a 24-year-old Palestinian ... and it was assumed that Senator Kennedy's well-known support for Israel was behind the assassination.'

Above: The coffin of Robert Kennedy is carried by family and friends.

April 2
Bombs Exploded in German Shop
Bombs placed by German terror group the Red Army Faction explode at a department store in Frankfurt.

April 7
Racing Driver Clark Killed
Former Formula 1 champion, Scotland's Jim Clark, is killed in a crash in a race in Germany.

May 14
Apple Records Founded
The Beatles found their own record label.

SOVIET TANKS ROLL INTO PRAGUE

SOVIETS INVADE CZECHOSLOVAKIA

After the Second World War, Czechoslovakia was tightly controlled by the U.S.S.R. For more than a decade, the country was subject to externally enforced restrictions on every aspect of life – social, economic, and political. Then gradually, during the 1960s, cultural changes began to emerge, and there was new freedom in the fields of music, literature, fashion, and the media. The Soviets disapproved of this Westernization, but Czechoslovakia's new leader, Alexander Dubček, who came to power in January 1968, brought about official reforms aimed at increasing political freedom. His aim was to establish basic human rights in the legal system and to bring an end to political persecution. The reforms were an attempt to create, in Dubček's own words, 'socialism with a human face', but his decentralization of the economy and democratization of the political system were met with increasing hostility from the U.S.S.R. The period that subsequently became known as the 'Prague Spring', for its reawakening of artistic and political freedom, came to an end in August 1968 when the U.S.S.R. led Warsaw Pact forces in an invasion of Czechoslovakia, with the declared intention of 'normalizing' what they saw as revolutionary forces. Alexander Dubček and other leaders of the reform were taken away to Moscow. The Soviet occupation of the country lasted for 20 years. The only reform to survive the Soviet counter-revolution was the division of Czechoslovakia into two separate republics, one Czech and one Slovak, but state administration remained strictly centralized.

Left: Prague is the capital of the Czech Republic, now a member of the E.U.

May 29
Manchester United Win European Cup
They beat Portuguese champions Benfica 4–1 in the final at Wembley Stadium, London. They are the first English club to win the trophy.

June 3
Warhol Shot
Artist Andy Warhol is shot and wounded by radical feminist Valerie Solanas.

October 2
Massacre in Mexico
Ten days before the start of the Olympic Games in the city, hundreds of student demonstrators are shot dead by police in Mexico City.

October 16
Black Power Salute
American sprinters Tommie Smith and John Carlos raise their arms in a black power salute during a medals ceremony at the Olympics.

1969

MEN LAND ON THE MOON

ONE SMALL STEP...

Right: Crowds in Trafalgar Square in central London watched the Moon landings on a giant T.V. screen.

Apollo 11 was the fifth mission of the Apollo Project and the third to take humans to the Moon. The space flight was launched on July 16, 1969, and it culminated in Commander Neil Armstrong and lunar module pilot Edwin 'Buzz' Aldrin walking on the Moon. The resounding success of the mission was heightened by its fulfillment of President Kennedy's statement of hope in 1961: 'I believe that this nation should commit itself to the goal, before this decade is out, of landing a man on the Moon and returning him safely to Earth.' The *Apollo 11* launch from the Kennedy Space Center in Florida was watched by thousands of people who had gathered around the site, as well as by millions more across the globe on television screens. On July 19 the spacecraft reached the Moon and orbited 30 times. The lunar module, named *Eagle* after the national bird of the United States, then separated from the command module and, on July 20, landed on the Moon, with Neil Armstrong and Buzz Aldrin inside. The module had just 25 seconds' worth of fuel remaining after a longer-than-expected descent, and when Neil Armstrong spoke the words, 'The *Eagle* has landed,' there was all-around relief at NASA's command base in Houston, Texas. Six hours later, in the early morning of July 21, Neil Armstrong descended from the lunar module and stepped onto the surface of the Moon. It was then that he uttered the now famous words: 'That's one small step for [a] man, one giant leap for mankind.' The moment was broadcast on T.V. to around 600 million people across the globe. It was filmed in 'slow-scan' mode, and then

> **'The lunar module had just 25 seconds' worth of fuel remaining after a longer-than-expected descent'**

January 12
Led Zeppelin 1
Seminal British rock band Led Zeppelin release their eponymous debut album.

January 20
Nixon Becomes President
Republican Richard Nixon becomes the 37th president of the U.S.A.

February 4
Arafat Becomes Leader of P.L.O.
Yasser Arafat is elected leader of the Palestine Liberation Organization.

April 22
Round-the-World Sailor Returns
British sailor Robin Knox-Johnston arrives back in Falmouth, England, 10 months after he had left to complete the first ever non-stop solo round-the-world voyage.

ONE GIANT LEAP...

a conventional T.V. camera filmed the slow-scan monitor. Although this meant that the images lost their quality and definition, few people cared: it was clear enough that men had landed on the Moon. While they were up there, Armstrong and Aldrin had various tasks to complete, such as depositing the Early Apollo Scientific Experiment Package, planting the American flag, collecting rock samples, and photographing the lunar module so that N.A.S.A. engineers could examine its condition. They also briefly spoke to President Nixon in the White House. Armstrong reported that moving around was easy, except for a tendency to slip on the fine Moon dust. The men had initially been allowed 34 minutes on the Moon's surface, but their tasks took longer than expected, so Houston decided to allow them a further 15 minutes. The astronauts then re-entered the lunar module and blasted off to be reunited with the command module *Columbia*, which pilot Michael Collins had maintained in orbit during their activities. On July 23, the three astronauts made a T.V. broadcast to the world, during which they thanked all those working behind the scenes, and Buzz Aldrin commented: 'We feel that this stands as a symbol of the insatiable curiosity of all mankind to explore the unknown ... Personally, in reflecting on the events of the past several days, a verse from Psalms comes to mind: "When I consider the heavens, the work of Thy fingers, the Moon and the stars, which Thou hast ordained, What is man, that Thou art mindful of him?"' *Apollo 11* splashed down to Earth on July 24, 1969. The astronauts had to endure three weeks in quarantine, but they were then paraded before the American people in a series of ecstatic celebrations.

Top left: The Earth seen from the Moon.
Left: The Saturn V rocket blasted all Apollo missions into space.

May 26
Lennon and Ono's Bed-In
John Lennon and Yoko Ono begin a week-long Bed-In in Montreal to protest against the Vietnam War.

June 28
Stonewall Riots
A series of demonstrations are held in New York City after police raid the Stonewall Inn in what is perceived as an attack on gay people.

July 1
Prince of Wales Invested
Prince Charles is invested as the Prince of Wales at Caernarfon Castle.

July 14
Football War
Following a soccer match in which El Salvador beat Honduras, riots break out in Honduras protesting against the 300,000 Salvadorean workers in the country. El Savaldoran troops invade in response. A ceasefire comes into effect six days later.

1969

CONCORDE UP!

On March 2, 1969, the supersonic airliner Concorde made its maiden flight. The Anglo-French project, in which the British had initially invested £155 million, produced a plane that could reach speeds of up to 1,300 mph (2,097 kph) – faster than the speed of sound. During the first flight, however, Concorde's French pilot maintained a moderate 300 mph (484 kph) and was airborne for only 27 minutes. The flight was considered a great success,

> **'The Anglo-French project ... produced a plane that could reach speeds of up to 1,300 mph (2,097 kph) – faster than the speed of sound.'**

however, and a British pilot completed his own test flight seven days later. Concorde made its first supersonic flight on October 1, 1969. Commercial flights were not launched until 1976, and these included a London–New York flight that took just three and a half hours. However, there had always been doubts about the commercial viability of Concorde, and it was estimated that it would end up costing Britain £900 million. Despite early excitement, the aircraft soon hit problems: heavy fuel consumption at a time when fuel prices were rising made it hugely expensive, and small fuel tanks prevented it from entering the trans-Pacific market. In 2003, Air France and British Airways announced that Concorde was no longer financially viable, and it made its final flight on October 23, 2003.

THE SUPERSONIC AGE

Left: Concorde's prototype went into construction in 1969.
Right: The in-service aircraft made a farewell tour of its routes in 2003.

August 9
Sharon Tate Murdered
A heavily pregnant Sharon Tate, wife of director Roman Polanski, and three of her friends, are murdered in Los Angeles by members of a cult led by Charles Manson.

August 15
Woodstock Begins
The Woodstock Festival in upstate New York begins.

September 1
Coup in Libya
King Idris is ousted in a military coup in Libya. Colonel Muammar al-Gaddafi takes power.

October 29
First Message Sent Over ARPANET
The forerunner of the internet is used for the first time.

October 31
Wal-Mart Founded
U.S. retail giant Wal-Mart is incorporated as Wal-Mart Stores, Inc.

BATTLE OF THE BOGSIDE IN NORTHERN IRELAND

TROOPS SENT TO NORTHERN IRELAND

Left: The Bogside area of Derry is still predominantly Catholic. Life is much more peaceful since the 1998 Good Friday Agreement.

Throughout 1969 there had been clashes between the Royal Ulster Constabulary (R.U.C.) and the nationalist residents of the Bogside area in Derry, who continued to oppose the government of Northern Ireland. The local population (predominantly Catholic) made every effort to resist the intrusion of the R.U.C., and there were several forced 'invasions' into the district, resulting in casualties on both sides. In July 1969, the Derry Citizens Defence Association (D.C.D.A.) was established to prepare for anticipated trouble on the occasion of the loyalist Apprentice Boys March

'On the eve of the Apprentice Boys March, women and children were evacuated and barricades were erected.'

in August. Nationalist leaders of the D.C.D.A. made it clear that the people of the Bogside would do everything within their power to keep out the R.U.C. On the eve of the march, women and children were evacuated and barricades were erected. The march went ahead as planned, on August 12, 1969, and there were clashes between the R.U.C. and nationalists in the Bogside, which soon escalated from stone throwing to full-scale rioting. For some time the people of Bogside stood firm and warded off the R.U.C., but by the evening the R.U.C. had breached the barricades. In an attempt to end the battle the Minister for Home Affairs at Stormont authorized the use of tear gas. Over the next two days, the debilitating gas was fired into the Bogside, and residents used homemade petrol bombs in retaliation. The residents took control of a block of flats and, from that position, rained down bombs on the R.U.C. Amid rumors that the Irish Army was coming to their aid, the residents held out, even when the R.U.C. began to use live ammunition. In the end, it was the British Army who stepped in to rescue the R.U.C., and the Battle of the Bogside promptly ended at 4 p.m. on August 14, 1969.

'The march ... soon escalated from stone throwing to full-scale rioting.'

November 9
Alcatraz Seized
A Native American group, led by Richard Oakes, occupies Alcatraz Island in San Francisco Bay. They hold the island until 1971.

November 14
Apollo 12 Launched
N.A.S.A. sends its second manned mission to the Moon.

November 21
U.S. Agree to Return Japanese Island
The U.S. and Japanese governments agree that Okinawa, a Japanese island controlled by the U.S. since the end of the Second World War, should return to Japanese sovereignty.

December 2
Jumbo Jet's First Flight
The first Boeing 747 flies from Seattle to New York City.

HAPPY ENDING FOR APOLLO 13 MISSION

MOON MISSION IN PERIL

Apollo 13 was due to be the third space mission to land men on the Moon. But on April 14, 1970, 56 hours into the mission, when the spacecraft was about 200,000 miles (320,000 km) from Earth, an onboard oxygen tank blew up. The explosion cut the electricity and water supply, and the astronauts – James Lovell, Jr., John Swigert, Jr., and Fred Haise, Jr. – could hear gas escaping. Mission control abandoned all thought of landing the astronauts on the Moon and instead concentrated on getting them home safely. The crew was forced to abandon the Service Module, where decreasing air pressure was making the atmosphere intolerable. They took refuge in the Lunar Module, *Aquarius*, and prepared to curve around the Moon and head back to Earth. However, the explosion had also disabled the navigation system, so instead the men had to rely on the Sun to guide them home. Had the explosion occurred after the lunar landing, when the Lunar Module would have already detached from the Service Module, there would have been no hope. As it was, the three men managed to survive on the Lunar Module's emergency battery power supply. Four days later, on Friday April 17, 1970, to the immense relief of the crew, mission control, and the watching world, the Command Module, *Odyssey*, splashed down safely in the Pacific Ocean. The Lunar Module and the Service Module had both been jettisoned before re-entry to the Earth's atmosphere. The crew was unharmed and was flown to American Samoa to be reunited with their families. The aim of the mission had been to conduct geological experiments to help establish the age of the Moon. Sadly, this was not accomplished, but the survival of the astronauts was of paramount concern.

Left: School children pray for the safe return of Apollo 13.

January
The Big Freeze
The coldest weather in years closes schools, shops, and airports across Europe, causing an influenza outbreak and a rise in the cost of heating oil.

January 15
End of War in Nigeria
Biafran rebels surrender, ending the war for independence in Nigeria.

March 1
Vietnam War Escalates
American war planes bomb the Ho Chi Minh trail in Vietnam, the main route between North and South Vietnam, made up of many intricate jungle paths.

HOSTAGE CRISIS IN MIDDLE EAST

On September 6, 1970, the first major act of Middle Eastern terrorism occurred when members of the Palestine Liberation Organization (P.L.O.) hijacked four commercial airliners. They flew three of the planes, with their hostages, to the Jordanian desert near Amman, and, after negotiations had secured the evacuation of all passengers in return for the release of P.L.O. terrorists in prison, they blew up the planes. The passengers were subsequently kept hostage for some weeks during negotiations. King Hussein of Jordan prepared to use military force against the P.L.O., but before he did so, he sought assurance from U.S. President Nixon that if Syria or Iraq came to the defense of the P.L.O. and attacked Jordan, America would lend military support. Henry Kissinger, U.S. Secretary of State, came up with an alternative plan: he suggested that King Hussein ask Israel for help in defeating the P.L.O. By joint agreement between King Hussein, President Nixon, and Israeli Prime Minister Golda Meir, the Israelis launched air strikes on Palestinian strongholds in Jordan. Around 2,000 P.L.O. fighters, as well as several thousand Palestinian civilians, were killed in the military action. Although Syria attempted to intervene on behalf of the Palestinians, they withdrew when faced with a joint U.S.-Israeli threat. King Hussein lost the support of his Arab neighbors. Although the P.L.O. had been ejected from Jordan, the group moved to Lebanon and grew stronger, thanks to Soviet support.

FOUR JETS HIJACKED

'The first major act of Middle Eastern terrorism occurred when members of the P.L.O. hijacked four commercial airliners.'

Left: Golda Meir was Prime Minister of Israel from 1969 to 1974.

April 10
Beatles Break Up
The world's most famous rock group holds a press conference to announce that they have disbanded, upsetting millions of fans around the world.

May 4
Students Shot
The U.S. National Guard fires on students demonstrating against the Vietnam War at Kent State University in Ohio, killing four.

May 8
Beatles' Last Album
The Beatles release their last album, *Let It Be*.

June 10
Younger Voters
President Nixon lowers the voting age in the U.S. from 21 to 18.

1970

WAR IN JORDAN

Following the Six-Day War with Israel in 1967, Jordan lost the West Bank of the Jordan River to Israel, displacing thousands of Palestinians who fled into Jordan. Yasser Arafat regrouped his militant Palestine Liberation Organization (P.L.O.) in Jordan and carried out military attacks on Israel, often prompting retaliations that, in turn, killed Jordanians. In response to the P.L.O.'s guerrilla tactics within his country, King Hussein of Jordan, who remained unpopular with Arab militants for his involvement in peace talks with Israel, authorized the shelling of Palestinian refugee camps in an attempt to flush the P.L.O. out of Jordan. In June 1970, this situation escalated into a state of civil war between Jordanian troops and Palestinian guerrillas, with the P.L.O. seizing control of the city of Amman. On June 9, several shots were fired at King Hussein's car, but he managed to escape unharmed, although his driver was wounded.

HUSSEIN IS SAFE

'The situation escalated into a state of civil war between Jordanian troops and Palestinian guerrillas'

U.S. IN CAMBODIA

At the beginning of 1970, U.S. President Nixon told the American people that the U.S. Army would withdraw from Vietnam as soon as possible. The North Vietnamese had long ago entered Cambodia despite the country's neutrality, and by March 1970, they had overthrown the Cambodian King, Norodom Sihanouk, and General Lon Nol was in power. Realizing that control of Cambodia would enable the North Vietnamese to carry out attacks on South Vietnam far more easily, President Nixon was forced to commit further U.S. troops to aid the Cambodians in repelling their invaders. His justification to the American people was that, if he did not commit troops to Cambodia, the lives of 150,000 American troops would be seriously endangered. Over the course of a 60-day action involving 30,000 U.S. troops, more than 10,000 North Vietnamese were killed and supply depots were seized. In June 1970, President Nixon announced that the mission in Cambodia had been successful, despite the fact that it had sparked further protests throughout the United States against the war.

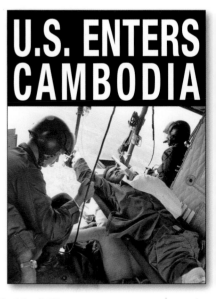

U.S. ENTERS CAMBODIA

'President Nixon was forced to commit further U.S. troops to aid the Cambodians'

August 26–30
Music Festival
About 600,000 people enjoy the largest-ever rock festival on the Isle of Wight, featuring Jimi Hendrix; The Who; The Doors; Chicago; Richie Havens; Joan Baez; Ten Years After; Emerson, Lake & Palmer; and Jethro Tull.

September 18
Jimi Hendrix Dies
Jimi Hendrix dies in London from a drug overdose. Born Johnny Allen Hendrix on November 27, 1942, one of the many songs he is remembered for is his electric guitar version of the 'Star Spangled Banner.'

October 15
New President of Egypt
Anwar Sadat becomes the third President of Egypt upon the death of Nassar. Sadat re-institutes the multi-party system in Egypt, and shares the 1978 Nobel Prize for Peace with Israeli Prime Minister Menachim Begin.

November 9
Charles de Gaulle Dies
Born November 22, 1890, de Gaulle led the Free French Forces during the Second World War and was the first President of the French Fifth Republic, from 1959 to 1969.

BANGLADESH FIGHTS FOR INDEPENDENCE

Since the 1947 partition of India created Pakistan as a separate state, there had been increasing differences between the people of West Pakistan and the people of the East. The two regions were at odds culturally, economically, and politically. West Pakistan dominated the new country politically and exploited the more populous East by diverting state funds to its own ends. West Pakistan also kept East Pakistan out of government by rigging the voting system so that the greater population in the East could not alter the balance of power. In the 1970 national elections, the Awami League, the East Pakistan political party led by Sheikh Mujibur Rahman, won a majority of seats in the National Assembly. However, the Pakistan People's Party of Western Pakistan refused to allow him to form a government. Instead they suggested creating roles for two prime ministers, one for the East and one for the West. In response, Rahman called a general strike in March 1971 and rallied his people to fight for independence from West Pakistan. On March 25, 1971, the Pakistan Army launched Operation Searchlight, a military crackdown on rebellion and nationalism in the East, which has in subsequent years been described as a genocide. The operation consisted of the systematic murder of thousands, or even millions, of Bengali civilians. Sheikh Mujibur Rahman declared Bangladesh (formerly East Pakistan) as an independent country, and on April 17, 1971, he formed a government-in-exile in Mujib Nagar, India, where masses of Bengali refugees had fled. In the civil war that followed, the collection of Bangladeshi guerrilla forces, known as Mukti Bahini, received support and training from India. By the end of 1971, Pakistan was increasingly afraid of Indian involvement in their civil war and tried to ward it off with a pre-emptive strike on Indian airfields. India promptly invaded Pakistan and, together with the Mukti Bahini, defeated them. In the 1972 Simla Agreement with India, Pakistan recognized Bangladesh as an independent country in exchange for the release of Pakistani prisoners of war.

Left: Mukti Bahini fighters threaten Razakars, who fought alongside the Pakistani Army.

January 25
Idi Amin Seizes Power
Idi Amin takes over as ruler of Uganda in a bloodless coup.

February 15
Concorde Flies
Supersonic Concorde's maiden flight takes place in France.

April 5
Mount Etna
In Sicily, a violent eruption of Mount Etna threatens villages and destroys an observatory.

April 24
March Against the War
Approximately 500,000 people march against the Vietnam War in Washington, D.C., along with about 125,000 protesters in San Francisco.

June 14
North Sea Oil
Norway starts production.

1971

BELFAST BAR BOMBED

On December 4, 1971, a bomb exploded in a crowded bar in Belfast, killing 15 people, including two children. It was one of the first major atrocities that launched the era often referred to as 'The Troubles'. Tramore Bar, more commonly known as McGurk's, was in a Catholic area, which baffled those who assumed that the Provisional Irish Republican Army (I.R.A.) had planted the bomb. The I.R.A., however, denied involvement, accusing a loyalist paramilitary group. The owner of the bar, Patrick McGurk, whose wife and daughter were killed in the blast, appeared on television with a public plea against retaliation: 'What's done can't be undone,' he said. After the bomb went off, fights between Catholics and Protestants broke out across the city. Despite the strange choice of target, for many years the belief continued that the explosion was caused by an I.R.A. bomb – the explanation given that it had gone off by mistake. It was not until 1977 that the driver of the getaway car confessed that the bomb had been planted by the loyalist paramilitary group the Ulster Volunteer Force. The driver was given 15 life sentences for his part in the crime, but no one else has since been arrested in connection with the bombing, despite calls by the victims' families to reopen the case.

VIOLENCE FLARES IN NORTHERN IRELAND

DECIMALIZATION FOR U.K

ALL CHANGE

'The United Kingdom and Ireland switched from the units of pounds, shillings, and pence to the decimal system.'

On February 15, 1971, the United Kingdom and Ireland switched from the units of pounds, shillings, and pence to the decimal system. Previously, £1 was made up of 20 shillings, and 1 shilling was made up of 12 pence. This system stretched back to Roman times, when a pound of silver was worth 240 silver pieces. Following decimalization, a pound consisted of 100 'new pennies'. The Americans pioneered the decimal system of money in 1786 when they established that $1 was worth 100 cents. The U.K. decision to go decimal had been delayed by discussions about scrapping the pound in favor of a smaller unit. However, in March 1966, James Callaghan, Chancellor of the Exchequer, announced the decision to make the change to decimal in 1971 and to retain the pound as the unit of currency. His announcement was greeted with cheers in the House of Commons. After Britain had made this change, several Commonwealth countries followed suit.

June 22–26
First Glastonbury
The first Glastonbury Festival, held on Worthy Farm in southwest England, was attended by only 1,500 people. Organized by Michael Eavis over the years, the first event was not a business success, although its headline act was T. Rex. The festival is now a tradition, famous for its mud and big acts.

July 3
Jim Morrison Dies
Jim Morrison, a legend in rock and roll, dies in Paris. Born in Florida on December 8, 1943, he is the charismatic lead singer and lyricist for The Doors.

August 16
Bombs in Britain
The I.R.A. starts its campaign of mainland bombing in Britain.

September
First Commercial V.C.R.
Although there were many variations preceding the V.C.R., Sony is credited with the world's first commercial videocassette recorder, using the Betamax format.

FIGHTING ON STREETS OF NORTHERN IRELAND

In July 1970, political parades and marches were banned in Northern Ireland for a period of six months in an attempt to stamp out growing violence. But the fighting continued in the streets, and the presence of the British Army did nothing to calm the situation. By the summer of 1971, the government at Stormont, under the last Northern Irish Prime Minister, Brian Faulkner, introduced a policy of internment without trial as an emergency measure. In total, 342 Republicans and Nationalists were arrested in dawn raids, and more than 200 of them were imprisoned without trial. Fighting in Belfast and Derry escalated, with gun battles in the streets claiming 12 lives. Following the 1971 bombing in the Tramore Bar (McGurk's) and the killings of 1972's Bloody Sunday, the British government announced that it would adopt an emergency measure of direct rule, dealing with security itself. This emergency measure was meant to last for a 12-month period but ended up lasting 25 years.

'The fighting continued in the streets, and the presence of the British Army did nothing to calm the situation.'

Above: The Parliament of Northern Ireland at Stormont was suspended in 1972.

October 1
Disney World
Walt Disney World opens in Florida.

November 15
World's First Microprocessor
The 4004, the world's first single-chip microprocessor, is released by Intel. This breakthrough allows the future embedding of intelligence in inanimate objects and, eventually, the personal computer.

November 24
Skyjack!
The world's only unsolved skyjacking takes place in a severe thunderstorm over Washington State. D.B. Cooper parachutes from a Northwest Orient Airlines plane with $200,000 ransom. Neither he nor the money is ever seen again.

December 19
A Clockwork Orange
Based on the novel by Anthony Burgess, Stanley Kubrick's influential and controversial film, portraying a decaying and violent society, is released. Kubrick withdraws the film from U.K. cinemas in 1973.

1972

UGANDAN ASIANS ARRIVE IN GREAT BRITAIN

UGANDAN ASIANS EXPELLED

In 1971, General Idi Amin seized power in Uganda by military coup, declaring himself President. In August 1972, he made the decision to expel the country's Asian population. At the time, around 80,000 Asians resided in Uganda. Resentment against Asians was growing because, through hard work and good business sense, they had made themselves the most commercially successful citizens. General Amin subsequently amended his expulsion order to include only those Asians who were not Ugandan citizens, which reduced the number to around 60,000. Since Uganda was a former British colony, the majority of the expelled Asians held British passports, and when they were forced from Uganda, the obvious choice was Great Britain. The situation was viewed with some alarm in Britain, particularly by its right-wing politicians, who argued against the need to accept the expelled Asians into Britain. However, in the end, around 30,000 Ugandan Asians did arrive in Britain, for the most part penniless, since they had been expelled without any compensation for the homes or businesses they were leaving behind. The expulsion made General Amin popular among many of the black majority, and members of the army, whom he valued highly, were rewarded with Asian property and businesses. The economy, however, went into drastic decline, with cement and sugar factories grinding to a halt.

> 'Resentment against Asians was growing because, through hard work and good business sense, they had made themselves ... commercially successful'

Left: Idi Amin claimed God had told him to expel Ugandan Asians.

March 4
An Offer You Can't Refuse
The film *The Godfather*, starring Marlon Brando and Al Pacino, is released. The film wins three Academy Awards and is later ranked second in American cinema history, behind *Citizen Kane*. Based on the book by Mario Puzo, the film is directed by Francis Ford Coppola.

March 24
Northern Ireland
British direct rule over Northern Ireland begins.

May 4
Greenpeace Emerges
The world's most well-known environmental activist group is renamed, having been known previously as the Don't Make a Wave Committee.

May 22
Nixon in Russia
Richard Nixon becomes the first American president to visit the U.S.S.R. He is not very warmly welcomed by President Nikolai Podgomy, Prime Minister Alexei Kosygin, and Foreign Minister Andrei Gromyko.

TERROR AT MUNICH OLYMPICS

MASSACRE AT OLYMPICS

On September 5, 1972, eight Arab terrorists with ties to Fatah, Yasser Arafat's branch of the Palestine Liberation Organization (P.L.O.), infiltrated the Olympic Village at the Munich Games and took nine Israeli athletes hostage. The terrorists had called themselves the Black September Organization after the 1970 Israeli airstrikes that killed thousands of Palestinians. After taking their hostages, the terrorists declared themselves Palestinians and demanded the release of 234 Arab terrorists held in Israeli jails, as well as the release of two held in a German prison and a guarantee of their own safe passage out of Germany. After hours of negotiations, the German authorities made it look like they agreed to fulfill the terrorists' request and arranged for helicopters to take them to an airfield. However, the German authorities had secretly positioned gunmen to kill the terrorists when they arrived at the airfield, while sparing the hostages. The rescue plan failed, leading instead to a shoot-out between the terrorists and the German authorities. One terrorist managed to set off a grenade in his helicopter, killing everyone onboard, while another shot dead the rest of the Israeli hostages. In all, 11 Israeli athletes and coaches, five terrorists, and one German policeman were killed. Three of the terrorists were captured alive and held in German jails, but they were later released following the hijacking of a German plane.

Right: Israeli swimmer Shlomit Nir at a memorial service for the murdered athletes.

Above: The Olympic Stadium in Munich, Germany.

May 22
Sri Lanka
Ceylon becomes the republic of Sri Lanka, with a new constitution.

May 26
Treaties Signed
Nixon and Brezhnev sign the SALT 1 Treaty in Moscow, as well as the Anti-Ballistic Missile Treaty.

June 8
Kim Phúc
The iconic image of nine-year-old Kim Phúc, running from her Vietnamese village Trang Bang, where a napalm bomb had just been dropped, makes a serious impact on efforts to stop the war.

June 17
Watergate Break-In
The Democratic National Committee headquarters in the Watergate Building, in Washington, D.C., is broken into by five White House operatives who are arrested, starting a chain of events that will lead to U.S. President Richard Nixon's resignation.

1972

MASS MURDER AT LOD AIRPORT

TERRORIST AIRPORT OUTRAGE

'The three men opened fire at random, killing 24 bystanders, including 16 Christian pilgrims from Puerto Rico.'

On May 30, 1972, three members of the Japanese Red Army carried out a terrorist attack on behalf of the Popular Front for the Liberation of Palestine at Lod Airport in Tel Aviv. Airport security forces were on the alert for a Palestinian attack and allowed the smartly dressed Japanese men with violin cases to pass them by. Once inside the airport, the three men opened fire at random, killing 24 bystanders, including 16 Christian pilgrims from Puerto Rico. One of the terrorists was shot by an Israeli security guard, another committed suicide by letting off a grenade, and the last was arrested.

BLOODY SUNDAY

In 1969, the Provisional Irish Republican Army (I.R.A.) began its campaign of violence against Unionists in Northern Ireland. Regiments from the British Army were sent to Northern Ireland to keep the peace, but their presence provoked further violence. Inspired by the Civil Rights movement in America, the Northern Ireland Civil Rights Association was formed and began to stage demonstrations. During one such demonstration in the Bogside area of Derry on Sunday January 30, 1972, 28 Civil Rights members were shot by soldiers of the British Parachute Regiment. Fourteen of the protestors died, six of them teenagers, and eyewitnesses claimed that all were unarmed and most were running away from the soldiers when they were shot. The incident became known as 'Bloody Sunday'. It bolstered the popularity of the I.R.A., and many Catholics in Northern Ireland who had previously supported the British government now shifted their loyalty to the Republic of Ireland. Two highly controversial inquiries failed to lay the blame squarely on the British government.

BLOODY SUNDAY

Right: British soldiers shelter from stones on Bloody Sunday 1972.

August
Going for Gold
U.S. swimmer Mark Spitz wins seven gold medals at the Munich Olympics.

August 11
Leaving South Vietnam
American ground troops withdraw from South Vietnam.

September
First Pocket Calculators
The world's first really pocket-sized electronic calculator is the Bowmar 901B, based on Texas Instruments Company components. It is the first with an L.E.D. display; the first hand-held to use a single integrated circuit; and the first electronic calculator to run on replaceable batteries. Hewlett Packard also have a pocket calculator in 1972, so-called because it is the exact size to fit into William Hewlett's shirt pocket. It is the first scientific calculator, with trigonometric and exponential functions.

December 23
Survivors Eat to Live
The 16 survivors of a plane crash in the Andes Mountains in Argentina are forced to eat the remains of the crash victims in order to stay alive in the freezing temperatures, without food or medical supplies, until rescued 10 weeks later.

U.S. LAUNCHES FIRST SPACE STATION

SKYLAB IN ORBIT

On May 14, 1973, the U.S. launched *Skylab*, its first space station, into space. It was to act as a space laboratory for only one year, but instead it remained in orbit around Earth for six years. During that time there were three manned missions to the *Skylab* space station, which enabled astronauts to conduct scientific research and undertake space walks. Around 2,000 hours of scientific and medical experiments took place on *Skylab*. It was during some of these experiments that the Sun's coronal holes were discovered. Other experiments investigated the astronauts' adaptation to long periods of microgravity.

Right: A re-creation of the inside of Sklylab.

'Around 2,000 hours of scientific and medical experiments took place on Skylab.'

Above: Skylab *was the second space station to be visited by a human crew.*

January 1
New Members for E.E.C.
The U.K., the Republic of Ireland, and Denmark join the European Economic Community (E.E.C.), later to become the European Union.

January 14
Aloha
Elvis Presley's television special, *Aloha from Hawaii*, is transmitted. It has over 1 billion viewers worldwide.

April 3
Can You Hear Me?
The first cellular telephone call is made by Martin Cooper, who conceived the original idea of the phone, in New York City.

April 4
Twin Towers
The World Trade Center is officially opened in New York City.

1973

TRUCE IN VIETNAM

As soon as he was elected in 1969, U.S. President Nixon made clear his intention to bring to an end the Vietnam War. However, it was not until October 1972 that he managed to persuade Communist North Vietnam to the negotiating table. The North had up to that point resisted negotiations, but a prolonged campaign of American air strikes had begun to have an effect. Although President Nixon was quick to agree terms with the North, the South Vietnamese President Nguyên Văn Thiêu was unhappy with the situation, which left the South vulnerable to attacks from the thousands of North Vietnamese soldiers still in occupation after the Americans pulled out. Peace negotiations broke down, and President Nixon launched one final military push in order to crush the North. On December 18, 1972, a massive bombing campaign began, targeting Hanoi. It succeeded in driving the North Vietnamese back to the negotiating table. This time an agreement was reached, and in Paris, on January 27, 1973, it was signed by all parties. However, once the American troops withdrew, North and South Vietnam continued to fight. Each country was determined to defeat the other. It was another two years before hostilities would end, with the North finally conquered the South. The American commitment to defending South Vietnam had failed.

'As soon as he was elected in 1969, U.S. President Nixon made clear his intention to bring to an end the Vietnam War.'

WATERGATE HITS NIXON

On June 17, 1972, a group of men broke into the Watergate Hotel, the site of the Democratic National Headquarters. Their aim was to uncover incriminating evidence against the Democratic Party and to bug their offices. The men were members of a security group known as the 'Plumbers', made up of former C.I.A. and F.B.I. men who worked for the Republican government of Richard Nixon and got their name because they 'fixed leaks' in the Republican administration. They had performed similar jobs before, but on this occasion they were careless, and a security guard alerted the police. All of the men were arrested, and it was then that their connections to the government began to emerge. Although President Nixon was elected to a second term, the scandal that would discredit him began to unfold. In May 1973, the Senate started to investigate, and when it was discovered that President Nixon taped all conversations that occurred in his office, Special Prosecutor Archibald Cox Jr. demanded that he hand over the tapes. Nixon stalled. By October, he still had not handed over the tapes, and when Cox continued to insist, Nixon had him fired. But he faced even tougher treatment from the next Special Prosecutor, Leon Jaworski. Nixon finally handed over some of the tapes, but two crucial ones were missing and some of them had erasures. By July 1974, Nixon was still refusing to cooperate, and Jaworski named him as a co-conspirator in the Watergate trial. The House of Representatives voted to impeach the President, and on August 8, 1974, Nixon resigned.

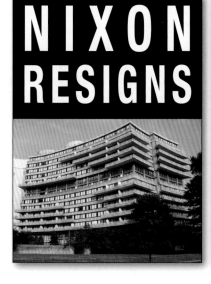

April 8
Picasso Dies
Pablo Picasso is one of the most recognized of the 20th-century artists, as a painter and sculptor, as well as for his lifestyle. Born on October 25, 1881, he was, among other achievements, the co-founder of the Cubist movement.

May 25
Tubular Bells
Mike Oldfield's successful album *Tubular Bells* is released.

September 11
Pinochet Takes Power
General Augusto Pinochet leads an American-backed junta after a military coup in Chile, during which President Salvador Allende commits suicide.

October 6
Yom Kippur War
Egypt and Syria attack Israel on Yom Kippur, the Jewish Day of Atonement. The war ends on October 26, when Israel wins, just as a U.N. ceasefire comes into effect.

WEST HIT BY CRIPPLING ENERGY CRISIS

On October 17, 1973, the members of the Organization of Arab Petroleum Exporting Countries (O.A.P.E.C.) proclaimed an oil embargo against the United States and other countries if they continued to support Israel in the Yom Kippur War. Countries affected included the U.S., U.K., Canada, Japan, and the Netherlands. The embargo coincided with a decision by O.A.P.E.C. to raise the price of oil as a way of stabilizing the exporters' incomes. This also came after considerable stress and rapid inflation in the world economy after the U.S. had pulled out of the Bretton Woods system, whereby only the dollar had been tied to the gold standard and other currencies had been tied to the dollar. The most hard-hit countries responded with a wide variety of initiatives to reduce their dependency on Arab oil. In order to immediately deal with depleted fuel supplies, in the U.K., Prime Minister Edward Heath introduced tough measures, including gasoline rationing. In the long term, the oil embargo changed Western policy towards energy use and conservation and led to more restrictive monetary policy to better fight inflation.

'The most hard-hit countries responded with a wide variety of measures to reduce their dependency on Arab oil.'

Right: Conservative Edward Heath was Prime Minister of the U.K. from 1970 to 1974.

October 12
Supplies to Israel
The U.S. begins Operation Nickel Grass, airlifting weapons and supplies to Israel.

October 20
Sydney Opera House
Queen Elizabeth II opens the Sydney Opera House, after 14 years' construction.

December 15
Jean Paul Getty III Found
After being kidnapped, Jean Paul Getty III is found alive in Italy after his grandfather pays about $2.8 million. The kidnappers had cut off one ear and sent it to the family, to prove they would kill their captive unless money was paid.

December 31
U.K. in Trouble
The U.K. is declared a State of Emergency as fuel supplies dwindle.

1974

THREE-DAY WEEK FOR THE U.K.

MINERS' STRIKE SHAKES THE U.K.

From January 1 to March 7, 1974, a three-day working week was declared by Conservative Prime Minister of the U.K. Edward Heath as an emergency measure to conserve electricity. Great Britain's electricity supply had been seriously reduced as a result of miners' strikes that followed the government's decisions in 1972 and 1973 to cap pay raises in an effort to halt rising inflation. Industrial action followed across the country, most notably among coal miners, whose unions claimed their pay was not keeping up with inflated prices. This industrial action had a disastrous effect on the country. Coal supplies rapidly declined, and in order to conserve what remained, the Prime Minister put into action a policy designed to keep the country running. The three-day week meant that commercial businesses could only operate on three consecutive days in a week. The ruling did not apply to essential services, and radio and T.V. broadcasting companies were also allowed to continue as normal, probably in order to keep up morale. However, even these industries had to close down at 10.30 p.m. Heath lost the 1974 election, and Labour's Harold Wilson became the next prime minister. Wilson followed through with the recommendation of a pay board appointed by Heath that the miners receive an exceptional 29% pay raise.

'Coal supplies rapidly declined, and in order to conserve what remained, the Prime Minister put into action a policy designed to keep the country running.'

Left: Harold Wilson was Prime Minister of the U.K. from 1964 to 1970 and 1974 to 1976.

February 4
Bankrobbing Heiress
Heiress Patty Hearst is kidnapped by the Symbionese Liberation Army, and goes on to rob a bank with them on April 15, declaring herself an urban guerrilla. Arrested in September 1975, her jail sentence is commuted by President Carter and she is later pardoned by President Clinton.

March 31
B.E.A. + B.O.A.C. = B.A.
The airline British European Airways (B.E.A.), founded in 1946, merges with the airline British Overseas Airways Corporation (B.O.A.C.), founded in 1939, to create British Airways (B.A.).

April 6
ABBA Wins
The Swedish group ABBA, an acronym formed from the first letters of the band's first names, wins the Eurovision Song Contest with the song 'Waterloo'.

June 26
Barcodes In
The universal product code, now called a barcode, is first scanned on a pack of Wrigley's chewing gum, at a supermarket in Troy, Ohio, U.S.A.

CYPRUS INVADED

The population of the Mediterranean island of Cyprus has long been mixed, with around 78% Greek-Cypriots, 18% Turkish-Cypriots, and the remainder Armenians, Maronites, and Latin-Cypriots. A former British colony, Cyprus had become an independent republic in 1960. For centuries, Greeks and Turks lived side by side in apparent harmony despite their religious differences. In fact, churches and mosques stand next to each other all over the island. However, during the 20th century, divisions and resentments began to surface. Then, on July 20, 1974, Turkey invaded Cyprus, declaring that the minority Turks on the island needed their protection. Turkey also claimed that the constitution of Cyprus as a republic was under threat. The Turkish military operation was in response to a Greek military-backed coup in Cyprus that deposed the Cypriot president with the apparent intention of annexing the island to Greece. Turkey launched a second attack in August 1974, this time seizing more than one third of the territory of Cyprus. In total, 200,000 Cypriots fled their homes in fear of the approaching Turkish Army, and over 2,000 are still unaccounted for, both Greek-Cypriot and Turkish-Cypriot. The Turks claimed the northern section of Cyprus as a federated Turkish state. Although this state has never been internationally recognized, over 100,000 new Turkish immigrants have settled in the region. The last major effort to settle the dispute was the U.N. Annan Plan of 2004. It gained the support of Turkish-Cypriots but was rejected by Greek-Cypriots.

'The Turkish military invasion was in response to a Greek military-backed coup in Cyprus that deposed the Cypriot president'

TURKEY INVADES CYPRUS

Left: A mosque in the Turkish portion of the island's capital, Nicosia.

July 1
Female Head of State
Isabel Perón becomes the interim President of Argentina until March 24, 1976, after the death of her husband Juan Perón, who died while in office. She is the first non-royal female head of state in the western hemisphere.

July 17
I.R.A. Bomb
A bomb explodes at the Tower of London, killing one and injuring 41.

August 9
Nixon in Disgrace
Richard Nixon resigns from the office of the President of the United States in order to avoid being impeached by Congress over his role in the Watergate scandal. Gerald Ford becomes President.

September 12
Haile Salasie Out
The Emperor of Ethiopia, Haile Salassie, is deposed and his son, Crown Prince Asfaw Wossen, is given the throne, reigning until 1975.

1974

PUBS BOMBED BY I.R.A.

The minority Catholics in Northern Ireland held a long-standing resentment toward the Protestants and the British authorities, who appeared to favor Protestants over Catholics. During the 1960s, there was growing support for the Provisional Irish Republican Army (I.R.A.), which opposed British rule in Ireland. After the British introduction in August 1971 of internment without trial for suspected terrorists, the I.R.A. campaign of violence increased and spread from Ireland to the mainland of Britain. Initially, attacks were aimed at military targets in Great Britain, but gradually they became more haphazard. Frequently, bombs were planted in public places to kill or injure civilians. The I.R.A. began to lose the sympathy of its less militant supporters. Following the Birmingham pub bombings of November 21, 1974, in which 21 people died, the British government brought in a Prevention of Terrorism Act that allowed for terrorist suspects to be held for extended periods before trial.

Right: An I.R.A. bomb exploded at the Earl's Court Boat Show in London in January 1974.

LUCAN MURDER

'Lady Lucan ran into the pub nearest her house with blood pouring from wounds on her head.'

On November 8, 1974, Richard John Bingham, 7th Earl of Lucan, disappeared after his children's nanny was found murdered in their home. The Lucans had separated, and Lord Lucan did not live at the house with his children and their mother. The police were alerted to the murder after Lady Lucan ran into the pub nearest her house with blood pouring from wounds on her head. Her version of events was that the nanny, Sandra Rivett, went down to the basement kitchen just before 9 p.m. to make a cup of tea and did not return. When Lady Lucan went to investigate, she found the basement in darkness and was attacked by a man. She managed to distract him and escaped. It has generally been assumed that Lucan murdered Sandra Rivett by mistake, believing that she was his wife. Her body was found in a sack in the basement. She had been beaten with a piece of lead pipe. Lucan's car was later discovered on the south coast of England. There were bloodstains on the seats and a length of lead pipe that matched the murder weapon. Lord Lucan has never been found, although various unconfirmed sightings have been reported. He was officially declared dead in 1999.

October 1
Golden Arches
The first McDonald's opens in London.

October 30
I Am the Greatest
Muhammad Ali regains his world heavyweight boxing crown, from the boxer George Foreman, in Zaire.

November 13
Amityville Horror
Ronald DeFeo Jr. murders his parents and his four younger siblings in Amityville, Long Island, U.S.A. The case is the inspiration for the book and film entitled *The Amityville Horror.*

November 24
Lucy
A skeleton of the hominid *Australopithecus aferensis* that lived between 3.9 and 2.9 million years ago is discovered in Ethiopia and named Lucy.

November 30
McCartney Soars
Paul McCartney and Wings release the album *Band on the Run.*

SOUTH VIETNAM SURRENDERS

After the U.S. withdrew from the Vietnam War, the battle continued to rage between North and South Vietnam for a further two years. However, when the U.S. also withdrew aid from South Vietnam in 1975, they could no longer cope alone. On April 21, 1975, Xuân Loc fell to the North Vietnamese. It was the last city protecting the capital, Saigon, and when it fell, the South Vietnamese President Nguyên Văn Thiêu fled the capital, eventually setting in Great Britain. By April 27, the North Vietnamese had surrounded Saigon. By April 30, the South Vietnamese had surrendered – the Vietnam War was over. Saigon became Ho Chi Minh City, and Vietnam became one country, ruled by the Communist North.

NORTH VIETNAM WINS WAR

Above: Saigon was named Ho Chi Minh City after a former North Vietnamese leader.

Right: A U.S. helicopter displayed in Vietnam.

Left: In 1975, Saigon's town hall was renamed the People's Committee Building.

March 1
Color T.V.
Color television transmissions begin in Australia.

April 4
Microsoft to Go
Bill Gates founds Microsoft in Albuquerque, New Mexico.

April 17
Cambodia Taken
The Communist Khmer Rouge forces take Cambodia.

June 12
Gandhi Guilty
Indira Gandhi, India's Prime Minister, is found guilty of electoral corruption.

June 20
Just When You Thought it Was Safe
The film *Jaws* is released, starring Roy Scheider and Richard Dreyfuss.

1975

THE JACKAL TAKES O.P.E.C. MINISTERS HOSTAGE

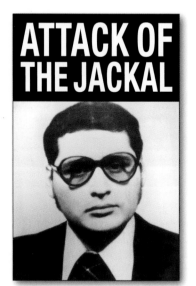

The notorious terrorist Ilich Ramírez Sánchez, better known as 'Carlos the Jackal', committed his most infamous act of terror when, in 1975 in Vienna, he organized the kidnapping of 42 members of the Organization of Petroleum Exporting Countries (O.P.E.C.). A Venezuelan by birth, he had converted to Islam, joined the Popular Front for the Liberation of Palestine in 1970, and committed himself to bringing down Western democracies. After attending terrorist training camp in Amman, Jordan, he was given the pseudonym Carlos and carried out a number of bombings in London and Paris. In December 1975, he was put in charge of a terrorist mission to kidnap O.P.E.C. ministers at their conference in Vienna, Austria. Part of the plan was that he and his team would execute Saudi Arabia's Oil Minister, Sheikh Ahmed Zaki Yamani, and Iran's Minister of the Interior, Jamshid Amouzegar, while keeping the others hostage. The group carried out the operation as planned, killing several police officers, security guards, and anyone else who tried to disarm them. However, they did not succeed in executing the Saudi and Iranian ministers, instead taking 42 hostages on a plane to Algiers. Carlos was eventually paid off by an unknown Arab ruler, and he released the hostages, escaping unhurt with the vast sum of money (rumored to be in the region of $20 million). He was finally extradited to France in 1994, and in 1997, he was sentenced to life imprisonment.

AUSTRALIA'S PRIME MINISTER DISMISSED

When Edward Gough Whitlam was elected Prime Minister of Australia in 1972, he immediately put into action a program of social and cultural reforms. He abolished conscription and withdrew troops from the Vietnam War. He was determined that Australia should develop a more independent foreign policy, instead of simply following the U.S. Domestically, he dramatically improved and expanded social services, put measures in place to ensure greater equality, particularly for women, and reformed the education system. He also introduced universal health insurance. Whitlam took a tough stance on racial discrimination and ended the race criterion in immigration applications. Whitlam achieved an incredible amount in a short space of time, but it all cost vast amounts of money, and Australia's economy suffered as a result: both inflation and unemployment increased. Though the Labour Party held the House of Representatives, the Senate remained hostile. In October 1975, the Senate refused to pass the Whitlam government's budget until an election was held in the House of Representatives. Whitlam refused to call an election, and when the Governor-General John Kerr heard of the deadlock, he dismissed Whitlam on November 11, 1975.

July 11
Terracotta Army Found
China's Terracotta Army is discovered by local farmers in Xi'an, Shaanxi province. Dating from the time of the first Chinese Emperor in 210 B.C.E., there are estimated to be more than 8,000 soldiers, 130 chariots, and 700 horses, most of which are still buried for their safekeeping.

July 17
Greetings in Space
The American and Soviet spacecraft dock in space, and the two commanders in charge of their vessels shake hands.

August 1
Helsinki Accord
The agreement officially recognizing Europe's national borders and respect for human rights is signed in Finland.

THATCHER LEADS CONSERVATIVES IN U.K.

Margaret Thatcher, who was to become Great Britain's first female Prime Minister, took over the leadership of the Conservative Party from Edward Heath in 1975 after the Conservatives lost the general election. After leaving Oxford University, she had become a research chemist and then a lawyer before going into politics. She had been a member of Parliament for Finchley in North London since 1959 and Secretary for Education in Heath's government. At the next general election, the Conservatives came to power, and Margaret Thatcher became Prime Minister in 1979. Her policies were famous for dividing the nation, and people either loved or loathed her. Her steely determination earned her the nickname of the 'Iron Lady' – a term that was first coined by the Soviets. Her domestic policies included privatization of state-owned companies, reduced taxes, and decreased spending on social services. She began to reform the system of welfare and reduced the power of the labour unions. Thatcher had a close political friendship with U.S. President Ronald Reagan, who shared her advocacy of a free-market economy.

Above: Margaret Thatcher with Prime Minister Ted Heath in 1974.

Though victory in the 1982 Falklands War against Argentina boosted her popularity, her introduction of the poll tax, which was regarded as penalizing the poor, and her anti-Europe stance lost her support during the late 1980s. She was forced to resign as Prime Minister in 1990 after a challenge to her leadership of the Conservative Party.

THATCHER WINS

Left: Thatcher's husband Denis was a loyal supporter and a self-confessed 'right-winger'.

September 16
Lebanon Conflict
Civil war breaks out in Lebanon.

October 29
Yorkshire Ripper
Peter Sutcliffe, later known as the Yorkshire Ripper, commits his first murder, in Leeds, England.

November 22
The Reign in Spain
The monarchy returns to Spain after the death of General Franco on November 20, with Juan Carlos declared King.

December
Step to Equality
The Sex Discrimination and Equal Pay Acts come into force in the U.K.

1976

350 DIE IN SOWETO RIOTS

VIOLENCE ERUPTS IN SOUTH AFRICA

One of the ways in which the white government of South Africa hoped to limit the power of black South Africans was to rule that only the Afrikaans language should be taught in black schools. The black population recognized this for what it was – an attempt to bar them from mainstream society and to prevent any escape from poverty through education. In Soweto, a township of Johannesburg where the majority of the black population lived in basic accommodation, protests broke out against the education ruling in June 1976. On June 16, 10,000 students marched through the streets, shouting, 'Down with Afrikaans!' When the police surrounded them, the protestors threw stones, and the police responded by firing into the crowds. The violence spread to the suburbs of Johannesburg, journalists were kept from the area, and Prime Minister Vorster declared, 'This government will not be intimidated, and instructions have been given to maintain law and order at all costs.' It is estimated that around 350 people died in the Soweto riots, which prompted a chain reaction of violence in the country, leading to more deaths. But the campaign against apartheid was strengthened by these public clashes, which aroused international sympathy for the plight of black South Africans.

> **'When the police surrounded them, the protesters threw stones, and the police responded by firing into the crowds.'**

Right: Johannesburg is the largest city in South Africa and the center of a wealthy gold and diamond trade.

January 21
Elegance in the Sky
Concorde begins commercial flights – and the age of supersonic travel has begun. Two flights take off from London and Paris at the same time, bound for Bahrain and Rio de Janeiro. Permission to fly in the U.S. is not granted until May 24, when the plane starts flights to Washington, D.C. and, in 1977, to New York City, its most successful route.

March 24
Perón Deposed
The Argentine military deposes President Isabel Perón.

April 1
New Prime Minister
James Callaghan becomes Prime Minister of the U.K., after Harold Wilson resigns in a live, unexpected television announcement.

WESTERNERS FLEE LEBANON

After the kidnap and killing of the incoming American ambassador, Francis E. Meloy Jr., along with the U.S. Economic Counselor Robert O. Waring, in Beirut on June 16, the American government called for Americans to leave the war-torn city. The men had been on their way to meet the new Lebanese President, and had just crossed what was called the Green Line, between Beirut's Christian and Muslim sectors, when they were taken by the Popular Front for the Liberation of Palestine. Their bodies were found a few hours later in Muslim west Beirut; they had been shot – casualties of Beirut's 14-month civil war. The British embassy in Beirut organized a road convoy to take Westerners to Damascus, but the route was considered unsafe and, after two attempts, the journey had to be called off. Instead of leaving from the British embassy, the refugees, consisting of about 270 Americans, 97 British, and other Westerners, gathered on the beach along with the 40-hour supply of food and water they had been advised to take, where an American navy ship rescued them on June 20.

BEIRUT EVACUATED

Left: U.S. president Gerald Ford oversaw the planning of the evacuation by the American military.

April 1
The Big Apple
Apple Computer Company is officially formed by Steve Jobs and Steve Wozniak.

May 25
May the Force be with You
The first *Star Wars* film, called *Star Wars* at the time, starring Harrison Ford, Carrie Fisher, and Mark Hamill, is released.

July 4
Born on the 4th of July
The U.S. celebrates its bicentennial, the 200th anniversary of the Declaration of Independence.

August 1
Lauda Critical
Racing champion Niki Lauda suffers extensive burns in the German Grand Prix in Nürburgring.

1976

OPERATION ENTEBBE

On June 27, 1976, as an Air France flight from Israel made a stopover in Athens, a group of armed hijackers, members of the Popular Front for the Liberation of Palestine, boarded the plane and ordered it to fly to Entebbe, Uganda. Ugandan dictator Idi Amin was a conspirator in the hijacking, and he provided armed guards for the plane while it was at the airport. The hijackers announced that, if 54 convicted terrorists were not released from jail, they would blow up the plane. From the 246 passengers, all non-Israelis and non-Jews were released, leaving 105 hostages. While the French and Israeli authorities bought time by negotiating, the Israel Defense Forces (I.D.F.) was planning a rescue operation. On July 3, the I.D.F. set off in five planes for Entebbe Airport. In addition to 200 paratroopers, the planes also carried a black Mercedes and some Land Rovers, which were to be used as a decoy by posing as a V.I.P. visit to the airport. The operation was almost perfectly executed. Just after midnight on July 4, the I.D.F. planes were heading home. Four hostages had been killed in the process, as well as one Israeli commander, eight hijackers, and many Ugandan soldiers.

Above: Ugandan dictator Idi Amin.

LIFE ON MARS?

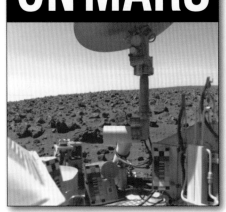

In 1975, N.A.S.A. launched its space program to Mars. The Viking program consisted of two space probes, *Viking 1* and *Viking 2*, each made up of an orbiter, which would photograph the surface of Mars, and a lander, which would conduct scientific tests on the planet's surface. The purpose of the mission was to discover as much as possible about the composition of the atmosphere and surface of Mars. The *Viking 1* lander touched down on Mars on July 20, 1976, while *Viking 2* landed on September 3. One of the main questions it was hoped the Viking mission could answer was whether there was life on Mars. The majority of the experiments indicated that the organic matter necessary for life was not present, but there was enough doubt cast by the limitations of equipment and conditions on the planet to leave the question unanswered.

Above: A full-scale model of the lander.

October 19
Chimps Threatened
The chimpanzee is placed on the endangered species list.

November 21
Rocky
The film *Rocky*, the first in the series of the same name, starring Sylvester Stallone, is released.

November 25
When the Band Stops Singing
Popular American-Canadian rock group The Band holds its farewell concert, *The Last Waltz*, in San Francisco.

December 8
Eagles Hit
The American rock band The Eagles release their album *Hotel California*, one of the top-ten bestselling albums.

HAPPY ANNIVERSARY

The celebrations for Queen Elizabeth II's Silver Jubilee commemorated the 25 years since she ascended the throne on February 6, 1952. The Queen marked her jubilee year by touring the Commonwealth, visiting 36 countries including Western Samoa, Tonga, Fiji, New Zealand, Australia, Tasmania, Papua New Guinea, Canada, and the West Indies. A week of celebrations in June opened with a beacon lit in Windsor, England, on June 6, launching a chain of lit beacons across the country. The next day, the Queen traveled in the Gold Stage Coach to St. Paul's Cathedral, London, for a service of thanksgiving, and later she appeared on the balcony of Buckingham Palace to greet the crowds. More than 1 million people lined the streets to watch the procession, and a further 50 million watched it on television. At a celebratory lunch, the Queen declared, 'I want to thank all those in Britain and the Commonwealth who, through their loyalty and friendship, have given me strength and encouragement during these last 25 years.' There were street parties all across the country. On Thursday June 9, the Queen took a ceremonial boat trip down the River Thames from Greenwich to Lambeth.

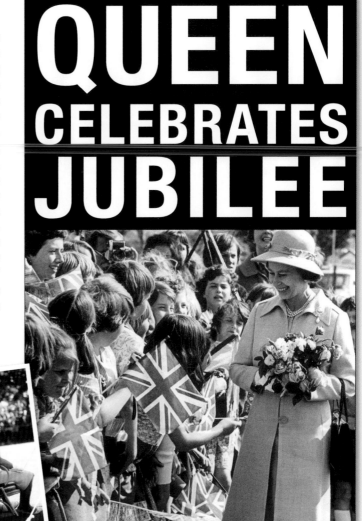

Above: An estimated 100,000 street parties were held in the U.K. in June 1977.

Above: The Queen in New Guinea in February 1977.

January 20
Carter Is President
Jimmy Carter is sworn in as President of the U.S.

January 31
Pompidou Centre
The Centre Georges Pompidou in Paris is officially opened by French President Valéry Giscard d'Estaing.

May
Baby Mammoth Found
A reindeer herder finds a young mammoth preserved in ice in northwest Siberia. The mammoth, with trunk and eyes intact and with some fur still on its body, is believed to have died about 10,000 years ago, at the time of the last Ice Age.

March 10
Planet Ringed
Three astronomers, James L. Elliot, Edward W. Dunham, and Douglas J. Mink, discover rings around the planet Uranus.

1977

JUMBO JETS COLLIDE

On March 27, 1977, two Boeing 747s – one K.L.M. and one Pan Am – collided just above the runway at Los Rodeos Airport in the Canary Islands. A series of unfortunate circumstances had come together to cause the world's worst aviation disaster, with 583 lives lost. The K.L.M. flight was taking mostly Dutch tourists to a vacation in the Canary Islands and was due to land at Las Palmas, the islands' main airport. The Pan Am flight was taking American tourists to the Canary Islands to begin a 12-day Mediterranean cruise. Both planes, along with various others, were diverted from Las Palmas Airport because of a terrorist bomb explosion in the airport and the threat of another to follow. At Los Rodeos Airport, to which both planes were diverted, the passengers left the plane but had returned by evening when the all-clear was given. By then, it was getting foggy, and the crews were eager to be on their way. The captain of the K.L.M. flight was especially determined that his crew should not exceed their maximum allowed flight time, as employment laws were very strict in Holland. Both planes were lined up and ready to depart. Due to poor communication between the two planes and air traffic control, with messages misunderstood or not heard, the K.L.M. plane took off before it was meant to and crashed head-on into the Pan Am plane, which was taxiing along the runway. Although the captain of the K.L.M. plane desperately tried to pull up, it still tore off the top of the other plane and both burst into flames. Most of the passengers were killed by the impact or fire. Only 90 people survived.

> 'A series of unfortunate circumstances had come together to cause the world's worst aviation disaster, with 583 lives lost.'

April 2
The Winner
Red Rum wins his third Grand National race at Aintree in England. The famous Grand National is held each year on a Saturday afternoon in April. Run over a distance of 4.5 miles (7.5 km), there are 30 fences to jump, and there are many injuries to the horses. Many British people who do not normally watch or bet on horse racing at other times of the year bet on this race. The winner is almost impossible to predict.

June 15
Spanish Elections
Democratic elections are held in Spain for the first time in 41 years.

July 5
Bhutto Out
Pakistani Prime Minister Zulfikar Ali Bhutto is ousted by the Chief of the Army Staff, General Zia ul-Haq, who imposes martial law.

July 13
The Lights Went Out on Broadway
New York City suffers a total blackout when the electric grids fails, leaving the city and its workers and inhabitants without power for 25 hours.

'THE KING' IS DEAD

On August 16, 1977, Elvis Aaron Presley was found dead on the bathroom floor of his Graceland home in Memphis, Tennessee. He was 42 years old. The official cause of death was given as 'cardiac arrhythmia', or irregularity of heartbeat. What was not made public was that the irregular heartbeat had been caused by an overdose of several prescription drugs. When this information leaked, Elvis Presley's father sealed the autopsy report, which will not be reopened until the year 2027, 50 years after the death. Elvis shot to fame during the 1950s with his good looks, sexy moves, and catchy rock-and-roll songs, which combined gospel, rhythm and blues, and country, thereby crossing racial divides. He received the nickname 'The King', and in 1950s America he was as much disapproved of as he was worshiped. He was often told to tone down his hip swinging at live concerts because of the effect on young girls, who fainted en masse. After his death, fans flocked to Graceland, which immediately became a pilgrimage site and remains a hugely popular tourist attraction to this day. At the same time, conspiracy theories began to emerge that Elvis had faked his own death, and the idea that he is still alive continues to surface today.

'He was often told to tone down his hip swinging at live concerts because of the effect on young girls, who fainted en masse.'

ELVIS DIES

Above: Elvis's grave is located in the grounds of his Graceland home, where he used to watch three T.V.s at once (left).

September 12
Steve Biko Dies
Civil rights leader and great anti-apartheid campaigner Steve Biko dies of head wounds while in police custody in South Africa. He coined the phrase, 'Black is beautiful'.

September 26
Laker's Skytrain
Freddie Laker, yet to be knighted, launches his inexpensive airline, Skytrain, in the U.K.

December 1
More Children's Television
Nickelodeon, the children's cartoon television channel, launches as the Pinwheel Network in Ohio, U.S.A.

December 25
Charlie Chaplin Dies
Charlie Chaplin, one of the world's great silent comics, as well as actor, director, producer, and musician, dies. He was born on April 16, 1889, in England.

1978

914 DIE AT JONESTOWN

Right: Bodies litter the ground at Jonestown following the mass suicide.

The People's Temple, a 'Christian' doomsday cult, was established in Indiana in the 1950s by James Warren Jones. At the time it was highly unusual for its multiracial congregation, and 'Jim' Jones preached a gospel of freedom, love, and equality that impressed upon its members the need to help the sick and the poor. This later developed into 'apocryphal socialism', which preached the imminent end of the world in a nuclear attack. After investigations began into Jones' claimed cures for cancer and heart disease, the Temple moved to California and then, amid further investigations of illegal activities, to Jonestown, Guyana, in South America. There, the Temple group leased 4,000 acres of jungle and formed the 'People's Temple Agricultural Project' to cultivate the land. It was there that Jones developed his theory of 'translation', whereby he and his followers would all die together and be transported to another planet where they would live in bliss. When Tim Stoen, a senior member of the Temple, left, he revealed that people were being held against their will in appalling conditions, and he started a group called Concerned Relatives. This group convinced Californian Congressman Leo Ryan to visit Jonestown to inspect conditions and practices. Congressman Ryan visited Jonestown on November 18, 1978, and when 16 members of the group decided to fly back to the States with him, they were all followed to the airport by Temple security guards who opened fire. Five people were killed, including Congressman Ryan. Jim Jones now knew that he was trapped. He managed to convince the majority of his followers to engage in a mass suicide by drinking poison. Most of them did, but some, who were clearly unwilling, were evidently murdered either with poison injection or by being shot. Only a few managed to escape into the jungle. The dead were numbered at 914: 638 adults and 276 children.

'Jones managed to convince the majority of his followers to engage in a mass suicide by drinking poison.'

January 23
No More Sprays
Sweden becomes the first country to ban aerosol sprays because of fears about damaging the Earth's ozone layer.

February 15
Ali vs Spinks
Leon Spinks makes history when he defeats Muhammad Ali in 15 rounds in Las Vegas, to take the World Heavyweight Champion title. Ali regains the title from Spinks in New Orleans on September 15.

February 15
Majority Rule
White Prime Minister Ian Smith of Rhodesia (now Zimbabwe), along with three black leaders, agrees to black majority rule in the country.

March 3
Rhodesia Attacks
Rhodesia attacks Zambia.

FIRST TEST-TUBE BABY BORN

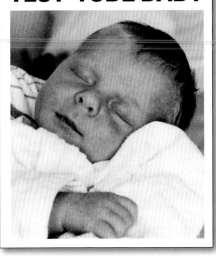

WORLD'S FIRST TEST-TUBE BABY

Above: The pioneering team of Steptoe and Edwards.

On July 25, 1978, Louise Brown, the world's first 'test-tube baby', was born in the U.K. Her mother, Lesley Brown, had been unable to conceive because of blocked fallopian tubes and had undergone experimental fertility treatment to become pregnant. The treatment was pioneered by Dr. Patrick Steptoe, a gynecologist, and Dr. Robert Edwards, a physiologist, who had begun experimenting with artificial conception in 1966. Their method involved removing eggs from a woman's ovary, fertilizing them with sperm in a glass (*in vitro*), and replanting them in the womb. However, until Lesley Brown's success, none of the 80 women who had trialed the method had been able to stay pregnant beyond a few weeks. On November 10, 1977, Lesley Brown underwent the treatment. She became the first woman to undergo a healthy pregnancy, and nine days before her due date, her daughter was delivered by caesarian section. Louise Brown was perfectly healthy and went on to have a child of her own. The success of the process gave new hope to millions of couples unable to conceive. For some, it also raised ethical issues. The main concern was whether the disposal of fertilized eggs, which is common practice in the process of in vitro fertilization (I.V.F.), is in effect disposing of human lives, if life can be counted as having started at the point of fertilization. There were also concerns at the time as to how this power to create life might be used in the future, by pre-selecting the gender or features of a child and disposing of fertilized eggs that do not meet these criteria.

STATESMAN MURDERED

ITALIAN MINISTER KILLED

As leader of the Christian Democracy Party in Italy, Aldo Moro had twice served as Prime Minister between 1963 and 1976. He had been out of office for two years when he was kidnapped on March 16, 1978; five bodyguards and a chauffeur were shot dead in the process. The left-wing Red Brigades gunmen who had kidnapped him demanded the release of 15 Red Brigades members, including their leader on trial in Turin, but Italian Prime Minister Giulio Andreotti refused to negotiate with them. Moro was held hostage for two months, during which time he made frequent appeals to the Italian government to negotiate with his kidnappers, as did his family and the Pope, but Andreotti remained firm. Aldo Moro's body was later found in the trunk of a Renault car in Rome, riddled with bullets, eight weeks after he had been kidnapped. The Red Brigades was a left-wing terrorist group formed in 1970 with the aim of overthrowing the capitalist government of Italy.

June
Charon Discovered
Pluto's largest moon, Charon, is discovered by astronomer James Christy.

July 8
Borg Again
Björn Borg wins the Wimbledon men's tennis singles for the third successive time, beating Jimmy Connors, who then goes on to beat Borg in the U.S. Open.

Walking Tall
Discovered accidentally in 1976, an archeological site in Laetoli, Tanzania, is excavated, revealing three different sets of footprints made by human ancestors that walked upright more than 3.6 million years ago.

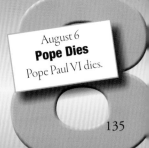

August 6
Pope Dies
Pope Paul VI dies.

1978

TANKER SPILLS CARGO OF CRUDE OIL

OIL SLICK HITS FRANCE

On March 16, 1978, the tanker *Amoco Cadiz* was en route from the Persian Gulf to Rotterdam, Holland, when it crashed against rocks off the coast of Brittany, France, spilling its cargo of 227,000 tons of crude oil. The tanker's steering system had failed, and although a German tug boat attempted to tow it, its massive weight could not be controlled. Despite the best efforts of the crew, the tanker ran aground on Portsall Rocks. It then gradually split in two as it crashed repeatedly against the rocks for two weeks, and its entire cargo emptied into the sea. The oil contaminated over 200 miles (320 km) of French coastline, and France sued the American company Amoco for compensation. After a lengthy legal battle, France was eventually awarded the equivalent of 190 million euros, less than half of the amount they had sued for. The oil slick destroyed vast amounts of marine life and had a long-term effect on local economies along the coast that relied on shellfish and oyster fishing. Although it was claimed that lessons had been learned, this was not the last oil slick to occur in the 20th century.

'Although it was claimed that lessons had been learned, this was not the last oil slick to occur in the 20th century.'

Left: The coast of Brittany, France, suffered long-term environmental damage from the spill.

August
Turin Shroud
The Turin Shroud goes on display for the first time in 45 years. The cloth is a very old, linen fabric marked with the image of a man's face. It is believed by some people to be the burial cloth that covered Jesus Christ.

September 17
Camp David Accord
Prime Minister Anwar Sadat of Egypt and Prime Minister Menachem Begin of Israel sign 'A Framework for Peace', witnessed by President Jimmy Carter.

September 28
Pope Dies
Pope John Paul I dies, after only 38 days as Pope.

October
Pope Chosen
Pope John Paul II takes office. Polish-born, he is the first non-Italian Pope in over 400 years.

I.R.A. BOMB KILLS MOUNTBATTEN

Admiral of the Fleet, the Earl Mountbatten of Burma, who was also Prince Philip's uncle, was murdered by the Provisional Irish Republican Army (I.R.A.) while on a fishing trip in Ireland on August 27, 1979. Lord Mountbatten had spent his life serving in the Royal Navy, and his funeral upheld British Naval traditions. His coffin, bearing an admiral's hat, his sword of honor, and his gold stick, was carried on a naval gun carriage through the streets, and his horse Dolly led the parade with her master's boots turned backward in the stirrups. The Earl's funeral procession through London, from Wellington Barracks to Westminster Abbey, to the sound of brass from the Royal Marine bands, was watched by thousands along the route. The manner of his death had shocked and greatly saddened the nation. Mountbatten had been on vacation with his family when a bomb placed in his fishing boat was detonated from the shore by members of the I.R.A. His 14-year-old grandson Nicholas died with him, as did his daughter's mother-in-law and Paul Maxwell, a 15-year-old local boy who was working as crew. Mountbatten's daughter, Lady Patricia, and her husband and another son, Timothy, were also in the boat and were seriously injured – so much so that Lady Patricia could not attend the funeral of her father or son. The great-grandson of Queen Victoria, Lord Mountbatten was christened Louis Francis Arthur Victor Nicholas Battenberg, but when George V created the House of Windsor, the name Battenberg was changed to Mountbatten.

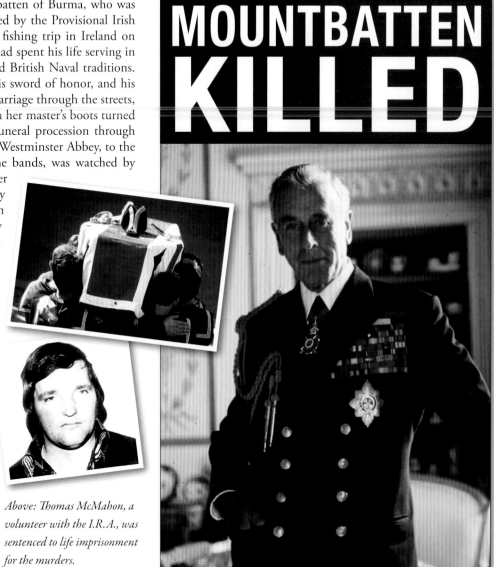

Above: Thomas McMahon, a volunteer with the I.R.A., was sentenced to life imprisonment for the murders.

MOUNTBATTEN KILLED

January 8
Vietnam vs Khmer Rouge
The Vietnamese defeat the Khmer Rouge ruling party in Cambodia.

February 1
Khomeini Is Back
The exiled religious leader and politician Ayatollah Khomeini returns to Iran.

March 28
Three Mile Island
The most serious nuclear civilian accident in the U.S. takes place, with the partial meltdown of a reactor at Midtown, a suburb of Harrisburg, Pennsylvania.

April 1
Republic of Iran
Iran is declared a republic.

May 4
Iron Lady Takes Power
Margaret Thatcher becomes the first female Prime Minister of the U.K., after the Labour government loses a general election.

1979

DEATH OF A NATION

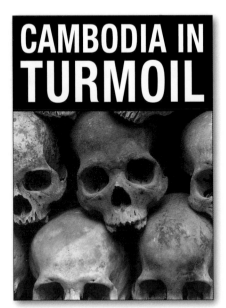

During the 1970s, Cambodia, known at the time as Democratic Kampuchea, was ruled over by a Communist government led by a former school teacher, Saloth Sar, who called himself 'Pol Pot'. The brutal regime ruled by terror, keeping themselves hidden away but constantly 'watching', letting the Cambodian people know that they were now their parents and must be obeyed. Pol Pot was the Secretary General of the Cambodian Communist Party, known as the Khmer Rouge, and under his dictatorship, millions of Cambodians died. Mentally unstable and paranoid, Pol Pot tried to carry out idealistic policies that involved evacuating the population out of the cities and into the countryside and abolishing money markets, private property, religion, and schools. Everyone was forced to wear a uniform and work in the fields for over 12 hours a day. Pol Pot was trying to follow the Soviet model of increasing agricultural output to generate funds for industrialization, but Cambodia had just come out of five years of civil war and the country was weak. A rejection of Western medicine, paired with widespread crop failure, led to millions of deaths as the workers in the countryside shipped their harvests to the city in order to fulfill their quota and ended up starving themselves. In January 1979, when Vietnamese forces invaded Cambodia, they uncovered fields full of the skeletons of the dead: millions of men, women, and children who had been brutally executed as enemies of the state.

SPY UNMASKED

Sir Anthony Blunt, an art historian, professor at the University of London, director of the Courtauld Institute of Art, and surveyor of the Queen's Pictures, was revealed in 1979 as a member of the Cambridge Spy Ring. While studying at Cambridge University, Blunt had joined the Cambridge Apostles, a secret society of Marxists. Blunt was recruited as a spy by the U.S.S.R. in 1934, joined the British Army in 1939, and in 1940 became a member of the U.K.'s security agency, MI5. He was knighted in 1956 for his work as surveyor of the British royal family's art collection. He had also carried out a secret mission for the royal family when he went to Germany after the war to recover incriminating letters sent by the Duke of Windsor to Adolf Hitler. When his fellow spies Guy Burgess and Donald Maclean defected to the U.S.S.R. in 1951, Blunt was questioned, but no concrete evidence against him was found. However, when, in 1979, another former Cambridge student claimed that Blunt had tried to recruit him as a spy, Blunt finally confessed. The Queen was informed, and she stripped him of his knighthood. After Prime Minister Margaret Thatcher publicly named Blunt, he fled to Europe, where he lived for some time. When he returned to London, he found that he had underestimated the strength of public feeling against him. On one occasion, he was booed out of a movie theater. Life in the public eye became intolerable, and his long-time partner tried to kill himself by jumping from a window. Blunt died in London in 1983.

June 1
Zimbabwe Born
Rhodesia is re-named Zimbabwe.

June 18
SALT-2
U.S. President Jimmy Carter and Soviet President Leonid Brezhnev sign the SALT-2 arms limitation treaty.

June 22
Sony Walkman to Go
Sony launch the portable Walkman in Tokyo, and change the way people listen to music forever.

July 11
Skylab Down
The U.S. space station *Skylab* re-enters the Earth's atmosphere, scattering debris in the Indian Ocean and over Western Australia.

July 16
Saddam Gains Power
Saddam Hussein becomes President of Iraq.

18 DIE IN I.R.A. BLASTS

'The deaths of the 18 British soldiers by two bombs in a carefully planned attack, was the largest single loss of life for the British Army since the Second World War.'

1979 was a year of Provisional Irish Republican Army (I.R.A.) terror. In addition to over 90 civilian murders carried out by the I.R.A. that year, the most infamous acts of terror were the killing of Lord Louis Mountbatten, on August 27, followed just hours later by the massacre of 18 British soldiers near Warrenpoint, South Down, close to Northern Ireland's border with the Irish Republic. The deaths of 18 British soldiers by two bombs in a carefully planned attack, was the largest single loss of life for the British Army since the Second World War. It was the first time in Northern Ireland that the I.R.A. used remote-controled bombs. There were no command wires: the bombs were detonated by radio waves from the top of a mountain, in a beautiful, rural, unpopulated area called the 'Narrow Water.' The first was an 800-lb (360-kg) bomb, hidden by bales of hay in a trailer by the side of the road, detonated as a three-vehicle convoy passed by. This killed six soldiers of the Second Battalion Parachute Regiment. The surviving troops immediately cordoned off the area and called for reinforcements. Members of the Queen's Own Highlanders flew in by helicopter from their base in County Armagh. Twenty minutes later, as their helicopter was leaving the scene with some of the injured men on board, the second bomb was detonated. The I.R.A. had known that the British Army would set up a command point, and had hidden a second bomb in milk pails against a gate lodge, the likeliest point for the command. Another 10 soldiers from the Parachute Regiment were killed, along with two from the Queen's Own Highlanders. The perpetrators escaped into the safety of the Irish Republic.

SOLDIERS MASSACRED

July 20
Sandinistas Win
The Sandinista rebels win the civil war in Nicaragua.

September 1
Jupiter Pictures Home
The space probe *Pioneer* sends back pictures of Jupiter.

November 30
Another Brick
Pink Floyd release their famous album *The Wall* in the U.K.

December 11
Mother Theresa
Mother Theresa is awarded the Nobel Prize for Peace for her work with the poor, in India and abroad.

December 27
The Red Army
The Soviet Union invades Afghanistan and seizes control.

1980

POLAND SEES LAUNCH OF SOLIDARITY UNION

STRUGGLE FOR DEMOCRACY

'The Gdansk Shipyard Strike sparked 20 further strikes, and the deputy prime minister was forced to negotiate with Walesa'

On August 14, 1980, unemployed Polish electrician Lech Walesa led a strike involving thousands of workers at the Lenin Shipyard in Gdansk. Although the secret police had tried to arrest him that same morning, Walesa managed to avoid them, and climbed over the shipyard wall to lead the strike. The strikers were protesting against low wages and a rise in food prices, but the most important change to come out of the strike was the creation of an independent trade union that was actually allowed to strike. It was the first time that such a union had existed in a Communist country. In fact, some years earlier in Poland, people had been killed by police for daring to strike. The Gdansk Shipyard Strike sparked 20 further strikes, and the deputy prime minister was forced to negotiate with Walesa, who emerged from the talks and announced to the cheering crowds of workers, 'We have an independent, self-governing trade union. We have the right to strike!' The right to strike was granted under the International Labor Organization, but had never before been exercised in a Communist country. Walesa's historic announcement marked the establishment of the Solidarity trade union in September 1980. A year later, when it was outlawed, a quarter of Poland's population belonged to the union. The Communist government, under pressure from their Soviet masters to crack down, declared martial law and arrested the movement's leaders, including Walesa. However, Solidarity continued to operate underground, with support from American trade unions and from Pope John Paul II. It was not until 1989, responding to Western encouragement and in the midst of economic depression, that Solidarity formed a government under Walesa in the first free elections to be held in the Communist bloc.

Left: The Gdansk shipyard, site of the strike that led to the formation of the Solidarity union.

March 4
Mugabe to Power
Robert Mugabe is elected Prime Minister of Zimbabwe.

April 10
Border Opens
The border between Spain and Gibraltar is opened again, having been closed since 1969.

April 18
Independence in Zimbabwe
Zimbabwe, following the troubled years after its declaration of independence, becomes truly independent.

April 29
Hitchcock Dies
Sir Alfred Hitchcock, eminent movie director, particularly noted for his suspenseful psychological thrillers, dies at the age of 81.

HUGE VOLCANIC ERUPTION

Mount St. Helens in the Cascade Mountains of Washington State is one of the most active volcanoes in North America. It is estimated that the Cascade Range has been volcanically active for 40,000 years, while Mount St. Helens itself has been active only for the past 2,500 years. It had not erupted for 123 years when, in March 1980, a series of small earthquakes in the region alerted volcanologists to impending trouble. They issued a warning to local authorities, who in turn evacuated the area. Scientists were able to set up equipment to monitor the volcano eruption in a way that had never before been possible, but even so it was impossible to gauge exactly when the volcano would erupt. On May 18, 1980, a research scientist named David Johnston was about 5 miles (8 km) from the main crater when he radioed to the Vancouver base, 'This is it!' Moments later he was killed under a heap of molten lava. An earthquake had triggered a volcanic eruption with about 500 times the force of an atomic bomb. Around 150 square miles (400 sq km) of forest were flattened by the flow of lava before it moved on to houses and cars. A cloud of ash darkened the sky and hung over several cities across northwestern America. In all, 57 people and 7,000 big-game animals died as a result of the eruption, although it could have been far worse if early evacuation had not been put into effect.

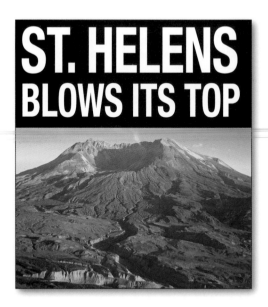

START OF IRAN–IRAQ WAR

Throughout the 20th century, border disputes between Iran and Iraq were commonplace, but since 1975 there had been relative peace. This came to an end with the 1979 Islamic Revolution in Iran, which brought Ayatollah Khomeini into power. Saddam Hussein's invasion of Iran in 1980 was prompted partly by fear of Khomeini's extreme religious regime, but also by his probable support of the oppressed Shia Muslims in Iraq. However, the official reason for the invasion was a dispute over the oil-producing regions along the border. In early 1980, Saddam executed the leaders of an Iranian-supported Shia group and deported other Shias of Iranian extraction to Iran. He then canceled the 1975 treaty between the two countries and announced that the Shatt al Arab region now belonged to Iraq. This launched full-scale hostilities between Iran and Iraq, but neither side was apparently able to clinch the swift victory it had expected. The war was to last for almost eight years, causing huge loss of life and permanent damage to both countries.

May 8
Tito Dies
Yugoslavia's long-serving president, Josip Tito, dies after 27 years in power.

May 21
The Empire Continues
The latest Star Wars movie, *The Empire Strikes Back*, is released.

May 22
Pac-Man
The world's best-selling arcade game, Pac-Man, is launched.

June 1
C.N.N. Takes to the Airwaves
Ted Turner's Cable News Network, commonly known as C.N.N., goes live in the United States.

1980

THE SIEGE BUSTERS

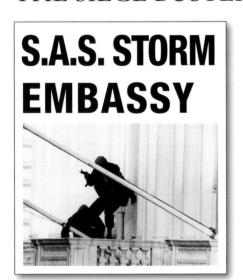

On April 30, 1980, six gunmen stormed the Iranian Embassy in Kensington, London. They were members of an Iranian rebel group that opposed the strict religious regime of Ayatollah Khomeini, and their demands included the release of 91 political prisoners held in Iran. The gunmen took a number of people hostage, including a policeman, members of the British media, and tourists, as well as Iranian Embassy officials. Four days into the siege, the terrorists dumped the body of an Iranian press officer outside the embassy and threatened to kill the rest of the hostages before blowing up the building. At this point, the British government decided it was time to act and sent 30 members of the anti-terrorist branch of the Special Air Service (S.A.S.) to carry out Operation Nimrod. The rescue mission, on May 5, was televised live and showed the masked rescuers entering the building, throwing grenades, and emerging 15 minutes later with 19 hostages. One hostage was killed and two were injured in what was otherwise seen as a successful mission. Five of the terrorists were killed, and the sixth was sentenced to life imprisonment. The S.A.S., whose motto is 'Who Dares Wins', had previously been an institution under threat, but the well-publicized mission catapulted them to fame as international heroes.

BEATLE SHOT DEAD

By 1980, John Lennon was living in New York with his second wife, Yoko Ono, and their five-year-old son Sean. They had recently moved to the Dakota apartment buildings and were under F.B.I. surveillance because of their pacifist activities, but they came and went freely without any security. On December 8, 1980, a mentally unstable man named Mark David Chapman asked John to autograph his latest album, *Double Fantasy*. Hours later, Chapman approached the Lennons outside their apartment building and called out John's name. John turned to face him and Chapman shot him five times. Lennon was rushed to a nearby hospital, but was pronounced dead on arrival. Chapman did not attempt to flee. When arrested by police he was holding a copy of J.D. Salinger's book *The Catcher in the Rye*. On December 10, John Lennon was cremated in New York. Thousands of fans gathered in Central Park, and a ten-minute silent vigil was held all over the world.

Right: The Dakota building in New York.

July
U.S. Boycotts Olympics
The U.S. Olympic team boycotts the summer Olympic Games in Moscow in protest at the Soviet war in Afghanistan.

July
Borg Wins ... Again
Tennis ace Björn Borg defeats John McEnroe in what is later described as the greatest men's singles final at Wimbledon. It is Borg's fifth successive Wimbledon singles title.

August 2
Bologna Bomb
A bomb planted by terrorists kills 85 people and wounds more than 200 at the train station in Bologna, Italy.

November
Who Shot J.R.?
More than 100 million people watch the season finale of the television show *Dallas* to learn who shot the famous character J.R.

PRINCE CHARLES MARRIES LADY DIANA SPENCER

On July 29, 1981, the 'fairy-tale' wedding of Prince Charles and Lady Diana Spencer took place at St. Paul's Cathedral in London. Hundreds of thousands of people flooded the streets, trying to catch a glimpse of the new princess, while an estimated 750 million watched on T.V. Twenty-year-old Lady Diana was taken to the cathedral in a glass coach. She wore a dress of ivory taffeta and antique lace, with a 25-ft (7.5-m) train, designed by David and Elizabeth Emmanuel. Lady Diana's walk down the aisle took three and a half minutes. After the Church of England ceremony, conducted by Archbishop of Canterbury Dr. Robert Runcie, the Prince and Princess of Wales traveled in an open-topped carriage through the streets to Buckingham Palace, where they appeared on the balcony and shared a kiss, to the delight of the crowds below. They then withdrew to a private wedding breakfast attended by 120 guests. Less than a year later, the princess gave birth to a son, William. A second son, Harry, was born two years later. By that time, the couple's marriage was already showing signs of strain. The couple officially separated in 1993.

'Hundreds of thousands of people flooded the streets ... to catch a glimpse of the new princess, while an estimated 750 million watched on T.V.'

ROYAL WEDDING

Left: St. Paul's Cathedral, the 17th-century church where Charles and Diana married amid huge public interest.

January 4
Yorkshire Ripper
The serial killer Peter Sutcliffe, known as the Yorkshire Ripper, is arrested at last, having killed 13 women and attacked another seven.

January 20
Movie-Star President
Former Hollywood actor Ronald Reagan is inaugurated as President of the United States.

February 9
Rock 'n' Roller Dies
Bill Haley, considered by many to be the first ever rock and roll musician, dies.

March 29
Run London Run
The first London Marathon, with 7,500 runners, takes place between Greenwich and Westminster.

1981

REAGAN SHOT IN ASSASSINATION ATTEMPT

SHOTS FIRED AT PRESIDENT

On March 30, 1981, the 70-year-old U.S. President Ronald Reagan, who had been in office only 69 days, was shot after leaving the Hilton Hotel in Washington, D.C. The president had been addressing an audience of union representatives, and as he turned to respond to waiting press upon leaving the building, he was shot by 25-year-old John Hinckley Jr. The White House Press Secretary, a policeman, and a Secret Service agent were also seriously injured by the gunman. President Reagan underwent an operation and recovered fully, going on to win a second four-year term in office. John Hinckley Jr., who had a history of stalking famous people, was diagnosed as mentally ill at his trial and was committed to a psychiatric hospital. His declared motivation had been a desire to impress the actress Jodie Foster, with whom he had a psychotic obsession.

'Ronald Reagan ... was shot after leaving the Hilton Hotel in Washington, D.C. ... The White House Press Secretary, a policeman, and a Secret Service agent were also seriously injured by the gunman.'

Left: Jodie Foster, the actress with whom Ronald Reagan's attempted assassin was infatuated.

May	May 11	June 5	June 12
New French Premier	**Bob Marley Dies**	**New Disease**	**Great Adventure**
François Mitterrand is elected President of France.	The musician and singer-songwriter Bob Marley, famous for the reggae music he made with his band The Wailers, dies of brain cancer in Jamaica at the age of 36.	The first cases of A.I.D.S. are announced.	The movie *Raiders of the Lost Ark*, starring Harrison Ford, is released to great acclaim.

UNSUCCESSFUL ASSASSINATION ATTEMPT ON POPE JOHN PAUL II

On May 13, 1981, a professional assassin named Mehmet Ali Ağca shot Pope John Paul II several times as he walked through St. Peter's Square in Rome. The Pope was hit by four bullets, two lodging in his lower intestine, one in his left hand, and one in his right arm, before the assassin was wrestled to the ground and disarmed. The Pope was rushed to hospital, where he was operated on and eventually recovered, despite having lost almost three-quarters of his blood. The real origins of the assassination attempt have never been discovered. Ağca, who received life imprisonment in an Italian court, gave so many different versions of events that investigators have never been able to pin down the real motive. Pope John Paul II forgave his would-be assassin and even visited the man in prison. In 2000, Ağca was extradited to Turkey, where he was also found guilty of other crimes, and his sentences are now running concurrently.

Right: St. Peter's Square in Rome, where Pope John Paul II was shot.

ANWAR SADAT MURDERED

When Egyptian President Anwar Al Sadat signed a peace treaty with Israel in 1979, he effectively signed his own death warrant. Although the move had won him a Nobel Peace Prize, it also implied that the Palestinian issue would not be resolved. Thus, he alienated himself from his Arab neighbors, as no Arab nation but Egypt had the military capacity to take on Israel. Meanwhile, Sadat cracked down on criticism in his own country by increasing censorship and jailing opponents. He also regularly falsified the result of political referendums to imply that he had his people's support. When, in June 1981, violence erupted between Muslims and Coptic Christians, culminating in mass slaughter in a Cairo slum, Sadat treated both sides with equal brutality. It was the final insult to his people. On October 6, 1981, while attending a military parade, Sadat was assassinated by a group of Muslim fundamentalists, with the aim of imposing Islamic rule in Egypt.

August 1
M.T.V.
The music channel M.T.V. is launched in the U.S.A.

August 24
Beatle Killer Sentenced
Mark David Chapman is sentenced to 20 years to life for killing John Lennon in Manhattan in 1980.

September 19
No Sounds of Silence
Simon and Garfunkel give a free concert in Central Park, New York, which is attended by half a million people.

December
Golan Heights Annexed
Israel announces that it will annex Syria's Golan Heights, captured in 1973.

1982

FALKLANDS WAR BREAKS OUT

TASK FORCE SENT TO FALKLANDS

Left: Captured Argentine troops were bewildered by the hostility of the Falkland Islanders, and by their own defeat.
Right: Many men were lost in naval battles during the Falklands War.

On April 2, 1982, Argentine forces invaded the British-controlled Falkland Islands in the South Atlantic. Ever since they had been claimed by Britain in 1833, the islands had been a source of dispute between Argentina and Great Britain. The Falklands, known as Las Malvinas to the Argentines, lie off the coast of Argentina but are English-speaking. The Argentine troops were surprised to find that the islanders did not view them as liberators. Although the British government had warned Rex Hunt, the Governor of the Falklands, some days earlier that the Argentines planned to invade, he could muster only 80 Royal Marines to defend the islands. Hunt initially rejected calls to surrender, but when 3,000 Argentine troops landed at Port Stanley, the handful of Marines were unable to withstand them. By the afternoon, Governor Hunt ordered British troops to surrender. Immediately, the British government under Prime Minister Margaret Thatcher prepared a naval force to retake the islands. During the war that followed, 655 Argentines and 255 British servicemen lost their lives before the Argentine troops finally surrendered on June 14, 1982. Margaret Thatcher then announced, 'We went to recapture the islands, to restore British sovereignty, to restore British administration. I do not intend to negotiate on the sovereignty of the islands in any way except with the people who live there.' The Falklands remain in British hands, and Argentine resentment still simmers.

> **'We went to recapture the islands, to restore British sovereignty, to restore British administration. I do not intend to negotiate ... in any way except with the people who live there.'**

February 5
Laker Collapse
Sir Freddie Laker's budget airline Laker Airways collapses, leaving approximately 6,000 people stranded in holiday destinations.

March 26
Vietnam Memorial
The groundbreaking ceremony for the Vietnam Veterans Memorial is held in Washington, D.C.

April 25
Israel Out of Sinai
Israel withdraws from the Sinai Peninsula in line with the Egyptian–Israeli Peace Treaty.

May 8
Villeneuve Dies
French-Canadian racing driver Gilles Villeneuve is killed in a qualifying race for the Belgian Grand Prix.

HOLLYWOOD PRINCESS DIES

On September 14, 1982, Her Serene Highness Princess Grace of Monaco died of fatal injuries after losing control of the car she was driving and plunging off the road into a ravine. The princess had been returning from her family's country house in France with her youngest daughter, Stéphanie, who also was injured. Princess Grace died of a brain hemorrhage the next day in hospital: it is believed that she may have suffered a minor stroke while driving, which is what caused her to lose control of the car. Before marrying Prince Rainier III of Monaco, Princess Grace had been the Hollywood movie star Grace Kelly, starring in two of Alfred Hitchcock's most successful movies, *Rear Window* and *Dial M for Murder*. Her husband and her three children, Caroline, Albert, and Stéphanie, were at her hospital bedside when she died. Princess Grace was buried in the royal family's vault after a service in St. Nicholas Cathedral in Monaco.

Above: The principality of Monaco.

PRINCESS KILLED IN CAR CRASH

BEIRUT MASSACRE

SLAUGHTER IN BEIRUT CAMPS

On September 16, 1982, hundreds – or possibly even thousands – of Palestinian civilians in two refugee camps in Beirut were slaughtered. The massacre occurred when the Israel Defense Forces (I.D.F.) allowed members of a Lebanese Christian group called the 'Phalangists' to enter the camps. Israel had invaded Lebanon three months earlier. Ariel Sharon, the head of Israel's Defense Ministry, was later found to be partially responsible for the slaughter because he was perfectly aware of the hostility that existed between the Palestinians and Lebanese Christians, especially following the assassination of the Phalangist leader only days earlier. For some time, the Phalangist militia had been supplied with arms by Israel in support of their fight against the Palestine Liberation Organization (P.L.O.). The I.D.F. had let the Phalangist militiamen into the Sabra and Shatila camps under the pretense of flushing out any P.L.O. terrorists hiding there. The final death toll is still a matter of dispute, and estimates range between 300 and 3,000, including many women and children. The United Nations condemned the slaughter as an act of genocide.

June 10
Call Home
The much anticipated movie *E.T.*, directed by Steven Spielberg, is released and becomes a box office smash hit.

June 21
Son and Heir
Prince William Arthur Philip Louis Windsor, first son of Prince Charles, is born, becoming second in line to the British throne after his father.

August 17
Compact Discs
The first commercial C.D.s are released to the public.

October 1
First C.D. Player
Sony launches the first compact disc player, the CDP101.

1982

LONG-TERM PROTEST AGAINST NUCLEAR WEAPONS

HUMAN CHAIN FOR PEACE

Right: Greenham Common protestors attempted to prevent the delivery of cruise missiles by sitting in the road.

In 1981, a group of women organized a march from Cardiff in Wales to the U.S. Air Force base at Greenham Common in England, to protest against the proposed storage there of cruise missiles. When they arrived at Greenham Common, four women chained themselves to the airbase gate in order to attract media attention. After the planned march came to an end, several of the women decided to set up a permanent peace camp there, which soon attracted increased support, and numbers grew. By January 1982 it was a fully fledged, women-only peace camp, and the seven gates of the base were named for the colors of the rainbow. The protestors were threatened with eviction but, encouraged by the Labour Party's moves toward disarmament, were determined to stay. The evictions began in May 1982, but those arrested were quickly replaced by others. Following a national call for support, many more women arrived, and on December 12, 1982, over 30,000 of them formed a human ring around the airbase. Approximately 2,000 women were arrested for their blockading action, but the encirclement and its consequences simply inspired further support. Despite these protests, the cruise missiles were still housed within the airbase, so the Greenham Common women decided to file a lawsuit against President Ronald Reagan. The protestors were denied a hearing, but they still gained massive publicity and support in the United States. British Prime Minister Margaret Thatcher continued to do everything in her power to evict the camp members, with considerable success, but their popular support continued to grow.

> **'Following a national call for support, many more women arrived, and on December 12, 1982, over 30,000 of them formed a human ring around the airbase.'**

October 29
'Dingo' Mother Jailed
Lindy Chamberlain, the Australian woman who claimed that her baby was taken by dingos, is jailed for murder. She is later exonerated of all charges.

November 10
Brezhnev Dead
Leonid Brezhnev, Premier of the Soviet Union, dies.

December 1
What a Thrill
Michael Jackson's album *Thriller* is released and eventually becomes the biggest-selling album of all time.

December 2
First Artificial Heart
Dr. Barney Clark, a dentist, becomes the first person to receive the Jarvik-7, an artificial heart, in an operation performed by surgeon William DeVries.

1983

COMMUNIST COUP PUT DOWN BY U.S. TROOPS

U.S. INVADES GRENADA

On October 13, 1983, there was a violent military coup on the Caribbean island of Grenada, in which the former deputy prime minister, Bernard Coard, mobilized the army in order to seize power and form a Marxist government. The coup was a matter of concern to neighboring Caribbean islands, but also to the U.S. government, largely because it was perceived as a Communist threat that had strong support from Cuba. U.S. President Ronald Reagan used the presence of around 1,000 American medical students in Grenada as a front for invading the island on October 25, 1983.

'The coup was a matter of concern to neighboring Caribbean islands, but also to the U.S. government, largely because it was perceived as a Communist threat that had strong support from Cuba.'

Reagan also claimed that neighboring Caribbean islands had appealed for American intervention. U.S. troops stormed in full force, and it took only two months to conquer Coard's military government. The Marxist regime was replaced with a U.S.-friendly government. The invading troops then departed, satisfied that they had demonstrated to the Communist leaders, both in the U.S.S.R. and in Cuba, that revolutionary politics could not be spread too close to American soil without inviting repercussions.

America's allies in Europe made clear their disapproval of the unilateral U.S. invasion, but by that time the mission had already been accomplished. Although the United Nations tried to pass a motion denouncing the American invasion, U.S. representatives at the U.N. managed to block it.

Left: Grenada looks like a tropical paradise, but it was the scene of violent upheaval when U.S. troops invaded to put down a Marxist coup.

January 3
Volcanic Eruption
Kilauea, a volcano on the island of Hawaii, starts erupting and is still erupting today.

March 5
Hawke Elected
Labour candidate Bob Hawke is elected Prime Minister of Australia.

March 23
Another Star Wars
U.S. President Ronald Reagan announces his first plans for an enemy missile intercept system, commonly known as Star Wars.

March 25
Moonwalking
Michael Jackson first performs his 'moonwalk'.

1983

SOVIETS DOWN PLANE

On September 1, 1983, Korean Air flight 007 was shot down by the U.S.S.R. after it strayed into Soviet airspace on its way from the United States to Seoul, South Korea. All 269 passengers were killed.

'The Soviets did admit that they had shot down the aircraft, but they argued in their defense that it had not contacted their air traffic controlers or responded to radio communications'

Due to a failed navigational system, the pilot of the Boeing 747 jetliner did not realize that he had strayed off course and was too close to a Soviet military complex and naval base. The following day, the Soviets did admit that they had shot down the aircraft, but they argued in their defense that it had not contacted their air traffic controllers or responded to radio communications, so they had reason for alarm. It had been too dark for the Soviet fighter pilots to see that the plane was a civilian passenger jet.

AMERICA'S FIRST FEMALE ASTRONAUT

Dr. Sally Ride was born in Los Angeles, California in 1951. After abandoning an early ambition to make a career in professional tennis, she enrolled at Stanford University, where she completed a bachelor's degree in English and physics, a master's degree in physics, and then a doctorate in astrophysics. In 1977, she was one of 8,900 people to answer a N.A.S.A. ad looking for potential astronauts, and was one of six women among the 35 people chosen. After completing her space flight training in August 1979, Dr. Ride acted as the on-orbit capsule coordinator on two space shuttle missions, but then, in 1983, she became the first American woman in space when she went on the *Challenger* mission that launched on June 18. The mission lasted for 147 hours and achieved several 'firsts', including the first use of a robotic arm in space to retrieve a satellite, a procedure that Dr. Ride had worked to develop. She took part in several other missions before retiring as a N.A.S.A. astronaut in 1987. Since that time, Sally Ride has been a professor of physics at the University of California, San Diego, and director of the California Space Institute.

Left: The launch of a space shuttle.

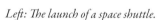

April 11
Gandhi the Oscar-Winner
Richard Attenborough's movie *Gandhi* wins eight Oscars.

May 14
Diaries Faked
The 'Hitler Diaries' are exposed as fakes, but are later published by *Stern* magazine.

July 15
New Computer Game
The innovative Nintendo Entertainment System is launched in Japan.

July 21
Cold in July
The lowest temperature on Earth is recorded at Vostok Station, Antarctica, when the mercury sinks to -128.6°F (-89.2°C).

ATTACK ON U.N. TROOPS IN LEBANON

During the 1980s, U.S. Marines were stationed in Beirut, Lebanon, as part of a U.N. peacekeeping force. Their aim was to stabilize the civil war-torn country, which was also suffering at the hands of the Palestine Liberation Organization and the Israeli Army. In the aftermath of the 1982 Israeli invasion of Lebanon, the U.N. stationed U.S., British, Italian, and French troops there in exchange for an Israeli withdrawal. On October 23, 1983, a suicide bomber drove a truck packed with explosives into the U.S. Marine barracks. As a result, 241 of the 300 U.S. troops sleeping inside were killed. Minutes later, there was a second blast at the compound that housed the French troops, and a further 58 military personnel were killed. The terrorists were part of a splinter group of Shi'a Islamist organization Hezbollah, which was a relatively small guerrilla operation at the time of the attacks. Three months later, President Ronald Reagan pulled the U.S. troops out of Lebanon, but the civil war continued to rage for another seven years. Joe Ciokon, a navy journalist who survived the blast, neatly summed up the attack: 'We walked into the middle of a family feud, and they all turned their guns on us.'

'241 of the 300 U.S. troops sleeping [inside the barracks] were killed. Minutes later there was a second blast ... and a further 58 military personnel were killed.'

BOMBINGS IN BEIRUT

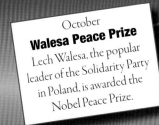

October
Walesa Peace Prize
Lech Walesa, the popular leader of the Solidarity Party in Poland, is awarded the Nobel Peace Prize.

October 13
Cellular Phone Network
The first U.S. mobile cellular telephone network is launched in Chicago by Ameritech Mobile Communications, now known as Cingular.

October 25
My Word
The software program Microsoft Word is released.

December 17
Harrods Bomb
I.R.A. terrorists bomb the world-famous Harrods department store, killing six people and injuring 90.

1984

GRAIN STORES FULL BUT THOUSANDS LEFT TO DIE

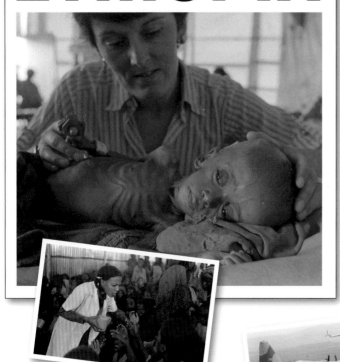

FAMINE IN ETHIOPIA

The famine that devastated Ethiopia between 1984 and 1985 had been building up for several years. The drought of 1981 had destroyed an entire harvest, which meant that supplies were already nonexistent when the lack of rain in 1984 threatened another bad harvest, with grain especially hard hit. There were early warnings of the potential famine, but Western aid was slow in coming and remained insufficient to deal with it. The Marxist military government in Ethiopia, under the leadership of Mengistu Haile Mariam, was spending vast amount on weapons, and Western governments feared that aid would only be diverted to pay for the ongoing civil war in Eritrea and Tigre. This made them reluctant to provide aid in early 1984 when aid agencies warned that thousands had already died of starvation and thousands more would do so if something was not done. Ironically, while Ethiopians were dying from lack of food, Europe was enjoying a grain surplus, but still food was not diverted, largely because the

'While Ethiopians were dying from lack of food, Europe was enjoying a grain surplus, but ... the West did not trust the socialist government to distribute it properly.'

West did not trust the socialist government to distribute it properly. Eventually, aid agencies were forced to buy European grain on the open market. In an attempt to shame Western governments into action, the international charity Oxfam donated $800,000 (£500,000) to Ethiopia, the largest single donation the charity had ever made. Meanwhile, widespread television coverage of people dying of starvation in Ethiopia was prompting an exceptional outpouring of private donations. In three days, the British public alone donated $8 million (£5 million), and within two months, the Western public had donated a total of $160 million (£100 million). In music, the Band Aid single 'Do They Know It's Christmas?', as well as two Live Aid concerts, raised millions more.

Above and right: Aid workers struggled to cope with the famine, even after food was flown in.

January 24
First Mac
Apple introduces its Macintosh computer.

February 7
Look, No Rope
Two astronauts on the tenth space shuttle make the first untethered space walk.

February 14
Olympic Ice Champions
British ice dancers Jayne Torvill and Christopher Dean score 12 perfect sixes for their interpretation of Ravel's *Bolero* in the 1984 Winter Olympics.

April 23
A.I.D.S. Identified
U.S. and French scientists identify the virus known as A.I.D.S.

BHOPAL DISASTER

POISON CLOUD KILLS THOUSANDS

On December 3, 1984, a leak in Union Carbide's pesticide plant in the city of Bhopal, India, caused toxic gas to escape, killing and disabling thousands of people. It was one of the worst industrial accidents in history. The toxic gas methyl isocyanate (M.I.C.) spread out across the city, burning eyes, lungs, and other organs on contact. Around 3,000 people died in the days immediately following the disaster. Tens of thousands more were permanently disabled, and it is estimated that another 20,000 people have since died as a direct result of the leak. After an investigation, Union Carbide (an American company) claimed that the leak had been caused by employee sabotage. Campaigners, though, claimed that cost-cutting measures had lowered safety standards. In 1989, Union Carbide paid $800 million (£470 million) in compensation to the Indian government. Victim support groups are seeking far more than this, and are pursuing a lawsuit against Union Carbide's boss, Warren Andersen, on charges of culpable homicide.

Right: Birth defects are very common among Bhopali children, even those born years after the disaster.

GANDHI SHOT BY HER OWN GUARDS

INDIRA GANDHI KILLED

'In the days following the assassination, riots broke out in the streets ... and more than 1,000 Sikhs were thought to have been killed.'

On October 31, 1984, the Indian Prime Minister, Indira Gandhi, was shot dead while walking in her own private gardens in New Delhi. The assassins were two Sikh bodyguards, motivated by their anger over the storming of the Golden Temple in Amritsar earlier that year in which 2,000 Sikhs had been killed. Prime Minister Gandhi had received death threats following the massacre at the Golden Temple, and only the day before the killing had said in a political rally, 'I don't mind if my life goes in the service of the nation. If I die today, every drop of my blood will invigorate the nation.' In the days following the assassination, anti-Sikh riots broke out in the streets of New Delhi. The police turned a blind eye, and 1,000 more Sikhs were thought to have been killed. Gandhi's son Rajiv succeeded her as Prime Minister. In 1989, Satwant Singh and Kehar Singh were hanged for her murder.

June 6
Temple Stormed
Indian government troops storm the Golden Temple at Amritsar, the Sikhs' holiest shrine, killing about 2,000 people.

June 22
Virgin Takes to the Air
Virgin Atlantic Airways' inaugural flight takes place.

July 28
Summer Olympics Boycott
The Soviet Union, along with 13 other countries, boycotts the Los Angeles Olympics on the grounds that the U.S. is using them for political purposes.

August 5
Burton Dies
Sir Richard Burton, renowned actor, dies at the age of 58.

1984

FIRST LINE-FREE SPACE WALK

The *Challenger* flight in February 1984 was to be the American space shuttle's tenth mission. Captain Bruce McCandless had waited 18 years to make his first space flight, and on February 7, five days into the mission, he became the first human to walk freely in space. McCandless stepped out of the shuttle without being secured by a safety line, as had always been common practice, using instead a manned maneuvering unit (M.M.U.). This groundbreaking step opened up new possibilities for the future of human activity in space.

Right: Bruce McCandless after his historic space walk.

I.R.A. HITS CONFERENCE

'Five people were killed by the blast, including one member of parliament, and 34 others were injured.'

In the early hours of October 12, 1985, a bomb went off at the Grand Hotel in Brighton, England, where the Conservative Party was holding its annual conference. The force of the explosion ripped off the front of the hotel and tore through eight floors. Five people were killed by the blast, including one member of parliament, and 34 others were injured. Prime Minister Margaret Thatcher and her husband escaped harm, but two members of her political cabinet were seriously injured. The Provisional Irish Republican Army (I.R.A.) immediately claimed responsibility, declaring, 'Today we were unlucky, but remember we only have to be lucky once; you will have to be lucky always.' Patrick Magee, thereafter known as the 'Brighton bomber', had planted the bomb in the hotel weeks earlier. He was sentenced to 35 years in prison, but was released in 1999 under the terms of the Good Friday Agreement. Failing to be swayed by the explosion, Margaret Thatcher insisted that the conference would proceed as planned the next morning. She began her opening address by declaring, 'This attack has failed. All attempts to destroy democracy by terrorism will fail.'

September 15
Another Son for Charles
Prince Henry Charles Albert David is born and becomes third in line to the throne, after his father Prince Charles and older brother Prince William.

September 26
Hong Kong
The U.K. and China sign an initial agreement that will give Hong Kong back to China in 1997.

October 16
Greenhouse Effect
Scientists warn that carbon monoxide pollution is causing the Greenhouse Effect.

November
Band Aid
Thirty-six of the best-known British and Irish musicians gather in a recording studio in Notting Hill, London, to record 'Do They Know It's Christmas?'

ROCKED WITH LOVE

The Live Aid Concerts, held in London and Philadelphia on July 13, 1985 to raise money for famine-stricken Africa, were the brainchild of musicians Bob Geldof and Midge Ure. Their original aim was to raise $1.6 million (£1 million), but in the end they raised a breathtaking $250 million (£150 million) to be donated to the starving multitudes in Africa. Around 90,000 people attended the events, and a further 1.5 billion people watched live television coverage that was broadcast to 100 countries. The idea for the concerts came from the success of the 1984 Band Aid single 'Do They Know It's Christmas?', another Geldof-Ure project, which itself raised $12 million (£8 million). The concerts ran for 16 hours across the two locations and brought together a record number of world-famous performers from both sides of the Atlantic, including Mick Jagger and Tina Turner, who performed a duet, David Bowie, Queen, Paul McCartney, Bob Dylan, Sting, Bryan Ferry, U2, Eric Clapton, Madonna, Elton John, and Dire Straits. The largest single donation came from the royal family of Dubai, who pledged $1.6 million (£1 million) in a phone conversation with Bob Geldof.

Left: The Live Aid concerts had an amazing array of stars from the music industry.

January 17
No More Red Phone Boxes
British Telecom announces that its iconic red telephone boxes will be phased out.

February 10
Mandela Rejects Freedom
Despite having been in prison for 21 years, Nelson Mandela rejects an offer of freedom from the South African government, saying he will not leave until apartheid has been abolished.

April 15
Black and White Can Marry
South Africa ends its ban on interracial marriage.

May 25
Deadly Cyclone
A tropical cyclone kills 10,000 people in Bangladesh.

1985

HELP FOR PEOPLE IN WAD KHOLI CAMP IN SUDAN

REFUGEES FLOOD INTO SUDAN

In January 1985, around 35,000 Ethiopians poured over the border into Sudan, fleeing the fighting and famine in their own country. After months of traveling, those who had survived ended up in the Wad Kholi camp, where a solitary doctor was suddenly faced with thousands of starving men, women, and children. At first, around 70 people died every day, half of them children, but once the charity Save the Children moved in with aid and medical staff, that number began to decrease. Thousands more Ethiopian refugees continued to pour into the camp, but their chance of survival increased thanks to massive private donations that succeeded in reaching their intended target.

> **'Around 70 people died every day, half of them children, but once the charity Save the Children moved in with aid and medical staff, that number began to decrease.'**

BAND MEMBERS KILLED IN COACH CRASH

R.A.F. COACH HITS PETROL TANKER

On February 11, 1985, a Royal Air Force coach carrying R.A.F. bandsmen on a tour of Germany was involved in a crash with a petrol tanker, killing 19 of its passengers. Although 24 of the bandsmen managed to scramble to safety, they were unable to help the 17 others who were trapped inside and overcome by the flames. It is thought that the rear emergency exit door was jammed.

June 17
Discovery Channel
John Hendricks launches the Discovery Channel in the U.S.A.

July 10
Rainbow Warrior Sunk
French agents sink the Greenpeace ship *Rainbow Warrior* in Auckland Harbour, New Zealand.

August 31
Titanic Found
Oceanographer Robert Ballard and his team find the wreck of R.M.S. *Titanic* on the ocean floor.

September 19
Mexico City Quake
An earthquake in Mexico City kills 9,000 people and destroys 95,000 homes.

DAM BURSTS IN ITALY

An earthen dam in northern Italy burst on July 20, 1985, taking the lives of hundreds of people. Onlookers described how a wall of mud and water 150 ft (45 m) high swept through the mountain village of Stava in the Dolomites, leaving destruction in its wake. It was the peak of the tourist season in the popular mountain resort when the dam gave way and the wave of muddy water crashed through crowded hotels and houses. Three hotels were completely wiped out; the guests were mainly Italian and Austrian, alongside other Europeans and Americans. The floodwaters flattened houses, uprooted trees, and buried cars over a 3-mile (5-km) stretch of land. The dam had been constructed 20 years earlier to hold back an artificial pond that was used to purify minerals excavated from a fluoride mine. It had just been examined for possible damage before it burst.

'It was the peak of the tourist season in the popular mountain resort when the dam gave way and the wave of muddy water crashed through crowded hotels and houses.'

BURST DAM KILLS HUNDREDS

Above: The Dolomite mountains of northern Italy, where the dam burst occurred.

October 2
Rock Hudson Dies
American film and television actor Rock Hudson, the first celebrity to admit publicly to having A.I.D.S., dies of the disease.

October 11
Orson Welles Dies
Famous film director and producer Orson Welles dies at the age of 70.

November 19
Reagan and Gorbachev
U.S. President Ronald Reagan and Soviet Premier Mikhail Gorbachev meet for the first time in Geneva.

November
Windows for the World
The Microsoft Corporation releases Windows 1.0, its first version of the program.

1986

MAJOR ACCIDENT AT CHERNOBYL POWER STATION

NUCLEAR DISASTER

Right: The town of Chernobyl was evacuated after the nuclear disaster.

On April 26, 1986, an accident occurred at the Chernobyl nuclear plant in Ukraine (then part of the U.S.S.R.) that killed 28 people immediately and had massive repercussions in the surrounding area for many years to come. Much of the panic at the time was due to unknown quantities: it was the first nuclear accident, so no one was sure what effect the leaked radiation would have or how far it would spread. The faulty design of the nuclear reactor caused an unexpected power surge during a routine test, and this led to an explosion that lifted off the reactor cover and released fission by-products into the atmosphere. A second explosion followed, causing 1,200 tons of graphite to burst into flames, releasing far more radioactivity into the atmosphere. An investigation found that, in addition to the design error, staff training was poor, and this was directly linked to the isolationist policies of the U.S.S.R. On the day of the disaster, 28 people, mainly firefighters, died as a result of their direct exposure to radiation, and 19 more died later, with many more suffering lasting damage. On May 2, around 45,000 local residents were evacuated from homes within a 6-mile (10-km) radius of the nuclear power plant. This zone was extended to 18 miles (30 km) within days. Initial rumors were exaggerated and did a lot to spread a culture of fear, mistrust, and fatalism. There have been long-term effects for the local population, such as an increased likelihood of contracting leukemia, but many of these effects have been found to be less drastic than originally anticipated. On the positive side, the Chernobyl incident was thought to be a contributing factor to the lifting of the 'Iron Curtain' around the U.S.S.R.

> **'The faulty design of the nuclear reactor caused an unexpected power surge ... and this led to an explosion that lifted off the reactor cover and released fission by-products into the atmosphere.'**

January 9
Kodak Out of the Picture
After losing a patent battle with Polaroid, Kodak quits the instant camera business.

January 20
Channel Tunnel Announced
The U.K. and France announce their intention of building a tunnel under the Channel.

January 23
Hall of Fame
The first inductions into the Rock 'n' Roll Hall of Fame are held, and include Chuck Berry, Elvis Presley, and Buddy Holly.

February 7
Duvalier Flees Haiti
Haitian President Jean-Claude Duvalier, known as Baby Doc, flees to France, causing widespread joy in Haiti and ending a dynastic rule that lasted 28 years.

SPACE SHUTTLE *CHALLENGER* EXPLODES OVER CAPE CANAVERAL

On January 28, 1986, the American space shuttle *Challenger* exploded one minute after liftoff, killing all seven astronauts on board. In Cape Canaveral, Florida, their family and friends watched in horror from the ground, while millions more watched live televised coverage, as the space shuttle burst into flames, showering the surrounding area with debris. An investigation found the cause of the explosion to be a leak through a faulty seal in one of the rocket boosters. On board were five men and two women, including a teacher, Christa McAuliffe, who had won a competition to join the crew. President Reagan led the nation in mourning for its national heroes. In a televised address the same evening he said,

'We will never forget them, nor the last time we saw them ... as they prepared for their journey ... and slipped the surly bonds of Earth to touch the face of God.'

'We will never forget them, nor the last time we saw them this morning as they prepared for their journey and waved goodbye and slipped the surly bonds of Earth to touch the face of God.' The tragedy dealt a massive blow to human space travel: although the *Challenger* had previously flown nine successful missions before the 1986 disaster, it was two years before N.A.S.A. resumed manned missions into space.

SHUTTLE EXPLODES

Left: The seven-member team pose with a model of the shuttle.

February 19
Mir Launched
The Soviet Union launches the Mir space station.

February 25
Marcos Defeated
President Ferdinand Marcos of the Philippines is overthrown.

March 11
Comet Back
Haley's Comet, visible once every 75 years, can be seen in the northern hemisphere.

April
Help to Quit Smoking
Nicorette chewing gum, designed to help smokers quit by providing nicotine in decreasing amounts, is put on the market.

1986

PREMIER SHOT DEAD IN STREET

The Swedish Prime Minister Olof Palme was shot dead as he left a movie theater in Stockholm, Sweden, with his wife Lisbeth on the night of February 28, 1986. Lisbeth was also shot, but her wounds were not fatal; Prime Minister Palme, however, was pronounced dead on arrival at hospital. A Social Democrat opposed to the political stance of what he called 'the Reagans and the Thatchers', Palme conducted his government informally and did not use bodyguards. He often walked unaccompanied around the streets of Stockholm, and the Swedish people were proud that theirs was a country where the Prime Minister was free to do so. Olof Palme was a firm supporter of the working classes, and a peace campaigner who took a strong interest in developing countries. At a time when the right wing dominated Western politics, Palme believed that the left wing was about to have its day, and often received criticism at home for his apparent Soviet sympathies. Christer Pettersson, a drug addict and petty criminal, was found guilty of his murder and sentenced to life imprisonment in 1989. However, the verdict was contested, and Pettersson was eventually released due to lack of evidence and motive. The crime remains unsolved.

SWEDISH P.M. SHOT DEAD

AIRPLANE HIJACKED

SLAUGHTER ON FLIGHT 073

On September 5, 1986, four hijackers disguised as airport security staff and armed with guns and grenades managed to board a Pan Am flight that was due to take off from Karachi Airport on its way to New York. They immediately fired shots to seize control of the plane, but the cabin crew had just enough time to warn the pilots, who escaped through a cockpit hatch, thereby grounding the plane at the airport. After seizing the passengers' passports, one hijacker, Zayd Safarini, grabbed Rajesh Kumar, a 29-year-old resident of California who had just gained U.S. citizenship, and made him kneel with his hands on his head. When Safarini's demands for a new flight crew were not met, he shot Rajesh Kumar in the head and threw him out of the plane. The hijackers then lost control and began shooting randomly at passengers. In the chaos that followed, Pakistani authorities entered the plane, also shooting. Although passengers tried to escape through emergency exits, 22 people were killed, most of them Indian or Pakistani, and a further 150 were injured. All of the hijackers were sentenced to life imprisonment. Their plan had been to fill the plane with explosives and fly it into the Israeli Defense Ministry.

April 15
U.S. Against Libya
The United States launches an airstrike against Libya.

May 16
Top Gun
The film *Top Gun*, starring Tom Cruise and Kelly McGillis, is released.

June 29
Branson Fastest
Entrepreneur Richard Branson breaks the transatlantic speed record in his powerboat.

August 19
Woman Found
Picasso's famous painting *Weeping Woman* is found in a locker in Melbourne, Australia, two weeks after being stolen.

1987

STOCKMARKET TAKES WORLDWIDE DIVE

On October 19, 1987, the world's financial markets suffered a sudden drop in value. It began with a crash on Wall Street that saw the Dow Jones lose 22.6% of its value (an equivalent loss of $500 billion/£300 billion). This led to a fall of 300 points on the F.T.S.E. Index, which is equivalent to an instant loss of $40 billion (£25 billion). In the U.S.A. the chairman of the New York Stock Exchange said, 'This is the nearest thing to a financial meltdown I've ever come across,' while President Reagan announced he was confident that the U.S. economy would survive. The crash came after a couple of years of fast growth in a 'bull' market – one characterized by hostile takeovers and relentless company mergers. The idea behind this type of market was that financial growth was limitless, and the way to keep it going was to keep buying companies. In order to raise the money to do this, many companies sold 'junk bonds', which are bonds that return high interest but also have a high risk attached. The investing public kept buying and buying these bonds with increasing greed, effectively buying nothing. As ever, when the bubble burst, panic set in: stocks were sold wholesale and values were wiped out. In this case, the fall was exacerbated by rising interest rates, a falling dollar, and fears of a looming war with Iran. Although it was the most drastic drop in the market's history, 'Black Monday', as it was called, did not lead to a depression, and it was not long before interest rates began to fall and investors began to buy again.

Right: Stockmarket traders worked at high speed – here on two phones at once – to offload stocks that had plummeted in value.

SHARES CRASH

January
Woman in Hall of Fame
Aretha Franklin is inducted into the Rock 'n' Roll Hall of Fame, the first woman to be so honored.

January 29
Reforms in Soviet Union
President Gorbachev begins reforms in the Soviet Union based on *perestroika* (restructuring) and *glasnost* (openness).

February 22
Andy Warhol Dies
Artist and filmmaker Andy Warhol, born August 6, 1928 in Russia and known for his involvement in the pop art movement, dies.

April
New Cartoon
The Simpsons cartoon appears for the first time on *The Tracey Ullman Show* in the U.S.A.

1987

U.S. AND U.S.S.R. AGREE TO CUT NUCLEAR ARSENALS

NUCLEAR WARHEADS CUT

'It was not until Ronald Reagan and Mikhail Gorbachev entered into negotiations that the arms race finally came to a real halt.'

Above: A mobile Russian missile launcher.

At the height of the Cold War, the U.S. and the U.S.S.R. held between them 30,000 nuclear warheads. In the 1970s, negotiations had opened up between U.S. President Richard Nixon and Soviet leader Leonid Brezhnev; these negotiations were known as the Strategic Arms Limitation Talks. These were aimed at limiting future weapons growth rather than reducing stockpiles, but they failed to achieve anything concrete. It was not until Ronald Reagan and Mikhail Gorbachev entered into negotiations that the arms race finally came to a real halt. After a 1986 summit between Reagan and Gorbachev, the Intermediate-Range Nuclear Forces Treaty was established, whereby both countries agreed to eliminate their ground-launched ballistic missiles, both nuclear and conventional, with a firing range of between 300 and 3,400 miles (480–5,440 km). Similar agreements had been discussed before, but the difference this time was that both countries agreed to let the other side carry out inspections to verify that the terms of the treaty had been met. As a result, by 1991 more than 2,500 weapons had been destroyed and subsequent leaders of both countries continued to agree to joint limitations.

June 19
Creationism vs Evolution
In a landmark ruling regarding a Louisiana state law, the U.S. Supreme Court rules that creationism does not have to be taught in public schools whenever evolution is taught.

June 22
Fred Astaire Dies
Fred Astaire, born May 10, 1899, film and stage dancer, known for partnering dancer Ginger Rogers, dies.

July
Barbie Convicted
Former Gestapo boss Klaus Barbie is convicted of crimes against humanity during the Second World War in Lyons, France, and jailed for life.

August 17
Rudolph Hess Dies
Rudolph Hess, Hitler's deputy at the start of the Second World War, is found dead in his cell, a suspected suicide, in Spandau Prison.

BRITISH NEGOTIATOR TAKEN HOSTAGE

Terry Waite had been an envoy of peace, negotiating for the release of hostages in Beirut, when he was taken hostage himself on January 20, 1987. As an envoy of the Archbishop of Canterbury, Terry Waite represented the Church of England on peace missions and had already successfully negotiated the release of several hostages held in Iran and Libya. In 1985, he became involved in negotiations to release four British hostages held in Lebanon by the extremist Islamic Jihad Organization. In January 1987, he went against advice and took the dangerous step of going alone with his contact, without guards or weapons, to meet the hostages. Blindfolded, he was taken on a four-day journey, supposedly to meet the hostages. It was only when he stepped down through a trapdoor and the door closed behind him that he realized he too had become a hostage. Terry Waite was held in Lebanon for a total of five years, four of which were spent in solitary confinement.

FERRY DISASTER

On March 6, 1987, a car ferry owned by the company Townsend-Thoresen (now part of P&O) capsized near Zeebrugge off the coast of Belgium, killing 190 people. The accident happened as a result of human error: the bow doors had been left open, and water began to pour into the car decks as soon as the ferry set sail. An inquiry discovered what it called a 'disease of sloppiness' at every level of the company's hierarchy. In 1989, a charge of corporate manslaughter was brought against P&O and, although the trial collapsed, it succeeded in establishing 'corporate manslaughter' as a possible criminal charge. Three individuals within the company were found guilty of manslaughter.

September 16
Climate Change
An international agreement to protect the ozone layer is signed.

October 15
Storms in Britain
Britain experiences its worst storms of the century, unforecast by meteorologists, killing 23 people.

December 18
Perl Created
Larry Wall creates the programming language Perl.

December 20
Disaster at Sea
The worst peacetime sea disaster takes place when a ferry sinks in the Tablas Straits in the Philippines, killing about 4,000 people.

1988

LOCKERBIE PLANE DISASTER

DISASTER AT LOCKERBIE

On December 21, 1988, Pan Am flight 103 exploded in mid-air and landed on the town of Lockerbie in Scotland. The flight was traveling from London to New York with 243 passengers onboard. All passengers onboard were killed, as well as 16 crewmembers and 11 people on the ground, bringing the total fatalities to 270. Onlookers described a massive fireball 300 ft (90 m) high, and the huge impact as the plane hit the ground caused debris to scatter for hundreds of miles. The plane landed in a residential area, crushing houses and cars. The investigation that followed revealed that a bomb had exploded onboard, and a murder inquiry began. Eventually, after a three-year joint investigation by the Scottish policing agency, the Dumfries and Galloway Constabulary, and the F.B.I., two Libyan intelligence agents were charged with the bombing. Abdel Basset Ali al Megrahi was jailed for life in 2001, but Lamin Khalifah Fhimah was found not guilty. Megrahi is currently serving his sentence in Greenock Prison in Scotland, despite frequent appeals for a retrial, and he continues to declare his innocence. Although Libya has never officially admitted carrying out the bombing, the government has accepted responsibility for the actions of its officials, and in 2002, Libya offered $2.7 billion (£1.7 billion) in compensation to the victims' families.

> '**Onlookers described a massive fireball 300 ft (90 m) high, and the huge impact as the plane hit the ground caused debris to scatter for hundreds of miles.**'

Right: The ditch made by the plane.

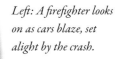

Left: A firefighter looks on as cars blaze, set alight by the crash.

January 26
Australia's Birthday
Australia celebrates its bicentennial.

February 5
Comic Relief
In the U.K., the first Comic Relief Red Nose Day raises millions of pounds for charity.

March 24
Vanunu Sentenced
Mordechai Vanunu is sentenced to 18 years in prison for advising *The Sunday Times* in London about Israel's nuclear program.

April
The Great Seto Bridge
The Great Seto Bridge, at 8.2 miles (13.1 km) the world's longest two-tiered bridge system, opens in Japan.

U.S. DOWNS IRANIAN AIRLINER

U.S. WARSHIP SHOOTS DOWN PASSENGER PLANE

The U.S. and Iran were unofficially waging war at sea in 1988. As the U.S. escorted Kuwaiti tankers in and out of the Persian Gulf, they shot down an Iranian civilian airliner, mistaking it for a fighter plane. The passenger jet, en route to Dubai, had veered 4 miles (6 km) off course, bringing it close to the battleground. A U.S. ship picked it up on radar and, after warning it several times by radio to change course and stay away, shot down the plane using a heat-seeking missile. The sky was hazy and the U.S. afterwards claimed that the military personnel involved had not seen the plane before they shot, and they believed it to be a hostile Iranian fighter jet. There were 290 people onboard, and all were killed. It was the first time the U.S. military had shot at a civilian plane. U.S. President Reagan called the incident a 'terrible human tragedy' and apologized to the bereaved families, but he maintained that the U.S. Navy had acted 'in a proper defensive action'. The Iranians referred to it as a 'barbaric massacre' and vowed to avenge their innocent dead.

EARTHQUAKE IN ARMENIA

EARTHQUAKE KILLS THOUSANDS

On December 7, 1988, an earthquake measuring 6.9 on the Richter scale devastated the Soviet state of Armenia, killing 25,000 people and leaving hundreds of thousands more homeless. Armenia, located between Turkey and Azerbaijan, is densely populated, and many people live in high-rise buildings, which heightened the scale of the disaster. The town of Spitak was entirely destroyed, with no hope to rebuild it. The U.S.S.R. was rocked by the tragedy, pleading for medical aid from the U.S. and pledging that the country would be rebuilt using low-rise buildings. The international community rushed to Armenia's aid, with France and America sending sniffer dogs, which successfully located many survivors in the rubble, India sending clothes and blankets, and Great Britain supplying excavating equipment.

'The U.S.S.R. was rocked by the tragedy, pleading for medical aid from the U.S. and pledging [to rebuild] using low-rise buildings.'

Left: A survivor in the aftermath of the quake.

April 11
The Last Emperor Wins
Bernardo Bertolucci's film *The Last Emperor* wins eight Oscars.

April 30
Eurovision Winner
Celine Dion wins the Eurovision Song Contest, which catapults her to international fame.

May 15
Soviet Withdrawal
The Soviet Union starts its troop withdrawal from Afghanistan, after eight years.

June
Mandela's Birthday Celebrations
Wembley Stadium in London holds a televised 70th birthday celebration for Nelson Mandela, imprisoned leader of South Africa's A.N.C., with celebrities from music, film, and comedy.

1988

TRAIN CRASH IN LONDON

RUSH HOUR DISASTER

It was the peak of the morning rush hour in London on December 12, 1988 when two commuter trains carrying more than a thousand passengers between them collided outside Clapham Junction station, killing 35 people. After the initial crash, a third train, which was empty of passengers, hit the wreckage, killing some of those who had survived the first crash. The accident happened just as the morning commuter train from Basingstoke to London Waterloo was nearing Clapham Junction. It slowed at a signal and the commuter train traveling from Bournemouth on the south coast ran into the back of it, hitting it at a speed of 40 mph (64 kph). Witnesses described carriages flying up into the air before crashing back to the ground. Several passengers with horrific injuries were given emergency surgery on the spot. The enquiry into the crash found that a signaling fault had been to blame, which was itself caused by a wiring error committed by a British Rail employee who had only had one day off in 13 weeks. As a result of the enquiry, British Rail employment practices came under strong attack. It was further recommended that automatic train protection (A.T.P.) systems be fitted to all trains to control their speed and stop them automatically at red lights. However, this recommendation was not implemented due to the prohibitive costs.

> 'The enquiry into the crash found that a signaling fault had been to blame, which was itself caused by a wiring error'

August
The Terminal Man
Mehran Karimi Nasseri, an Iranian refugee, lives at Terminal One in De Gaulle Airport, Paris, from August until July 2006, after his papers are stolen and he is refused entry into Britain.

August 20
Iran-Iraq War Ends
With an estimated 1 million dead, the Iran-Iraq War ends.

October 13
Turin Shroud a Fake
The Turin Shroud is declared a fake.

November 8
Bush Elected
George H.W. Bush is elected President of the United States.

CLEVELAND SCHOOL MASSACRE

On January 17, 1989, Patrick Edward Purdy opened fire with an AK-47 assault rifle, killing five children and wounding 29 others at Cleveland Elementary School in Stockton, California. Purdy, who had exhibited increasing sociopathic and violent behavior, fired more than 100 rounds of ammunition into the school playground before shooting himself in the head with a pistol. All of the children killed were of Southeast Asian background and the majority wounded were also from ethnic minorities. Subsequent police investigation found that the 24-year-old harbored a deep hatred towards immigrants, particularly those from Cambodia, India, Pakistan, and Vietnam, all of whom now lived in Stockton.

'Despite a previous criminal record and alleged mental health problems, Purdy purchased both weapons shortly after being released from jail.'

This incident, one in a long line of school shootings, led journalists and sociologists to question how the current system was dealing with racial hatred and mental health problems as well as how Purdy was able to buy his weapons with ease. Despite a previous criminal record and alleged mental health problems, Purdy purchased both weapons shortly after being released from jail. This attack led to public and political support for tighter gun control in California which, combined with increased media attention, led to the 1989 ban on assault weapons.

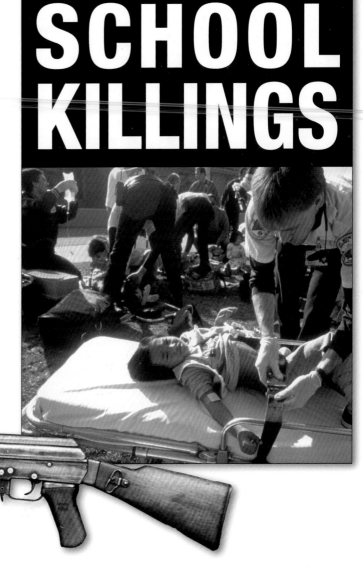

Right: An AK-47 assault rifle, similar to the weapon used by Purdy in the attack.

January 24
Ted Bundy Executed
Serial killer Ted Bundy is electrocuted in the electric chair in Florida, U.S.A. He is thought to have killed at least 30 women.

February 2
Sky T.V.
Sky Television plc is launched in Europe.

February 14
Fatwa Declared
Ayotollah Khomeini declares a fatwa against Salman Rushdie, author of *The Satanic Verses*.

February 15
Soviet Troops Exit
The last Soviet troops leave Afghanistan.

1989

OIL TANKER RUNS AGROUND IN ALASKA

'Around 30 million tons of oil were spilled, which led to the death of about 250,000 seabirds, as well as thousands of otters, seals, and eagles'

On March 24, 1989, the Exxon oil tanker *Valdez* hit a reef in Alaska's Prince William Sound, resulting in a massive oil spill. The environmental disaster caused extensive damage to the coastline, as well as birds and fish. Third Mate Greg Cousins was steering the vessel when a miscommunication over navigation led him to run aground on Bligh Reef, puncturing the hull. The reaction to the spill was far from effective, since there were insufficient chemical dispersants available and the equipment used to clear the oil manually was faulty. In all, around 30 million tons of oil were spilled, which led to the death of about 250,000 seabirds, as well as thousands of otters, seals, and eagles. The captain of the ship was charged with negligence amid rumors that he had been intoxicated. Exxon was forced to pay billions of dollars in damages to the Alaskan communities whose lives had been shattered by the spill, and the *Valdez* was banned from Alaska, even after it underwent a complete overhaul and changed its name.

SOCCER FANS CRUSHED TO DEATH

The 1989 FA Cup semi-final between Liverpool and Nottingham Forest was held at the Hillsborough Stadium in Sheffield, England. It was to become the site of the worst human disaster in soccer's history as 96 Liverpool fans were killed. A series of policing errors led to too many fans being let into a crowded terrace, where they were penned in by fences and crushed to death. The game had been under way for some minutes before the crush was noticed, and an enquiry after the disaster was heavily critical of the police, who were slow to recognize the seriousness of the situation and at first treated the crush as a public order problem. The disaster had a huge emotional impact on the British public, who saw it all unfold live on their TV screens. The Hillsborough tragedy led to a complete redesign of soccer stadiums in England and the removal of fencing around terraced areas.

June
Solidarity
The Polish Solidarity Party is elected to power, the first time in 42 years a non-Communist is elected.

July 5
Seinfeld Premieres
The hit television show *Seinfeld* is first shown.

July 12
I'll Have What She's Having
When Harry Met Sally, a popular film starring Billy Crystal and Meg Ryan, is released.

July 14
Happy Birthday, France
France celebrates the 200th anniversary of the French Revolution.

BERLIN WALL PULLED DOWN AS EAST AND WEST GERMANY REUNITED

After being separated for 28 years by guarded fortifications, in November 1989 East and West Germans were finally reunited. The 27-mile-long (43-km) Berlin Wall had been erected in 1961 by the Communist government of East Germany as a means of preventing East Berliners from escaping to the West. During the years that followed, many would-be refugees had been shot dead attempting to cross it, but a liberalization of governments in Hungary and Czechoslovakia had allowed East Germans to reach West Germany through other borders. In order to call a halt to such 'back door' emigration, on November 9, 1989, the Communist government of East Germany announced that the crossing points would be opened and East Germans would be free to travel to the West. No sooner had the government made the announcement than crowds flocked to the crossing points to be met by cheering supporters on the other side. Still more began to climb the wall itself from both sides, pulling it down

'Crowds flocked to the crossing points to be met by cheering supporters on the other side. Still more began to climb the wall itself from both sides, pulling it down piece by piece.'

piece by piece with their bare hands. The West German Chancellor Helmut Kohl welcomed the move and called for a meeting with East German leader Egon Krenz. Krenz had replaced the Communist hardline leader Erich Honecker and had opened the way for democratic reforms. However, when East and West Germany officially reunited a year later, Egon Krenz was arrested on charges of manslaughter for the deaths of all those who had tried to cross the wall and been shot by guards.

Right: Germans from East and West Berlin celebrate the end of the divide.

TEAR DOWN THE WALL

October 17
Quake Kills
An earthquake in San Fransisco kills 63 people.

December 3
Out of the Cold
The end to the Cold War is declared.

December
Chile Elections
Chile holds its first free elections in 16 years.

December 25
Ceausescu Executed
Nicolae Ceausescu, the former dictator of Romania, is executed by firing squad.

1990

IRAQ INVADES KUWAIT

WAR IN THE GULF

On August 2, 1990, Iraqi leader Saddam Hussein ordered his soldiers to invade the Gulf state of Kuwait. A total of 200,000 Iraqi soldiers easily succeeded in taking over Kuwait City, sealing it, and blocking off all lines of communication. The Emir of Kuwait fled to Saudi Arabia, but his brother was killed along with hundreds of others in the first days of fighting. The Iraqi justification for the invasion was that Kuwait had seized an unfair monopoly on the world oil market. Saddam Hussein claimed that Iraq was owed compensation for oil Kuwait had sold that came from a disputed oil field on the border of the two countries. Iraq also owed Kuwait over $60 billion that Kuwait had lent in support of Iraq's eight-year war with Iran, and was reluctant to pay it back. Despite the U.N.'s call for an immediate and unconditional withdrawal from Kuwait, and international condemnation of the invasion, Saddam Hussein refused to back down. The U.S.S.R., Iraq's main arms supplier, immediately stopped the sale of arms to the country but refused to be involved in any military intervention. The U.N. rejected Saddam Hussein's claim that Kuwait was now part of Iraq. Days later, the U.S., under President George Bush Sr., launched Operation Desert Shield. By October 1990, British and French troops had joined U.S. troops in the region, and they were soon also backed by Egypt, Syria, and Morocco. By January 1991, when the Allies launched Operation Desert Storm, there were 580,000 Allied troops against 540,000 Iraqi troops. Several air and land attacks by the U.S. and its allies during January and February eventually succeeded in convincing Saddam Hussein to withdraw his troops from Kuwait. On February 27, 1991, President Bush announced the liberation of Kuwait.

Right: Some of the Iraqi troops captured during the war.
Above right: General Norman Schwarzkopf, commander of coalition forces.

January 31
McDonalds in Moscow
After 14 years of negotiation, the first McDonalds restaurant opens in Pushkin Square, Moscow. It continues to be the busiest McDonalds in the world.

February 14
Solar System Snapped
Following its launch in 1977, *Voyager 1* traveled through the Solar System, taking breathtaking pictures of the entire Solar System in February 1990.

April 1
Prison Riot
Britain's longest prison riot, at Strangeways Prison in Manchester, lasts for 25 days. Two men die.

NELSON MANDELA FREED

Nelson Mandela, the anti-apartheid leader and Deputy Chairman of the African National Congress (A.N.C.), was released from prison on February 11, 1990 after 27 years' incarceration at Robben Island prison. His release followed the softening of the apartheid regime under South African President F.W. de Klerk, which had seen the ban lifted on the A.N.C. Following his release, Mandela addressed crowds of supporters in Cape Town, declaring, 'Our march to freedom is irreversible. Now is the time to intensify the struggle on all fronts.' Nelson Mandela had been convicted of treason and sabotage against the apartheid government in 1964 and sentenced to life imprisonment. After his release, he and F.W. de Klerk worked together toward fair, multiracial elections in South Africa.

'Mandela addressed crowds of suppporters in Cape Town, declaring, "Our march to freedom is irreversible."'

RIOTS ON THE STREETS OF LONDON

On March 31, 1990, 100,000 people joined a demonstration in central London against the government's new 'poll tax'. The poll tax had been unpopular ever since it was first introduced, on the grounds that it taxed individuals the same amount regardless of their circumstances. The March demonstration started out as a peaceful protest, but according to police, one group of around 3,000 demonstrators launched a purposefully targeted violent attack on the police. It began when protestors staged a sit-in outside of the governmental offices of Whitehall, near the entrance to Downing Street, and refused to move. The resulting arrests led to placards and cans being thrown at the police. The violence escalated: bricks and other missiles were aimed at police, fires were started and windows were broken, and there was looting of the stores around Trafalgar Square in central London. In all, 113 people were injured and 340 were arrested. The poll tax controversy contributed to Prime Minister Margaret Thatcher's downfall the same year. The following year, the poll tax was replaced by the council tax, which was based on the value of property.

April 9
First Free Elections in Hungary
Decades of Communist rule come to an end with the newly formed Hungarian Democratic Forum forming a new government.

May 20
Hubble Space Telescope Scans the Skies
Within weeks of its launch, a defect in the telescope's mirror is discovered, resulting in blurry images. The problem is not repaired until 1993.

May 22
Microsoft Releases Windows 3.0
The third release of the Windows operating system features more advanced graphics and an improved user interface. It goes on to sell over 10 million copies in the next two years.

June 8
Soccer World Cup Kicks Off in Italy
West Germany meet Argentina in the final, winning 1–0, with Argentina's Pedro Monzon becoming the first player ever to be sent off in a World Cup Final.

1990

CHANNEL TUNNEL COMPLETED

THE FRENCH CONNECTION

3001

Left: Workers on the British section of the Channel Tunnel.

In 1981, the French and British governments invited bids from private companies for the construction and maintenance of an undersea tunnel connecting France and Great Britain. By 1986, British Prime Minister Margaret Thatcher and French President François Mitterrand announced that work was ready to begin. Tunneling began from both ends simultaneously. Sophisticated laser surveying techniques meant that, when the two sides met in the middle in December 1990, there was only a $3/4$-inch (2-cm) error. However, the meeting of the tunnels did not signal the start of under-Channel transportation. The project was supposed to cost $7 billion (£4 billion) at the start, but it ballooned out of proportion and ended up costing $20 billion (£12 billion) by the time it opened for use in 1994. Further problems surfaced for the British rail network when it emerged that Eurostar trains, which could reach 186 mph (300 kph) on the Continent, were limited in their speed by the British system of rails. The required upgrade of the British line was finally completed in 2007, reducing the journey time from London to Paris to 2 hours 15 minutes.

June 21
Quake Kills Thousands in Iran
An earthquake hits an area northwest of Tehran, causing 40,000 fatalities and making half a million homeless.

October 3
Germany Re-Unified
The former state of Communist East Germany joins the Federal Republic of Germany, and Berlin is re-unified.

November 22
Margaret Thatcher Forced Out
Following an internal leadership contest, the United Kingdom's first female prime minister leaves office after 11 years in charge.

December 25
'World Wide Web' Invented
While working at C.E.R.N. (the European Organization for Nuclear Research), British computer scientist Tim Berners-Lee creates the first hypertext link, the basis for the entire World Wide Web.

FORMER PRIME MINISTER OF INDIA ASSASSINATED

'The assassin had held the basket of flowers out to Rajiv Gandhi, dying herself in the attack.'

On May 21, 1991, Rajiv Gandhi, the former Prime Minister of India, was campaigning for the Indian National Congress (or Congress Party) on the second day of democratic elections in India when a bomb hidden in a basket of flowers exploded inches from his body, killing him instantly. At least 14 others were also killed by the blast. The assassin was a female member of the Tamil Tigers, a guerrilla force fighting for an independent homeland for the Tamil people in Sri Lanka. The assassin had held the basket of flowers out to Rajiv Gandhi, dying herself in the attack. The assassination was presumed to be revenge for India's military intervention in Sri Lanka from 1987 to 1990, which had been initiated by Gandhi in an effort to impose peace. The 1991 election proved to be one of the most violent in India's history, with over 200 people killed in the lead-up. Rajiv Gandhi had become a member of parliament in 1980, taking the seat of his brother Sanjeev, who had been killed in an air crash. Rajiv Gandhi subsequently became Prime Minister after the death of his mother, Indira Gandhi, in 1984. Although he had rejuvenated and modernized the Congress Party, it fell into disgrace under his successor P.V. Narasimha Rao and lost the elections in 1996. Rajiv Gandhi was the grandson of Jawaharlal Nehru, who was the first Prime Minister of an independent India.

Right: Rajiv Gandhi's family pray at his memorial on the anniversary of his death.

February 26
Iraqi Troops Leave Kuwait
Saddam Hussein orders the withdrawal of Iraqi troops from Kuwait.

March 13
Clean-up Bill
Oil firm Exxon agrees to pay $1 billion to clean up the oil spill from its tanker the *Exxon Valdez* in Alaska.

April 17
Stock Market Milestone
The Dow Jones Industrial Average closes above 3,000 for the first time ever, having recovered from a value of 1,738 following the 1987 crash.

June 12
Yeltsin Elected
Boris Yeltsin becomes the first elected President of Russia, with a 57% share of the vote.

1991

THE END OF THE SOVIET UNION

GORBACHEV RESIGNS

With the creation of the Commonwealth of Independent States (C.I.S.) in December 1991, the former U.S.S.R. (or Soviet Union) was dissolved as 11 Soviet states broke away from the Union. The President of the U.S.S.R., Mikhail Gorbachev, was opposed to the breakup of the Soviet Union because he felt it did not reflect the popular choice. The C.I.S. had been formed by a secret agreement between Russia, Ukraine, and Belarus. On December 25, 1991, Gorbachev announced his resignation. The Soviet red flag depicting the hammer and sickle was lowered over the Kremlin, replaced instead by the Russian Federation's tricolor flag. Boris Yeltsin, as the new President of the Russian Federation, took over leadership of the Kremlin and also took the U.S.S.R.'s permanent seat in the United Nations. Mikhail Gorbachev had transformed the U.S.S.R., distancing it from its Communist roots and introducing democracy. He has been credited with establishing free elections, a free press, freedom of worship, and free enterprise, as well as improving human rights and ending the Cold War with the U.S. His keys words for reform were *perestroika*, meaning restructuring, and *glasnost*, meaning openness.

Right: Boris Yeltsin was Russia's first elected President.

July 11
Lights Out
The longest solar eclipse for 141 years takes place, in which the Moon comes between the Earth and the Sun. Best viewed from the Baja Peninsula in Mexico, it lasts 6 minutes and 52 seconds.

July 22
Milwaukee Murderer Captured
Serial killer Jeffrey Dahmer is arrested, leading to his indictment on 17 murder charges.

July 31
Nuclear Cap
The U.S. and Russia sign the START treaty, reducing the number of nuclear weapons in their stockpiles by a third.

August 25
Schumacher Makes F1 Debut
Michael Schumacher races for the first time in Formula 1 in the Belgian Grand Prix. He retires on the first lap, but goes on to become one of the greatest drivers of all time.

1991

I.R.A. ATTACKS LONDON

MORTAR BOMBS HIT DOWNING STREET

On February 7, 1991, the Provisional Irish Republican Army (I.R.A.) launched three mortar bombs at No. 10 Downing Street, the home and private office of the British Prime Minister. Prime Minister John Major was holding a government cabinet meeting in the Cabinet Room when a white van parked on Whitehall, the street that crosses the end of Downing Street, and launched three mortar bombs at No. 10. One of the bombs exploded in the garden, blowing in the windows of the Cabinet Room, but remarkably no one was hurt. Major had to move to a temporary residence in Admiralty House while Downing Street was repaired, but he made it his priority to carry on business as usual, undeterred by the attack.

Above: Prime Minister John Major survived the attack.

GUNMAN KILLS 22 IN TEXAS DINER

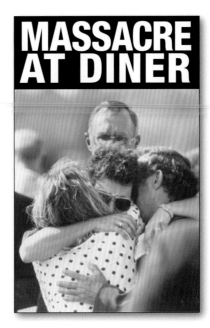
MASSACRE AT DINER

On October 16, 1991, a man named George Jo Hennard drove a pickup truck through the window of Luby's Cafeteria in Killeen, Texas, and began firing at diners. He killed 22 people before turning the gun on himself when police arrived on the scene. The restaurant was unusually full because it was National Boss's Day, and many employees were taking their bosses out for lunch. The surviving witnesses described how Hennard continually reloaded his gun, walked up to his victims, talked to them, and then shot them in the head. The 35-year-old man lived alone in his parents' house in the town of Belton 20 miles (32 km) away. There was no known motive for the massacre, believed to have been driven by delusional psychosis, but in terms of death toll, it was the deadliest rampage in America at the time. Following the tragedy, Texas changed its laws to allow citizens to carry concealed firearms on their person. This move was driven by Suzanna Gratia Hupp, who was at the restaurant with her parents but had left her handgun in the car, as required by law. Both of her parents were shot in the massacre.

'In terms of death toll, it was the deadliest rampage in America at the time.'

September 19
Frozen Find
Two hikers in the European Alps discover a 5,000-year-old frozen, mummified corpse, christened Ötzi, after the Ötztal region in which he is discovered.

November 5
Robert Maxwell Found Dead
The body of newspaper baron Robert Maxwell is found floating in the Atlantic off the coast of Tenerife.

November 24
Farewell Freddie
Queen frontman Freddie Mercury dies, the day after announcing that he is H.I.V. positive. A tribute concert five months later is attended by over 70,000 people and raises money for A.I.D.S. charities.

1992

YUGOSLAVIA BREAKS UP

YUGOSLAVIA TORN APART BY WAR

Historically, the area covered by the Socialist Federal Republic of Yugoslavia has been beset by ethnic conflict. President Josip Broz Tito had allowed self-determination among the federal states – Bosnia and Herzegovina, Croatia, Macedonia, Montenegro, Serbia, and Slovenia – as well as for Kosovo and Vojvodina, autonomous regions within Serbia. However, many Serbs were unhappy that the Albanian majority in Kosovo was in control of a region that was felt to be part of Serbia. Before Tito's death in 1980, he had made it a part of the Yugoslavian constitution that each of the eight leaders of the regions should take it in turns to be president for one year. This arrangement weakened and fragmented the government. By the end of the 1980s, Slovenia and Croatia were seeking independence. Meanwhile, Serbia sought to rein in the independent province of Kosovo, and the Albanian majority in Kosovo was looking to become a republic in its own right. Tito had somehow held all the factions together, but since his death, nationalism

> 'Tito had somehow held all the factions together, but since his death, nationalism and separatism had grown.'

and separatism had grown. The Serbian leader Slobodan Milošević reduced Kosovan independence so that he himself could choose its representatives. Albanians went on strike in protest, and Slovenia and Croatia supported their calls for republic status. Milošević tried to maintain a united Yugoslavia by force. On June 25, 1991, amid the first rumblings of war, Slovenia and Croatia declared their independence. The Serb population in Croatia formed their own Serbian republic within Croatia. Then, in September 1991, Macedonia declared its independence. In November 1991, the Bosnian Serbs in Bosnia and Herzegovina voted to remain part of Yugoslavia, but the result of a national referendum was the opposite, and the republic declared its independence in April 1992, with Bosnian Serbs forming their own republic within Bosnia. Yugoslavia was tearing itself apart.

February 7
Maastricht Treaty Signed
The 12 members of the European Community sign the treaty in the Dutch town of Maastricht, creating the European Union and laying out a framework for closer monetary and economic cooperation.

February 20
British Soccer's Premier League Formed
The 22 teams from the existing First Division break away to form the new Premier League, becoming the world's most watched and most lucrative football league.

April 12
Euro Disney Opened
The second Disney theme park outside the U.S.A. opens on a 5,000 acre (20 sq km) site near to Paris. In 1995 the park is renamed Disneyland Paris.

April 29
Los Angeles Race Riots
The acquittal, by an all-white jury, of four white police officers captured on video beating black motorist Rodney King prompts several days of rioting in which 55 people die.

I.R.A. BOMBS LONDON

On April 10, 1992, a truck-bomb exploded outside the Baltic Exchange on St. Mary Axe Street in London's financial district. It was one of several bombs planted by the Provisional Irish Republican Army (I.R.A.) as part of an ongoing campaign in London. The Semtex bomb, planted characteristically in a white van, tore off the front of the building and severely damaged several other buildings nearby. Three people were killed in the blast. In total, the damage cost around $800 million (£500 million) to repair. Originally, English Heritage, the organization responsible for the management of historic buildings in England, insisted that the 1903 Baltic Exchange building should be restored with its facade exactly as it had been. This would have proved too expensive for the Baltic Exchange, and the company was forced to sell the building. When English Heritage realized the full extent of the damage, however, they withdrew the statement. The building was completely destroyed in 1998, and on its site now stands the building commonly referred to by Londoners as the 'Gherkin'.

BOMB EXPLODES IN THE CITY

Left: The 'Gherkin', the building that replaced the Baltic Exchange.

EL AL PLANE CRASHES IN AMSTERDAM

On October 4, 1992, El Al cargo flight 1862, traveling from New York to Tel Aviv via Amsterdam, crashed into a nine-story apartment block on the outskirts of Amsterdam, killing 43 people, including three crewmembers, one passenger, and 39 people on the ground. Shortly after takeoff from Amsterdam, the pilot made an emergency radio call reporting that two of his four engines had failed. He attempted to turn back to make an emergency landing, but the plane came down, crashing into the apartment block and hitting 50 apartments. The 114 tons of cargo, reported to include one ingredient used to make up the nerve gas sarin, burst into flames on the ground. The crash occurred at 6.30 p.m. when many of the apartments were occupied. It was the worst air disaster ever in Holland and the first crash in El Al's history. It was initially feared that fatalities would be much higher, causing many newspaper reports to exaggerate the death toll.

PLANE CRASHES ON APARTMENTS

June 3
Rio Earth Summit
The U.N. Conference on Environment and Development is unprecedented in its size and impact, with over 100 governments attending and 10,000 journalists covering the event.

July 25
Barcelona Olympics Starts
Spain hosts the Games of the 25th Olympiad, at which the ban on professional athletes competing is lifted. Gymnast Vitaly Scherbo of Belarus becomes the first athlete to win six gold medals in one Games.

September 16
Black Wednesday
The British pound is forced out of the European Exchange Rate Mechanism following a collapse in its value. The British government increases interest rates from 10% to 15% and spends billions of pounds attempting to prop up the currency, but to no avail.

November 11
Church of England O.K.s Women Priests
The Anglican Church votes (by a very narrow margin) to allow women to become ordained as priests.

1992

PRINCE AND PRINCESS OF WALES SEPARATE

CHARLES AND DIANA SPLIT

After several years of press speculation, the British Prime Minister John Major announced on December 9, 1992 that Prince Charles, the heir to the British throne, and Princess Diana would separate. Major emphasized that the separation was amicable and that the couple would continue to meet over the care of their two sons. There had already been rumors of extramarital affairs on both sides, and the couple were increasingly leading separate lives. They did not divorce until 1996, when the Queen apparently urged them to finish the matter properly. Diana was allowed to retain her title of 'Princess of Wales' and to keep her residence in Kensington Palace, but she had to give up the title 'Her Royal Highness', as well as any claim to the throne. What had initially seemed like a fairy-tale romance before all the secrets began to emerge, turned into a battle fought through the media.

> 'There had already been rumors of extramarital affairs on both sides, and the couple were increasingly leading separate lives.'

November 20
Blaze at Windsor Castle
A fire rages through the Queen's Berkshire residence, damaging 100 rooms and threatening the monarch's priceless art collection. Firefighters battle for 15 hours to bring the blaze under control.

December 9
U.S. Marines Fly into Somalia
A U.S.-led multi-national operation is designed to prevent looting and corruption that was preventing aid supplies from getting through, but ends in failure in 1995 as U.N. forces withdraw, leaving Somalia with no government.

June 23
Yitzhak Rabin Takes Office
Two years after taking power in Israel, Rabin receives the Nobel Peace Prize for his part in the Oslo Accords, which reinvigorate the Middle East peace process.

November 3
Bill Clinton Wins U.S. Presidential Election
Democrat Bill Clinton wins with 43% of the vote, defeating incumbent Republican President George Bush.

75 DIE IN WACO SIEGE

The Branch Davidian Seventh Day Adventists came into existence in 1955 as a separatist branch of the Davidian Seventh Day Adventists, who had themselves broken away from the Seventh Day Adventists. David Koresh was a leader of the breakaway 'Branch', and in 1993, he brought their name to international media attention. On February 28, 1993, a siege began at Mount Carmel, the site of Koresh's Branch Davidian compound just outside of Waco, Texas. The U.S. government's Bureau of Alcohol, Tobacco, and Firearms (A.T.F.) was investigating claims that the Branch Davidians had a store of illegal weapons, and had decided to launch a raid on the compound. Koresh (real name Vernon Wayne Howell) apparently knew that the raid was coming and emerged unarmed to greet the A.T.F. agents, who were coming with a search warrant. A.T.F. agents opened fire as soon as they entered the compound, and in the exchange of fire, four agents and six Branch Davidian members were killed. The raid turned into a 51-day siege by the F.B.I. and A.T.F., with Koresh and his followers refusing to leave their 'Ranch Apocalypse'. Negotiations began via telephone, and Koresh agreed to a peaceful evacuation if his message could be broadcast on national radio. However, he later backtracked on this, saying that God had told him to wait, and releasing only 19 children. It was not known if those who remained inside did so willingly, but the F.B.I. decided to treat it as a hostage situation. One faction of the F.B.I. thought negotiation was the best way forward, while others thought that force was necessary. The F.B.I. used aggressive tactics to drive out the cult members, including playing loud, distorted music and disturbing sounds such as the squeals of a rabbit being slaughtered. They then cut off water and electricity supplies. The F.B.I.'s tactics were later criticized because they could have been part of what drove the sleep-deprived, wounded religious sect to their final act. The F.B.I. did not know how to deal with the Davidians' religious zeal, nor with the apparent willingness of the 21 children left inside to stay. Experts on apocalyptic religious cults tried to convince the F.B.I. that their aggressive siege tactics would only convince cult members that they were facing an end-of-the-world situation, making a violent outcome more likely. On April 19, 1993, the F.B.I. launched an assault on the compound. The agents went in firing tear gas and announcing that no shots would be fired. When the Davidians allegedly opened fire on the F.B.I., however, the agents returned fire. The Davidians had barricaded themselves into a building, and when the F.B.I. began to break in, several Davidians are believed to have set fire to it. In total, 75 Davidians died, 50 adults and 25 children, either buried under the collapsing building, burned alive, or 'mercy' shot by their own people.

SIEGE AT WACO

January 19
I.B.M. Announces Record Loss
I.B.M. reveals a $4.97 billion loss for 1992, which at this point is the largest ever single-year corporate loss in United States history.

February 11
Queen Pays Up
The Queen becomes the first British monarch to pay income tax, although the exact size of her fortune remains a closely guarded secret.

February 17
Haitian Ferry Disaster
The ferry *Neptune*, carrying 1,500 people, sinks 50 miles (80 km) west of Port-au-Prince, drowning over 500 passengers.

February 26
World Trade Center Bombed
A car bomb placed in an underground car park at the Twin Towers in New York explodes, killing six people and injuring hundreds.

1993

I.R.A. TARGETS LONDON AGAIN

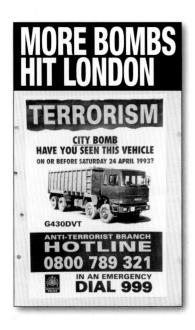

On April 24, 1993, the Provisional Irish Republican Army (I.R.A.) detonated a bomb in a truck in Bishopsgate, at the heart of London's financial district. The explosion killed one person, injured 44, and caused around $1.6 billion (£1 billion) worth of damage. There were fewer casualties than might have been expected because it was a Saturday and police had already spotted the abandoned Ford truck in which the one-ton bomb had been hidden. The police had also received warnings from the I.R.A. to clear the area. The only person killed was a press photographer for the *News of the World*, who ignored warnings to evacuate. The incident, the latest in a string of I.R.A. bomb attacks in London, prompted the City of London to set up a so-called 'ring of steel', involving tight security measures around the square mile of London's 'City' business area, with routes into the City guarded by armed police. By 1993, the peace talks for Northern Ireland were hanging in the balance, with Prime Minister John Major publicly refusing to enter negotiations until the I.R.A. called a ceasefire, arguing that 'those who use violence for political aims exclude themselves by their own actions'. He insisted that business should continue as usual in the City as much as possible, later writing of the event: 'They hardened our attitude, whereas they believed that their actions would soften it.'

JOINT PRIZE FOR SOUTH AFRICAN PEACE

Nelson Mandela and F.W. de Klerk were awarded the Nobel Peace Prize in 1993 for working together to reverse the hatred caused by the apartheid policies of South Africa. They were awarded the prize as recognition of 'their work for the peaceful termination of the apartheid regime, and for laying the foundations for a new democratic South Africa.' As leader of the National Party, F.W. de Klerk became President of South Africa in 1989. He quickly called for an end to racial segregation. It was de Klerk who lifted the ban on the African National Congress (A.N.C.) and authorized Mandela's release. He subsequently entered into negotiations with Mandela and the A.N.C. to create a one-person, one-vote democratic system, which gave black citizens equal rights to whites. Although the two men worked together and created an iconic moment in South Africa's history by presenting a united front that had seemed unimaginable, the process of negotiation after that time was not easy. South Africa was collapsing economically, and de Klerk's historic political decision changed that. The joint actions of Mandela and de Klerk opened the way for a more hopeful future.

March 12
Storm of the Century Batters U.S.

A huge cyclonic snowstorm affects 26 U.S. states along the eastern seaboard, killing over 300 people and causing over $6 billion of damage. Some areas see 3.5 ft (1.1 m) of snow, producing drifts of up to 35 ft (11 m).

March 22
Pentium Chips Launched

Intel Corporation ships the first Pentium microprocessors, giving a speed boost to P.C.s and paving the way for the multimedia capabilities of modern computers.

March 29
Pacino Claims First Oscar

Having been nominated as Best Actor five times previously, Al Pacino finally picks up the coveted statue for his role in *Scent of a Woman*. He is also nominated for a Best Supporting Actor award for his role in *Glengarry Glen Ross*.

April 6
Russian Nuclear Accident

An explosion at the Tomsk-5 Nuclear Plant in Russia spreads nuclear contamination over a 78-mile (125-km) radius.

OIL TANKER DISASTER

The oil tanker *Braer* ran aground on the southern end of the Shetland Islands, which lie north of Scotland, on January 5, 1993. While traveling from Norway to Canada, the *Braer* was hit by hurricane-force winds, causing it to lose power and leaving it to the mercy of a violent sea. When it was clear that a collision was inevitable, the crew was airlifted to safety, while the tanker smashed against rocks in Quendale Bay. The *Braer* was carrying twice as much oil as the *Exxon Valdez* had been when it had run aground in Alaska four years earlier.

'Almost every last drop of the oil spilled out into the North Sea.'

Built in 1975, the ship did not have the double hull of more recent tankers, which might have prevented the spillage of the whole of its 85,000 tons of oil. Almost every last drop of the oil spilled out into the North Sea. Although local authorities had been prepared for such a disaster, fully aware of the rough conditions around their coastline, emergency measures were not enough to prevent an ecological catastrophe. The Shetland Islands are renowned worldwide for their marine and bird life, much of which suffered permanent damage as a result.

TANKER RUNS AGROUND

Right: A seal struggles in the oily water off the Shetland Islands.

May 27
Florence Bombing
A car bomb parked next to the Uffizi Museum in Florence kills five people, including the museum's curator, and damages many priceless works of art, destroying three Renaissance paintings.

April 30
Tennis Ace Stabbed
Women's number one Monica Seles is stabbed in the back at a match in Hamburg, Germany, by a deranged Steffi Graf fan. She returns to tennis in 1995, winning the Canadian Open.

September 13
Oslo Accords Signed
In a historic photo opportunity, Yasser Arafat and Yitzhak Rabin shake hands on the White House lawn, in the presence of U.S. President Bill Clinton.

October 19
Pakistan Elects Bhutto Again
Benazir Bhutto is elected for a second term as leader of Pakistan. She serves until 1996 before being removed following corruption charges.

1994

U.S. SENDS TROOPS INTO HAITI

On September 19, 1994, 20,000 U.S. troops landed in Haiti to oversee the return to power of Jean-Bertrand Aristide. Aristide, a Roman Catholic priest, had become president in Haiti's first free elections in 1991, but in the same year he was removed from power in a military coup. The coup had been supported by many of the country's economic elite, and it prompted a mass exit of many Haitians by boat. For three years, a three-man military junta treated the population with ruthless brutality – it is still not known how many people died – until the U.N. approved the use of force to return the elected leader Aristide. The U.S. responded to the call, and on September 18, 1994, just before the U.S. was preparing to use force against the military dictators, a diplomatic delegation led by former U.S. President Jimmy Carter negotiated a voluntary handover of power. Aristide was returned to power without any bloodshed, although the peace was not to last.

'Former U.S. President Jimmy Carter negotiated a voluntary handover of power.'

January 7
Skating Star Attacked
Top U.S. ice skater Nancy Kerrigan is attacked with a metal crowbar one month before the Winter Olympics. Investigations reveal that rival skater Tonya Harding's ex-husband is behind the attacks. Kerrigan goes on to win a silver medal in the Olympics.

February 12
The Scream Snatched
Thieves break into Oslo's National Art Museum and steal Edvard Munch's iconic painting *The Scream*. A ransom demand for $1 million is received but museum authorities refuse to pay, with the painting finally being recovered on May 7.

March 13
Nessie Photo Faked
The most famous alleged photo of the Loch Ness Monster, dating from 1934, is proved to be a fake after a relative of one of the men involved in creating it confesses. The picture was created by adding a head and neck onto a toy submarine and floating it in the lake.

March 21
Schindler's List Scoops Oscars
Steven Spielberg's film about a German businessman trying to save Jews from the Holocaust cleans up at the Oscars, picking up seven awards, including Best Director, Best Picture, and Best Original Score.

1994

NELSON MANDELA ELECTED PRESIDENT OF SOUTH AFRICA

Despite the lifting of apartheid, violence remained a part of everyday life in South Africa. A new constitution was drafted in November 1993, establishing a timescale for elections in April 1994 and a five-year transitional government. Nelson Mandela and the African National Congress (A.N.C.) tried to encourage new investment in South Africa, but due to the ongoing unrest, foreign investors viewed the country as unstable. A few political parties still demanded a whites-only homeland and declared that they would boycott the elections. The U.N. provided personnel to oversee the elections, which were also being monitored by international mediators. Eventually, on March 31, 1994, President F.W. de Klerk was forced to declare a state of emergency in Natal and Kwazulu, where he deployed 3,000 troops to allow free elections to take place. Elections went ahead on April 26, 1994, with over 22 million voters turning out. Voting was extended to April 29, and tensions remained high, but by May 6, the Independent Electoral Commission gave the result of a 'substantially fair and free' election. The A.N.C. had won 62% of the votes, and Mandela was elected President.

RWANDAN GENOCIDE BEGINS

In Rwanda, from April 6, 1994, militia formed of ethnic Hutu began a campaign of brutality against the ethnic Tutsi population, killing 800,000 men, women, and children with machetes and clubs. Historically, the Tutsi, though only accounting for 15% of the population in the small Central African country, had been the aristocratic ruling class. Particularly during the era when Rwanda was a Belgian colony, the Tutsi minority had ruled over an 85% majority of Hutu peasants. However, as soon as the Belgians left in 1962, the Hutu majority took power and began to systematically oppress the Tutsis. Over 200,000 Tutsi fled to neighboring countries and set up a guerrilla force known as the Rwandan Patriotic Front. In 1990, this guerrilla force invaded Rwanda, forcing the Hutu president to sign a power-sharing agreement. Ethnic tensions continued to rise, as a U.N. peacekeeping force watched over the fragile ceasefire. When, on April 6, 1994, two Hutu presidents were shot down in a plane, Hutu militia went on a killing spree, targeting Tutsi civilians. After ten Belgian soldiers were tortured and murdered, the U.N. began to evacuate their personnel. A frenzy of cruelty was unleashed, and the churches and hospitals where Tutsis had taken refuge began to be specifically targeted. The U.N. planned to send forces back in, but they were too late. The genocide only stopped when Tutsi guerrilla groups from neighboring countries defeated the Hutus in July 1994. One tenth of the total population had been killed.

April 8
Kurt Cobain Found Dead
The body of Kurt Cobain, songwriter and lead singer of Nirvana, is discovered at his Lake Washington home. He died from a single gunshot wound to the head. A suicide note is found nearby.

May 1
Ayrton Senna Killed in Race Crash
Three-time Formula 1 champion Ayrton Senna is killed in an accident at the San Marino Grand Prix. His car leaves the track at a speed of 192 mph (309 kph) and crashes into a concrete wall.

May 6
Chunnel Opens
The Channel Tunnel between England and France is officially opened by the Queen and French President François Mitterrand. The tunnel allows trains to travel from London to Paris in 3 hours.

1994

TERRORIST STANDS TRIAL

THE JACKAL IS CAUGHT

Ilich Ramírez Sánchez, the Venezuelan-born international terrorist kwown popularly as 'Carlos the Jackal', was finally captured in Sudan on June 4, 1994 and extradited to France to face trial. Ramírez Sánchez converted to Islam and joined the Popular Front for the Liberation of Palestine, although first and foremost he styled himself as a revolutionary rather than an advocate of one particular cause. He was wanted for several terrorist crimes, ranging from bombings in London and Paris to taking 42 hostages at an Organization of Petroleum Exporting Countries (O.P.E.C.) meeting in Vienna in 1975. He was also thought to have been the mastermind behind the murder of the Israeli athletes at the Munich Olympics in 1972. However, there is no proof of his involvement in all the atrocities attributed to him, and his own almost certainly exaggerated boasts have confused the issue further. During the Cold War, Ramírez Sánchez had found sanctuary in Eastern Europe before settling in Damascus, Syria. By 1990, the Syrians had forced him to become inactive, eventually expelling him in 1991. He moved to Khartoum, Sudan, where he was protected for three years before the Sudanese authorities agreed a deal with France to hand him over. He was given over to French agents after coming into hospital for a routine operation. After three years spent in solitary confinement in a Paris jail, Carlos the Jackal was sentenced to life imprisonment for killing two French intelligence agents. He had always been proud of his notoriety and remained unapologetic to the end.

DEADLY EARTHQUAKE HITS LOS ANGELES

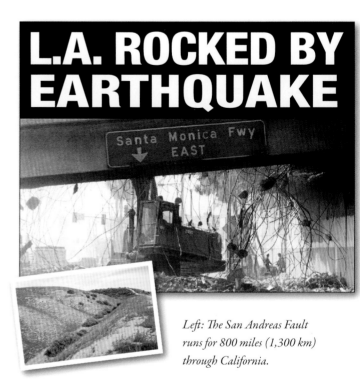

Left: The San Andreas Fault runs for 800 miles (1,300 km) through California.

In the early hours of January 17, 1994, Los Angeles was rocked by a massive earthquake that measured 6.6 on the Richter scale and lasted for 40 seconds. In that short space of time, it caused $30 billion (£18 billion) worth of damage and killed 60 people. The San Fernando Valley was the worst hit, with over 3 million people affected and emergency services working around the clock to rescue people from collapsed buildings. Because of the damage to many hospital buildings, surgeons were forced to operate in the open air. The mayor of Los Angeles declared a state of emergency and imposed an evening curfew. President Clinton visited the city the week after the quake and asked Congress to raise $6 billion (£4 billion) for the relief effort.

July 8
Kim Il Sung Dies
Kim Il Sung, President of North Korea, dies. The longest-serving dictator of the 20th century, he had held power for 46 years and was succeeded by his son Kim Jong Il.

September 28
Baltic Ferry Disaster
The car ferry M.S. *Estonia*, sailing from Estonia to Sweden, sinks in the Baltic Sea, killing 852 people. An inquiry finds the cause of the accident to be crew error and the design of the ferry's doors.

November 5
Reagan Reveals Alzheimer's Diagnosis
Former U.S. President Ronald Reagan announces that he has been diagnosed with Alzheimer's disease, a degenerative form of dementia.

December 11
Chechnya Invaded
Russian President Boris Yeltsin orders troops and tanks into the southern Russian republic of Chechnya. Chechen separatists fight a 20-month war with Russia during which 100,000 people are killed.

BOMBING IN OKLAHOMA CITY
KILLS 168 PEOPLE

On the morning of April 19, 1995, a bomb exploded outside the Alfred P. Murrah Federal Building in Oklahoma City. It was 9.05 a.m., and most employees had already arrived at work, many having first dropped off their children at the building's daycare center. The bomb ripped off the front of the building, and by the time rescue workers had finished sifting through the rubble weeks later, the bomb had claimed 168 victims, including 19 children. The bomb had been planted by U.S. citizen Timothy McVeigh, a former army sergeant, who was pulled over by police hours later for driving without a license plate and carrying an unlicensed weapon. It was only when he was about to be released that someone recognized his similarity to the sketch of one of the bomb suspects. Since leaving the army, McVeigh had developed increasingly paranoid political views, and he was convinced that the U.S. government was becoming a controlling dictatorship. He belonged to various white-supremacist groups, and traveled the country attending gun shows and selling bumper stickers that said, 'Fear the Government that Fears your Gun'. The bombing of the Oklahoma City Federal Building, where the Alcohol, Firearms, and Tobacco Agency had offices, had first been suggested to him when he spent time at an anti-government, white-supremacist compound known as Elohim City on the Arkansas-Oklahoma border. Although he was thought to be part of a wider conspiracy and certainly had accomplices, Timothy McVeigh was found guilty of planting and detonating the bomb, and he alone was executed by lethal injection on June 11, 2001.

Left: The memorial to victims of the bombing in Oklahoma City.

January 1
World Trade Organization Founded
The W.T.O. is a global body designed to establish rules of trade between nations. It has over 150 members, representing 95% of global trade.

February 21
Solo Balloon Flight Across Pacific
Adventurer Steve Fossett lands his hot air balloon in Saskatchewan, Canada, becoming the first person to make a solo flight across the Pacific Ocean.

May 1
Chirac Elected President of France
Jacques Chirac, the Gaullist candidate, is elected the new President of France, taking over from socialist François Mitterrand.

1995

ROGUE TRADER FELLS BANK

BARINGS BANK COLLAPSES

Nick Leeson, who came from a working-class London background, had first landed a job in the banking industry in the 1980s and, specializing in Far Eastern currency markets, had worked his way up to becoming Barings Bank's star Singapore trader. By 1993, he was working in Singapore and had earned the bank $16 million (£10 million), taking a $220,000 (£130,000) bonus and $80,000 (£50,000) salary. It seemed that nothing could stop this rising star. But in 1994, Leeson's luck began to turn. By the end of the year, his losses for the bank stood at $360 million (£208 million). Then the Kobe earthquake in Japan in January 1995 changed the Far Eastern currency market, and Nick Leeson's star began to fall. He requested more and more money to dig himself out of the crisis, and when the bank did an audit later that year, losses amounted to $1.2 billion (£800 million), which Leeson had managed to conceal by fraud. He went on the run to Borneo and then Frankfurt, but he was eventually extradited by Germany back to Singapore, where he was sentenced to six and a half years in prison. The executives who should have been overseeing him either resigned or were fired. Barings Bank, Great Britain's oldest merchant bank and the personal bank of the Queen, collapsed and was bought for just under $2 (£1) by the Dutch financial group I.N.G.

ISRAELI PREMIER ASSASSINATED

RABIN ASSASSINATED

On November 4, 1995, Israeli Premier Yitzhak Rabin was assassinated by a right-wing Zionist who opposed Rabin's peace negotiations that had resulted in the Oslo Accords. Yitzhak Rabin had been participating in a rally celebrating the Oslo Accords in Tel Aviv when Yigal Amir shot him three times. Rabin had declined to wear a bulletproof vest that day. The Oslo Accords, signed in Washington, D.C. in September 1993 in the presence of Palestine Liberation Organization (P.L.O.) Chairman Yasser Arafat, Israeli Premier Yitzhak Rabin, and U.S. President Bill Clinton, set out a framework for future peaceful relations between Israel and a Palestinian state, allowing territorial trade-offs to a Palestinian Authority. The agreement involved the withdrawal of the Israel Defense Forces (I.D.F.) from parts of the Gaza Strip and the West Bank, and it was the first time a face-to-face agreement had been reached between Israel and the Palestinians. The assassination shocked the people of Israel, who held rallies and renamed parts of the city after their respected leader.

July 13
Chicago Heatwave
The Midwestern U.S.A. experiences a week of record temperatures ranging from 90° to 106°F (32°–41°C), causing 465 deaths.

July 15
Srebrenica Massacre
Bosnian Serbs seize the former safe haven of Srebrenica, where thousands of Muslim refugees are sheltering from the Balkan conflict under the protection of Dutch peacekeepers. Mass graves are later discovered and it is thought that up to 8,000 Muslim men were killed by Serb soldiers.

August 24
Microsoft Launches Windows 95
The successor to Windows 3 is launched with great fanfare, including an advertising campaign built around the Rolling Stones song 'Start Me Up', a reference to the new 'start' button built into the interface.

September 3
Ebay Founded
Computer programmer Pierre Omidyar founds the online auction site, and the first item sold is a broken laser printer. Ebay now boasts over 84 million users worldwide.

EARTHQUAKE HITS KOBE, JAPAN

JAPANESE EARTHQUAKE KILLS THOUSANDS

An earthquake with a magnitude of 7.2 on the Richter scale hit Japan on January 17, 1995, devastating entire cities and killing thousands of people. The most powerful earthquake to hit Japan for 47 years struck in the early morning, just as commuters were beginning their journeys to work. The worst-affected city was the port of Kobe, home to around 1.5 million people, where apartment blocks fell to the ground and a raised freeway collapsed, throwing 50 cars off the edge. Damaged water and gas pipes obstructed rescue operations, and electricity was cut off in many areas. At the end of all rescue attempts, it emerged that 6,433 people had died. A further 27,000 had been injured, and 45,000 homes had been destroyed. It was one of the most disastrous earthquakes in Japan's history. Prime Minister Tomiichi Murayama set up an emergency committee and sent troops to help with the rescue operation. The cost of rebuilding Kobe reached the $100 billion (£60 billion) mark, and the city found it difficult to rebuild its population, many of whom left for good after the quake.

Right: the Earthquake Memorial in Meriken Park, Kobe.

'At the end of all rescue attempts, it emerged that 6,433 people had died. A further 27,000 had been injured, and 45,000 homes had been destroyed.'

October 24
Solar Eclipse Over Asia
A total solar eclipse can be seen from Iran, India, Thailand, and Southeast Asia.

November 19
Toy Story Premiered
The first entirely computer-generated animated film is produced by Pixar Animation and features the voices of Tom Hanks and Tim Allen. Since its release it has grossed over $190 million.

December 4
Beatles Release New Single
Fifteen years after the death of John Lennon, The Beatles release a new single, 'Free as a Bird'. Based around a vocal recording of Lennon, the track was created by the surviving three Beatles and producer Jeff Lynne.

December 14
Balkan War Ends
Bosnia, Serbia, and Croatia sign the Dayton Accord in Paris to bring the three-year conflict to an end. The deal is brokered by U.S. President Bill Clinton and is followed by the arrival of a N.A.T.O. peacekeeping force.

1996

I.R.A. BOMBS LONDON

MORE BOMBS HIT LONDON

During 1996, the Provisional Irish Republican Army (I.R.A.) stepped up its bombing campaign on mainland Great Britain. The first target was the Docklands area of London, the redeveloped commercial district, which was hit by a bomb on February 10. This bomb marked the end of a 17-month ceasefire during which British, American, and Irish leaders had failed to reach an agreement on a peaceful end to the Irish 'Troubles'. Two men, both newsagents, were killed, and 39 others were injured by the blast, which brought down a six-story building and damaged several others.

In 1998, James McArdle was jailed for 25 years on the charge of conspiracy to cause an explosion, but he was released under the terms of the Good Friday Agreement in 2000. Just over one week after the first explosion, another bomb went off on a double-decker bus in central London. Only one person was killed, the I.R.A. bomber Edward O'Brien who had been transporting the bomb to another location when it accidentally went off. Then, in June 1996, soon after peace talks had resumed, another I.R.A. bomb went off in a busy shopping district of Manchester. This time there were no fatalities, but many people were seriously injured by the flying glass that resulted. British Prime Minister John Major insisted that peace talks would continue.

> **'This bomb marked the end of a 17-month ceasefire during which British, American, and Irish leaders had failed to reach any agreement on a peaceful end to the Irish "Troubles".'**

Left: Gerry Adams, leader of Sinn Fein.

January 20
First Palestinian Election
Polls open in the first ever election for a Palestinian President and parliament. Yasser Arafat wins the poll for President, taking 88% of the vote.

February 10
Chess Computer Defeats Grand Master
Chess computer Deep Blue defeats world chess champion Garry Kasparov for the first time. Although the I.B.M. machine wins one game, Kasparov wins the overall match.

March 20
British Beef in B.S.E. Panic
The British Government announces that the disease B.S.E. (Bovine Spongiform Encephalopathy, more commonly known as Mad Cow Disease) found in British cattle, could be transmitted to humans.

March 25
'Year of the Independents' at the Oscars
Anthony Minghella's *The English Patient* takes nine awards, making it the third most decorated film in the history of the Oscars.

BOMBING AT 100TH OLYMPICS, ATLANTA

ATTACK AT THE OLYMPICS

Above: The Atlanta Olympics was successfully completed despite the blast.

At the end of the first full week of the 1996 Summer Olympic Games in Atlanta, Georgia, U.S.A., an event that had already been riddled with logistical problems was rocked by a bomb blast. The bomb went off in the early hours of July 27 in Centennial Olympic Park, where tens of thousands of fans were attending an evening rock concert. The explosion killed two people: an American woman and a Turkish cameraman, who suffered a fatal heart attack. America was already feeling vulnerable to the threat of terrorism following the T.W.A. plane explosion that had killed 230 people only ten days earlier. The Centennial Olympic Park bomb blast brought home to the watching world that even a 30,000-strong security presence could not protect people from terrorism, despite the chief organizer's claim before the games that, 'The safest place on this wonderful planet will be Atlanta during the time of our Games.' In April 2005, Eric Robert Rudolph pleaded guilty to planting the bomb.

EVIDENCE OF LIFE FOUND ON MARS

FOSSIL FOUND IN MARTIAN ROCKS

'The complex organic compounds within the rock point toward biological origins'

In August 1996, N.A.S.A. scientists announced that they had discovered evidence of fossil life on the planet Mars. Their claim was based on the discovery of a meteorite in an Antarctic ice field in 1984. According to extensive analysis, this specific chunk of rock had been ejected into space from Mars during an asteroid impact 15 million years ago, and it then orbited as a small planet before being buried in the Antarctic Ocean 13,000 years ago. The complex organic compounds within the rock point toward biological origins, which suggests the existence of life within the rock at one time. The life-forms present in the rock are simple micro-organisms that are similar to bacteria and are believed to be around 3 or 4 billion years old.

Left: the microscopic image of the possible bacteria.

April 3
Unabomber Arrested
Police in the U.S.A. arrest the man behind an 18-year bombing campaign that killed 3 people and injured 23 others. The nickname 'Unabomber' came from the initial letters of his most common targets – universities and airlines.

July 19
Bosnian Serb President Radovan Karadžic Resigns
The President resigns after being indicted on war crimes charges, and the issue of an international arrest warrant. He is not apprehended until 2008, when he is discovered in Belgrade.

July 25
Paris Underground Bombing Campaign
An explosion on the Paris Metro underground rail system marks the start of a bombing campaign by the Armed Islamic Group. The attacks continue until October, killing eight people and wounding hundreds.

1996

GUNMAN MASSACRES PRIMARY SCHOOL CHILDREN

On March 13, 1996, a man entered an elementary school assembly hall in Dunblane, Scotland, firing bullets all around him and killing 16 children and their teacher. It was 9.30 a.m., and the five- and six-year-old children had just started a P.E. class when Thomas Watt Hamilton, a local man, walked in and showered them with bullets before turning the gun on himself. Hamilton had once been a scoutmaster but had been fired after concerns about his behavior around young boys. His suspicious behavior had put him on police registers, and he was known to have a license for six guns. However, an inquiry ruled that his actions on that day in March could not possibly have been predicted. The tragedy shocked and devastated the local tight-knit community. The Snowdrop Campaign, launched after the Dunblane Massacre, as it has come to be known, has since successfully tightened gun control in Great Britain, making it illegal to buy or own a handgun. Campaigners also aimed to set up a centralized database of gun owners in the U.K.

'The tragedy shocked and devastated the local tight-knit community.'

JET CRASHES AS FUEL TANK EXPLODES

On July 1, 1996, T.W.A. flight 800 left New York bound for Rome via Paris, but minutes later the plane exploded in mid-air, killing all 230 people onboard. Although several emergency vehicles reached the spot where the plane had crashed into the Atlantic Ocean within minutes, there were no survivors to be rescued. The first assumption was that the explosion had been caused by terrorist sabotage, and the F.B.I. launched a simultaneous investigation with the aviation authorities. The F.B.I. interviewed several witnesses, many of whom claimed to have seen a streak of light approach the plane before the explosion, and there were suggestions that an external missile had caused the explosion. However, detailed examination of the wreckage could not find any evidence to support this theory, nor the theory that a bomb onboard had caused the explosion. At the end of its investigations, the National Transportation Safety Board concluded that the probable cause was an explosion in the center wing fuel tank.

August 28
Prince Charles and Princess Diana Divorce
The royal couple's marriage officially comes to an end with the granting of a decree nisi. Diana loses her royal title (Her Royal Highness) and is now known as simply Diana, Princess of Wales.

September 7
Tupac Shakur Gunned Down
The 25-year-old American rapper is killed in a drive-by shooting following a feud between East and West Coast gangs and rappers. New York rapper Notorious B.I.G. is shot dead in a revenge attack six months later.

November 6
Bill Clinton Wins Second Term
Incumbent U.S. President Bill Clinton wins a second term after a presidential race against Republican Bob Dole, taking 48% of the vote.

November 7
Huge Cyclone Hits India
The storm hits the eastern coast of India, leaving fishing villages marooned after waves surge as far as 3 miles (5 km) inland, with wind speeds of up to 140 mph (230 kph). Over 1,000 people are thought to die.

COMET HALE-BOPP PASSES EARTH

Referred to as the 'Great Comet', the most spectacular astronomical sight of 1997 was the appearance of the Hale-Bopp comet in the night sky. The comet came closest to Earth on March 22, 1997, and its closest approach to the Sun, when it showed at its brightest, was on April 1, 1997. Amateur astronomers Alan Hale in New Mexico and Thomas Bopp in Arizona separately discovered the comet on the same day in 1995. A comet's head, known as the 'coma', is made up of dust and gas, but at its center is a solid nucleus of rock, dust, and ice. Observations conducted from N.A.S.A. observatories estimated that Hale-Bopp's nucleus is between 19 and 25 miles (30–45 km) in diameter. By comparison, the comet that is thought to have struck Earth 65 million years ago, probably causing the extinction of the dinosaurs, is estimated to have been 6 to 9 miles (10–12 km) in diameter. After the 1997 appearance, it is calculated that the Hale-Bopp comet will disappear from sight again until the year 4397.

'NEW LABOUR' WIN

In May 1997, at the age of 43, Tony Blair became the youngest Prime Minister of Great Britain for 200 years. Following a law degree at Oxford University and several years as a lawyer in London, Blair had entered the House of Commons in 1983 as a Member of Parliament (M.P.) for Sedgefield in County Durham, England. At the age of 30, he was the youngest Labour M.P. in the House of Commons. In the build-up to his election as Prime Minister, Tony Blair had pledged the complete reform of the Labour Party, changing politics in an attempt to broaden the party's appeal beyond its base in the trade union movement. Within the shadow government cabinet, Blair had found a close ally in Gordon Brown, and the two rapidly moved up party ranks together. When the death of Labour leader John Smith in 1994 left the job open, the Labour Party was divided over whether so-called modernizers such as Blair should take over. Blair eventually won and rebranded the party 'New Labour'.

March 26
Heaven's Gate Cult Mass Suicide
The San Diego cult believe that the Hale-Bopp comet is a sign that they should leave their earthly bodies behind to join a spacecraft flying behind the comet. Thirty-nine members of the cult commit suicide by drinking a deadly cocktail of vodka and barbiturates.

April 12
Plot to Kill Pope Foiled
Twenty anti-tank mines are found under a bridge in Sarajevo, Bosnia, on the Pope's planned route around the city. The devices are discovered the day before the Pope is due to arrive, but the visit goes ahead as planned.

April 13
Tiger Woods Becomes Youngest Ever Winner of U.S. Masters
At the age of 21, Tiger Woods also becomes the first black golfer to win a major tournament, with a winning margin of 12 strokes.

1997

PRINCESS KILLED IN HIGH-SPEED CRASH

DIANA KILLED IN CAR CRASH

'The Princess was alive when she was removed from the scene of the crash, but two hours of surgeons' efforts failed to save her life.'

In the early hours of August 31, 1997, Princess Diana was killed in a car crash in Paris. The nation awoke to the news, and there was an unmatched outpouring of public grief, with thousands flocking to Kensington Palace, where she resided, to lay flowers. The Princess had left the Ritz Hotel in Paris with her companion Dodi Fayed, son of the Harrods owner Mohammed al Fayed, when her car was pursued aggressively by paparazzi. This was not unusual, but on this occasion her driver, who was subsequently discovered to have taken both drugs and alcohol, dramatically increased his speed, and the car crashed in a tunnel downtown. The Princess was alive when she was removed from the scene of the crash, but two hours of surgeons' efforts failed to save her life. The Prince of Wales was with the rest of the royal family at Balmoral Castle in Scotland, where he broke the news of their mother's death to his sons, Princes William and Harry. Buckingham Palace issued a statement saying that the Queen and the Prince of Wales were 'deeply shocked and distressed'. Mohammed al Fayed, whose son was also killed in the crash, claimed that Diana had

Above: The Pont d'Alma tunnel in Paris, where the fatal crash took place.

April 22
Embassy Siege In Peru
A four-month siege at the Japanese Embassy in Peru is brought to an end when the building is stormed by security forces. All 12 of the Túpac Amaru rebels inside the embassy are killed, with all but one of the 72 hostages freed.

June 30
First Harry Potter Book Published
London publisher Bloomsbury issues the first of J.K. Rowling's novels for children, entitled *Harry Potter & the Philosopher's Stone*. The series of books has subsequently sold over 400 million copies.

July 1
Hong Kong Handed Back to China
British governor Chris Patten transfers control of Hong Kong back to the Chinese authorities after more than 150 years of British rule.

Left: Mohammed al Fayed, father of Diana's companion Dodi.

been engaged to Dodi, and he was convinced that the royal family had them killed. However, despite a major inquest into the crash, only Henri Paul, the driver, has been found to be at fault. The paparazzi photographers were not officially charged, although their behavior opened up widespread criticism of the increasingly aggressive tactics used by the tabloid press. Princess Diana was given a full state funeral at Westminster Abbey; around 1 million people lined the streets in order to witness the passing of her funeral procession.

'Despite a major inquest into the crash, only Henri Paul, the driver, has been found to be at fault.'

Right: Henri Paul, the driver, who had been drinking.

Above: (From left to right) Earl Spencer, Princess Diana's brother; Princes William and Harry, her two sons; and Prince Charles, her ex-husband, attend the funeral.

July 4
N.A.S.A. Probe Lands on Mars
The Pathfinder probe was launched in December 1996, and arrives on Mars seven months later, delivering a robotic vehicle capable of traveling over the Martian surface to analyze the geology and climate of the red planet.

July 15
Gianni Versace Murdered
The Italian fashion designer is shot dead outside his Miami mansion by Andrew Cunanan. Versace was the fifth victim in a murderous four-month rampage that ended when the gay prostitute shot himself with the same gun used to kill Versace.

September 5
Mother Teresa Dies
After a lifetime caring for the sick and needy, Mother Teresa dies at the headquarters of the order she founded in Calcutta. The Missionaries of Charity forsake all modern conveniences, beg for food, and are allowed home to visit their families once every five years.

1997

MAMMAL CLONED FOR FIRST TIME

SHEEP SUCCESSFULLY CLONED

'D.N.A. tests revealed that Dolly is identical in every way to the sheep from which she was cloned and shows no genetic similarity to the surrogate mother sheep.'

On February 11, 1997, a group of scientists in Edinburgh announced that they had successfully cloned a ewe using the cell of another adult sheep. Dolly the sheep had actually been born on July 5, 1996, but the announcement was delayed so that her development could be monitored before it was made public. The cloned sheep was created by inserting a single cell from another sheep's udder into an egg, which was then implanted into a surrogate mother sheep. Dolly's birth marked the first time a mammal had successfully been cloned from an adult cell, rather than from an embryo, as with previous experiments. D.N.A. tests revealed that Dolly is identical in every way to the sheep from which she was cloned and shows no genetic similarity to the surrogate mother sheep. The cloning raised ethical questions and sparked fears of human cloning, but Dr. Ian Wilmut, who led the team of scientists, insisted that the cloning of human beings was a 'repugnant' idea, as well as being illegal. P.P.L. Therapeutics, which has bought the rights to the cloning experiments, say that the groundbreaking work will help research into currently incurable genetic diseases. In 2003, Dolly was put down when it was found that she had a fatal lung disease. Her preserved body is on display at the National Museum of Scotland.

September 12
Scotland Votes for own Parliament
A referendum in favor of devolution means that Scotland will have its own parliament for the first time in over 300 years.

September 26
Quake Shakes Italy
A double quake in central Italy badly damages the Basilica of St. Francis in Assisi, killing four people and destroying a priceless series of frescoes by the medieval artist Cimabue. The church is restored at a cost of $50 million and reopens in 1999.

December 17
Landmine Treaty Signed
122 governments sign the treaty banning antipersonnel landmines, known as the Ottawa Treaty. Over 150 countries have now ratified the treaty, but superpowers such as Russia, China, and the United States have not signed.

TALIBAN BANS TELEVISION

By 1994, Afghanistan had been divided up by the various conflicting groups within its borders. At the same time, the powerful Mujahideen commanders had established themselves as warlords, and in the southern city of Qandahar, they routinely terrorized the local population. Under former Mujahid Mohammed Omar, a mullah in the Qandahar province, other former Mujahideen opposed to the warlords established a group that called themselves 'taliban', meaning seekers or students. Their aim was to establish Islamic law and order, or at least their own interpretation of it. The Taliban began by attacking the notorious warlords in a series of successful military campaigns. They took control of Qandahar and demilitarized it, before moving on toward Kabul. Pakistan soon made an ally of the Taliban, and Osama bin Laden found a safe haven for his Al-Qaeda troops with them. Their strict, oppressive regime forced women to wear burkas and forbade them to work outside of the home. Every aspect of 'modern' life was banned, including music, dancing, and, in 1998, television. On July 8, 1998, Afghans were given two weeks to hand in their televisions.

U.S. AND U.K. BOMB IRAQ

On December 16, 1998, the U.S. and Great Britain launched a three-day bombing attack on Iraq known as Operation Desert Fox. Iraqi leader Saddam Hussein was accused of obstructing weapons inspectors, and U.S. President Clinton had threatened the use of force if Saddam's regime did not fall into line with United Nations resolutions. Coalition forces bombed 100 targets with the aim of 'degrading' Saddam's capacity to produce weapons of mass destruction, but as President Clinton acknowledged, 'there will be unintended Iraqi casualties'. Coalition forces blew up various suspected chemical and biological weapons plants, as well as residential sites housing Saddam's secret police. After the three-day attack, the Iraqi Deputy Prime Minister stated that 62 military personnel had been killed, but there were also civilian casualties. Iraq's actual weapons capacity remains a highly disputed question.

Left: U.S. President Bill Clinton, who ordered the bombing.

January 11
Algerian Massacre
Islamic extremists kill over 400 people in an attack on two villages in the northwest of Algeria, as part of an ongoing civil war that claims over 100,000 lives.

February 3
N.A.T.O. Jet Brings Down Cable Car
A low-flying N.A.T.O. jet severs the cable holding a cable car in the Dolomites, causing the deaths of the 20 people inside. The pilot is jailed in 1999 for conducting unauthorized maneuvers.

May 15
Frank Sinatra Dies
Ol' Blue Eyes passes away after a year of ill health following a heart attack in 1997.

1998

AL-QAEDA ATTACKS

On August 7, 1998, bombs exploded outside the U.S. embassies in Nairobi, Kenya, and Dar es Salaam, Tanzania. The terrorist attacks, which killed 224 people, prompted the first military action by the U.S. against Osama bin Laden, who was engaged in a public campaign of violent terrorism against the U.S. From a wealthy family in Saudi Arabia, Osama had first become involved in anti-Western, militant Islamism when he helped to finance the Afghans in resisting the Soviet invasion in 1979. It was there that he formed his own army, known as Al-Qaeda. After his expulsion from Saudi Arabia and Sudan for terrorist activities, Osama bin Laden took refuge in Afghanistan, under the fundamentalist Taliban regime, and issued a fatwah, or religious declaration, calling for the death of Americans. In the 1998 attack on the U.S. Embassy in Nairobi, 213 people were killed and many more were seriously injured when 2,000 lb (900 kg) of T.N.T. explosives were detonated from a van outside the embassy's doors. U.S. President Clinton ordered a military strike against Al-Qaeda training camps in Afghanistan on August 20, 1998. In November, the U.S. charged Osama bin Laden and 21 others with the bombing of the embassies.

PEACE AT LAST FOR NORTHERN IRELAND

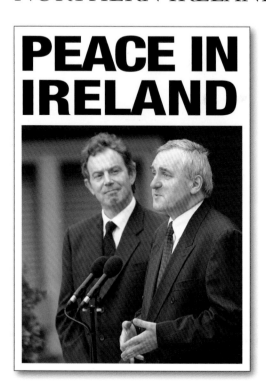

After 30 years of bloody conflict and two years of peace talks, on April 10, 1998, Great Britain and Ireland finally reached an agreement over Northern Ireland. The solution, known as the Good Friday Agreement, was seen as a triumph for British Prime Minister Tony Blair and his Irish counterpart Bertie Ahern. The agreement involved the creation of a Northern Ireland Assembly and significant links between Northern Ireland and the Republic of Ireland. The proposals set out in the agreement were sent to every household in Northern Ireland to be voted on in a referendum in May 1998, and the people voted a resounding 'yes'.

April 15
Pol Pot Dies

The former dictator of Cambodia dies of a suspected heart attack, a year after he is deposed as the leader of the Khmer Rouge.

May 6
Apple Launches the iMac

Following the return of founder member Steve Jobs to head up the company, Apple announces the product that is to revolutionize their fortunes over the next five years. Created by British designer Jonathan Ive, the iMac's clean simple lines and iconic design are a huge hit.

May 28
Pakistan Nuclear Tests

Tension between India and Pakistan is heightened when Pakistan tests five nuclear devices under the mountains near its border with Afghanistan.

November 7
New Court of Human Rights

The European Court of Human Rights opens in Strasbourg, France. All 47 member states of the Council of Europe are bound by its judgements.

STUDENTS GO ON ARMED RAMPAGE AT SCHOOL

13 SHOT AT SCHOOL

On April 20, 1999, two teenagers, Dylan Klebold and Eric Harris, walked into their high school, their trench coats loaded with guns, knives, and explosives, with the intention of killing as many people as possible before committing suicide. In the end, they killed 12 students and one teacher before killing themselves. The Columbine High School massacre left the suburban Colorado community not only shocked and angry, but also utterly confused. No one could figure out why these two apparently fairly typical teenagers from stable homes had committed such a horrific crime. According to documentary evidence that the boys left behind, Klebold and Harris had been planning the attack, in which they hoped to kill as many as 500 of their peers, for more than a year. Diaries created a confusing image of the two boys downloading recipes for explosives and making them, at the same time as worrying about who they should take to the prom. The two boys had been friends for several years, and although they found it difficult to fit in at their high school, they were not otherwise abnormal. The only clue that could provide any possible motive was a general sense of hatred that they both felt toward the world and toward people in general. The objects of their hatred, however, were often contradictory: they hated both minorities and racists, for example. Even after working on the case for a year, the lead investigator was unable to give any clear-cut answers: 'There's not an easy answer,' she said, 'I can't tell you why it happened.'

'In the end, they killed 12 students and one teacher before killing themselves.'

January 25
Colombia Quake
One thousand people are killed when an earthquake measuring 6 on the Richter scale hits Colombia. Many older buildings are unable to withstand the tremors, which leave 200,000 homeless.

March 8
Joe DiMaggio Dies
Known as 'The Yankee Clipper', and one-time husband of Marilyn Monroe, he played baseball in the 1940s and 1950s but latterly became known for his charity work.

April 30
Nail Bombs Hit London
A nail bomb explodes in a busy city center pub in Soho, London's gay district, killing two people. The bomb is the third in a series targeting minority groups. David Copeland, a self-confessed Nazi, is later imprisoned for the attacks.

1999

MONETARY UNION

NEW EUROPEAN CURRENCY

On January 1, 1999, 11 European countries replaced their national currencies with the newly created euro, a single European currency. The previous day, exchange rates between the old currencies and the euro had been permanently fixed. Germany, France, Italy, Spain, Holland, Belgium, Austria, Portugal, Finland, Ireland, and Luxembourg all made the switch. Greece qualified to join the euro two years afterward, with Slovenia (2006), Malta (2007), Cyprus (2007), and Slovakia (2008) joining later. All the participating countries had to meet criteria that had been established by the 1992 Maastricht Treaty. Although the individual national currencies of the first 11 countries remained in circulation for another three years, acting as smaller denominations of the euro, commerce between banks and stock market trading immediately adopted the euro as its sole currency. The actual circulation of euro coins and bills started on January 1, 2002, known as 'E Day', when the old currencies became invalid.

EUROPE AT WAR

N.A.T.O. ATTACKS SERBIA

On March 24, 1999, N.A.T.O. launched the second military action in its history when it began a bombing campaign against Belgrade, the Yugoslav capital. N.A.T.O. was acting to end the oppressive treatment of Albanians in Kosovo by Serbians under President Slobodan Milošević. Operation Allied Force was carried out entirely from the air to avoid loss of any N.A.T.O. personnel. For several years, Milošević and his Serbian forces had been carrying out a policy of ethnic cleansing, during which 850,000 Albanians were forced from their homes. Some fled into the neighboring countries of Albania and Macedonia, but others were simply displaced within Kosovo, where they were at the mercy of violent Serbian militia. The war ended on June 11, 1999, when the Yugoslav government agreed to withdraw Serbian forces from Kosovo, which nonetheless remained part of Serbia. Milošević saw the outcome as a victory, but he fell from power a year later and was eventually indicted for war crimes.

Above: Prijedor, in Bosnia, an area 'ethnically cleansed' by Serb forces.

June 1
Napster Launched
Shawn Fanning creates software that allows computer users to swap music files across the Internet via a central directory. The service quickly becomes hugely popular, with millions of files shared for free among users.

June 14
Thabo Mbeki Elected President of South Africa
Nelson Mandela's successor is sworn in as head of South Africa's second democratically elected government. The A.N.C. takes two-thirds of the seats in the parliament.

June 19
Horror Writer Stephen King Injured
The bestselling author is hit by a motorist while walking in Maine, U.S.A. Earlier in the year he had been working on a novel in which the protagonist dies after a car accident.

July 23
Woodstock 99 Festival Held
Thirty years after the original Woodstock Festival, an anniversary event takes place. Over 200,000 people attend.

KING HUSSEIN OF JORDAN DIES

King Hussein of Jordan, who had been a stabilizing force for peace in the Middle East during his 46 years of rule, died on February 7, 1999. He had been suffering from lymphatic cancer for some time, and he eventually died of heart failure at the age of 63. His son, Prince Abdullah, was sworn in as his successor, but there were fears about what would happen in the region once the great peacemaker was gone. U.S. President Clinton described King Hussein as 'a man who believed that we are all God's children, bound to live together in mutual respect and tolerance' and that, when peace finally comes to the Middle East, 'his name will be inscribed upon it'.

TOTAL ECLIPSE OF THE SUN

On August 11, 1999, a total eclipse of the Sun was visible from the U.K., a phenomenon which had not occurred since 1927 and will not do so again until 2090. The eclipse was total along a path stretching from the North Atlantic to India, and in the U.K. it was visible for longest from Cornwall on the southwest tip of the coast of England and in the Scilly Isles off the coast of Cornwall. The partial phase was visible from all over Britain. The total eclipse lasted for around 2 minutes, with the longest visibility in Romania, where it lasted 2 minutes and 23 seconds. The spectacular phenomenon occurs when the Sun, Moon and Earth coincide in a straight line during their orbits around each other. The Sun is about 400 times larger than the Moon, but it is also about 400 times farther away, so when all three lie in a straight line with the Moon at the center, the Moon blocks out the Sun's light to the Earth in certain pathways. All over the world, people flocked to witness this once-in-a-lifetime sight, many traveling great distances to ensure the best possible chance of seeing it.

May 2
Oliver Reed Dies

Notorious actor Oliver Reed dies during a break in the filming of Ridley Scott's *Gladiator*.

May 28
'Last Supper' Returned to Public View

One of Leonardo da Vinci's most famous paintings is returned to public display in the church of Santa Maria delle Grazie, Milan, after over 20 years of restoration work.

December 30
Beatle Stabbed in his Home

Former Beatle George Harrison and his wife Olivia are attacked in their mansion by an intruder.

December 31
World Welcomes New Millennium

People around the world prepare to celebrate the beginning of a new millennium, with spectacular firework displays and parties planned all over the globe.

2000

CROWDS AROUND THE WORLD
CELEBRATE A NEW MILLENNIUM

THE NEW MILLENNIUM

'The global computer crash that had been predicted in the years leading up to the millennium eve did not occur, though billions of dollars had been spent in an effort to prevent the potential crisis.'

Right: Crowds watch the London fireworks on December 31, 1999.

The dawn of the new millennium was celebrated across the world by people of all nationalities and all religions. In London, around 2 million people lined the banks of the River Thames to witness a spectacular firework display. Meanwhile, the Queen and the Prime Minister, Tony Blair, celebrated in the newly built Millennium Dome in Greenwich, at a party to which 6,000 members of the public had also been invited. In New York, 4 tons of confetti were dropped on the 3 million party-goers, and in Sydney Harbor, the crowds were treated to what was later agreed to be the most spectacular firework display of all. Among other symbolic moments, Nelson Mandela revisited his former prison cell on Robben Island and handed a candle to a child in a ceremony of hope and resolution. In Bethlehem, the believed site of Christ's birth 2,000 years ago, 2,000 doves of peace were released, and in Rome, the Pope encouraged his audience to work hard for peace over the next 1,000 years. The first dawn of the new millennium broke over the Pacific Islands, in Tonga and Fiji, but the Pacific Island of Samoa was the last place to experience the dawn of the third millennium, around 25 hours later. The global computer crash that had been predicted in the years leading up to the millennium eve did not occur, though billions of dollars had been spent in an effort to prevent the potential crisis.

Left: The Millennium Dome in London was built for the celebrations.

January 31
Doctor Convicted
In the U.K., Dr. Harold Shipman is convicted of murdering 15 patients.

February–March
Mozambique Floods
Devastating floods in Mozambique kill 800 people.

March 26
Putin for President
Vladimir Putin is elected President of Russia, bringing in economic reforms.

April 3
No to Microsoft
U.S. software giant Microsoft is ruled to have violated competition laws.

VOTE COUNTING CONTROVERSY FOR U.S. PRESIDENTIAL ELECTION

BUSH ELECTED PRESIDENT

The 2000 U.S. Presidential election saw the Governor of Texas, George W. Bush, running against Democratic contender Al Gore. The election was close across the states, but when it reached the Florida ballot, which would prove to be the deciding state, the counting ran into problems which buried the outcome in controversy. Early signs prompted news stations to call a victory for Bush in Florida, which made Gore concede defeat, but the final result in Florida was slim enough to require a mandatory recount by machine – and Gore withdrew his concession. The Gore camp now called for a manual recount. When the process was already under way, Bush appealed to the U.S. Supreme Court to stop the recount. On December 12, 2000, the Supreme Court ruled that the recount was unconstitutional and should stop. Florida was called for Bush, who became President. Later detailed analysis uncovered a string of irregularities in the Florida voting process that year, including ambiguous forms that caused many people to vote for another candidate, Pat Buchanan, instead of their intended candidate of Al Gore.

HUMAN GENOME DECODED

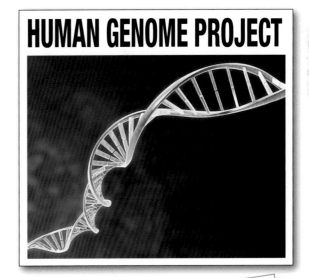

HUMAN GENOME PROJECT

In what was declared one of the most important scientific breakthroughs of all time, on June 26, 2000, scientists announced that they had decoded the human genome. The process involved reading the 300 billion 'letters' that are strung out along the spirals of deoxyribonucleic acid (D.N.A.) at the core of human cells. The researchers announced that 85% of the code had been accurately sequenced, and they expected to have completely deciphered the entire code within three years. The discovery had far-reaching consequences for dealing with genetic diseases, as it continues to be the hope that 'faulty' genes will be identified and corrected before causing problems. However, some people fear that the information that will become available about individuals' genetic make-up might prompt genetic discrimination. The ability to read the code of the human genome in effect means that the full instructions for creating a human being will be available for the first time.

May 25 — Israeli Withdrawal Israel withdraws its troops from Southern Lebanon.

July 25 — Concorde Crashes 113 people die as Air France flight 4590, a Concorde aircraft, crashes.

August 3 — Mob Violence Rioting erupts about suspected sex offenders in Portsmouth, U.K.

August 12 — Submarine Sinks Russian submarine K-141 *Kursk* sinks. All 118 men on board perish.

September 26 — Protests at I.M.F. Anti-globalization protests take place at the International Monetary Fund (I.M.F.) and World Bank summits.

2000

ENVIRONMENTAL DISASTER FOR KENTUCKY

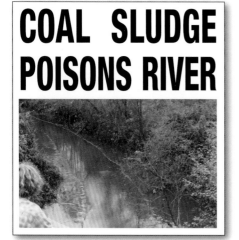

On October 11, 2000, in Martin County, Kentucky, U.S.A., a large-scale environmental disaster occurred when a mass of coal sludge broke through an underground mine and spilled out into the Tug Fork River. A total of 306 gallons of black waste flooded the river, polluting hundreds of miles of waterways and contaminating the water supplies of 27,000 residents. All aquatic life in the river was destroyed. The extent of the pollution was 30 times greater than that of the 1989 *Exxon Valdez* oil tanker spill, and it took years to repair. Fears began to circulate that the same thing would happen with other underground mines in the region, filling local waterways with coal sludge.

Right: Coal sludge wiped out aquatic life in Coldwater Fork and Wolf Creek, Kentucky.

FIRE ON SKI TRAIN KILLS 155 PEOPLE

On November 11, 2000, a ski train was traveling through a tunnel in the Alps when a fire broke out, killing 155 people. The train was preparing to leave a ski resort near Salzburg, Austria, when some drops of oil from the train's cable caused the overheated filament of a faulty fan heater in the rear driver's cabin to catch on fire. The train set off up the mountain and soon entered a tunnel, where the spreading fire caused it to grind to a stop. The doors were firmly shut, preventing the passengers from escaping as the fire moved through the train. Only 12 passengers in the rear car managed to smash a window with their skis and boots and escape down the mountain. The remaining passengers, who were mainly Austrian, but also included Germans, Japanese, British, and Americans, were either burned or suffocated to death. When the doors finally opened, the passengers who were able to climb out soon collapsed from smoke inhalation. Employees of the lift company, its suppliers, and the Austrian Transport Ministry were all charged with negligence.

October 12
Al-Qaeda Blast
The U.S.S. *Cole* is hit by Al-Qaeda suicide bombers in Yemen, killing 17 crew members.

November
Inspections for Iraq?
New proposals for United Nations Security Council weapons inspections are rejected by Saddam Hussein's Iraq.

November 2
Space Station Is Manned
The first crew reaches the orbiting International Space Station.

December 24
Indonesia Bombings
Terrorists from Al-Qaeda and Jemaah Islamiyah bomb churches in Indonesia.

TALIBAN REGIME TOPPLED IN AFGHANISTAN

After the September 11, 2001, attacks in New York and Washington, D.C., U.S. President George W. Bush declared a 'War on Terror'. Having identified Osama bin Laden, founder of the terrorist organization Al-Qaeda, as the mastermind of the attacks, the U.S. demanded that the Taliban regime in Afghanistan, which was known to have offered Osama safe haven, turn him over. When the Taliban refused, the U.S. joined with the Northern Alliance, the homegrown resistance forces in Afghanistan, to bring down the Taliban's oppressive, Islamic fundamentalist regime. In October 2001, the U.S. and allies began by targeting Al-Qaeda training camps and Taliban military headquarters. By November, with the suppport of U.S. bombings, the Northern Alliance ground troops had succeeded in capturing the Afghan capital, Kabul. By December, the Taliban had surrendered the major city of Kandahar. The remainder of Taliban and Al-Qaeda troops fled, initially into the Hindu Kush Mountains bordering Pakistan, and then on to hidden retreats within Pakistan. From there, they have maintained a violent revolt against the new Afghan government. U.S. and N.A.T.O. troops remain in Afghanistan.

TALIBAN DEFEATED IN AFGHANISTAN

'The remainder of Taliban and Al-Qaeda troops fled, initially into the Hindu Kush Mountains bordering Pakistan, and then on to hidden retreats within Pakistan.'

Above: Ruined buildings surround a mosque in Kabul.

Left: British soldiers in the Afghan desert, in 2002.

January 15
Information for Everyone
Wikipedia, the free online encyclopedia, is launched.

January 20
George Bush Sworn In
George Walker Bush is sworn in as President of the United States.

January 26
Gujarati Earthquake
More than 12,000 die when an earthquake hits Gujarat in India.

February 12
Getting Near
The Near Earth Asteroid Rendezvous (N.E.A.R.) *Shoemaker* lands on the asteroid 433 Eros.

February 16
Bombing Raids on Iraq
British and U.S. forces bomb Iraq's air defense network.

2001

PLANES HIT TWIN TOWERS

Above: The steel skeleton of the South Tower days after the attacks killed 2,603 people in the towers and on the ground.

Left: Around 17,400 people were in the World Trade Center at the time of the attacks.

February 19
Foot and Mouth Crisis Begins
Foot and mouth disease breaks out among sheep and cattle in the U.K.

April 1
Milošević Surrenders
Former Yugoslavian President Slobodan Milošević is to be tried for war crimes.

April 1
Same-Sex Marriage
Same-sex marriages are legalized in the Netherlands.

June 1
Massacre in Nepal
Prince Dipendra of Nepal kills nine members of his family.

June 19
U.S. Missile Hits Iraq
A U.S. missile kills 23 people when it hits a soccer field in Iraq.

WAR ON THE WORLD

On September 11, 2001, 19 Islamic-extremist terrorists linked to the Al-Qaeda ('The Base') organization hijacked four passenger planes and crashed them all, killing all passengers onboard, as well as thousands of other civilians. The terrorists took control of the commercial planes and crashed two of them into the twin towers of the World Trade Center in downtown New York, bringing down the entire complex, destroying two other buildings nearby, and killing thousands of people inside. Some victims were killed instantly on the planes' impacts; others were trapped inside the buildings, with some leaping to their deaths from the windows to escape the flames. Both towers had collapsed within two hours. A third plane was crashed into the Pentagon, the headquarters of the Department of Defense, located in Arlington, Virginia, killing 125 people working in the building. The fourth plane came down in a field in rural Pennsylvania after its passengers and crew attempted to take control. They prevented the plane from crashing into its intended target in Washington, D.C. America responded to the horrific attacks by declaring war on Afghanistan (see p.283), where the Taliban regime had harbored Al-Qaeda terrorists – specifically, Osama bin Laden, their leader. In 2006, building work began on Freedom Tower on the site of the World Trade Center in Manhattan. It will be joined by three other towers and, when it is completed in 2011, will be one of the tallest buildings in America. In total, 2,974 fatalities resulted from the September 11 attacks (known as '9/11' in the U.S.A.), including 411 emergency workers who were killed in rescue attempts.

'The terrorists took control of the commercial planes and crashed two of them into the twin towers of the World Trade Center in downtown New York'

THE HUNT FOR BIN LADEN

July 2
Have a Heart
American Robert Tools receives the world's first self-contained artificial heart in Tennessee.

September 18
Anthrax Attacks
Five people die as letters containing anthrax spores are sent to news media offices in the U.S.

November 10
China Gets Membership
The World Trade Organization admits the People's Republic of China.

November 22
Pope Sends Email!
Pope John Paul II sends the first papal email.

December 13
Attack on Indian Parliament
Tension mounts between India and Pakistan after an attack on the Indian Parliament.

2002

THE U.K.'S QUEEN ELIZABETH THE QUEEN MOTHER DIES

On March 30, 2002, Queen Elizabeth the Queen Mother died in her sleep at Windsor Castle, England, at the age of 101. The Queen was at her mother's bedside when she passed away. Ten days of national mourning followed before the funeral on April 9. The Queen Mother's body remained at Windsor Castle for three days before being taken to Queen's Chapel at St. James's Palace in London, and then onward, in ceremonial procession, to Westminster Hall before the funeral at Westminster Abbey. The funeral was conducted with full ceremony, creating a majestic spectacle that was viewed by more than 1 million people who had lined the processional route. The Queen Mother's coffin was eventually laid to rest beside that of King George VI, her husband, at St. George's Chapel in Windsor. The Queen Mother's younger daughter, Princess Margaret, had died seven weeks earlier, and her cremated ashes were buried with her mother's coffin. Public sympathy for the Queen was heightened by this double loss in such a short space of time, and by the time of her Golden Jubilee in the summer, nationalistic pride in the royal family was at a peak. The Queen Mother, born Elizabeth Bowes-Lyon, and her husband had been unexpectedly thrust onto the public stage by the abdication of the King's brother, Edward, and they had never expected to be king and queen. The Queen Mother could be credited with making the royal family more accessible, accountable to the nation for their behavior as individuals and as an institution. She invented the now familiar 'walkabout', a way for royals to meet their people face-to-face, and during the wartime Blitz, when many were abandoning London for the country, she insisted that the royal family should remain in the city. She took on public duties fully and was always present to support her shy husband, and later her daughter, Queen Elizabeth II.

Right and far right: The Queen Mother's grandchildren and great-grandchildren attend her funeral.

January 1
Euro in Europe
Twelve European countries issue euro notes and coins.

February 27
Indian Riots
Hundreds perish in riots in India after 57 Hindus die when their train is burned by a Muslim mob.

May 26
Life on Mars?
The space probe *Mars Odyssey* finds traces of water ice deposits on the surface of Mars.

June 15
Near Miss!
Near Earth Asteroid 2002 MN misses Earth by just 75,000 miles (120,000 km). If it had hit the planet, it could have flattened up to 800 sq miles (2,000 sq km).

ENRON AND WORLDCOM SCANDALS EXPOSE FRAUDULENT BUSINESS PRACTICES

Two of the world's most successful companies, Enron and WorldCom, collapsed in late 2001 and early 2002, exposing a high level of fraud and corruption at the heart of their management. While Wall Street banks earned millions of dollars in fees and loan interest, hiding the true state of the companies' finances, thousands of investors were conned into sinking money into them by means of fraudulent activity set up by banks and company bosses. Ken Lay (right), the boss of Enron, began by making it look like his company was far more profitable than it actually was in order to boost its share prices. During the 1990s, various banks, including Citibank and J.P. Morgan, staged fake transactions in order to create false income on Enron's accounts. These transactions included pouring $125 million into an offshore company, which then supposedly bought gas from Enron. The scam, however, was that no gas actually changed hands, and the $125 million 'loan' from Citibank appeared as income for Enron. By 2000, Enron was in serious debt, but the banks continued to prop up the company by painting a false picture of its finances. In 1999, the financial services firm Merrill Lynch created a network of fake companies and persuaded investors to pour money into them. This gave Enron an apparent $1 billion profit in 2000, when in fact it made a loss. WorldCom boss Bernie Ebbers managed his fraudulent activity differently. Ebbers convinced the banks to lend money to WorldCom and to employ supposedly unbiased 'star analysts' to hype up WorldCom shares. In this way, as share prices went up, the banks were paid back, plus interest, and WorldCom's shares continued to rise. In 2002, the auditing firm Arthur Anderson uncovered an accounting error in Enron's books that led to further investigations, a fall in share prices – and, ultimately, to bankruptcy. This then led to further thorough corporate investigations, during which WorldCom was also exposed. The companies' bosses were tried, and the bankers responsible were either fired or fined. Meanwhile, thousands of investors lost a total of $240 billion.

MAJOR BUSINESS SCANDAL

'The scam, however, was that no gas actually changed hands, and the $125 million "loan" from Citibank appeared as income for Enron.'

August
Severe Floods
Dozens are killed and thousands made homeless as floods hit Central Europe.

September 5
Violence Continues in Afghanistan
Interim Afghan President Hamid Karzai escapes an assassination attempt. On the same day, 30 die in a car bomb in Kabul, Afghanistan.

September 26
Joola Capsizes
A Senagalese passenger ferry called the *Joola* capsizes, killing 1,863 people.

October 2
Sniper Attacks
The so-called Beltway Sniper strikes in the U.S. Eleven people are shot in the attacks.

2002

HOSTAGES DIE IN RUSSIAN THEATER SIEGE

850 TRAPPED IN THEATER

On October 23, 2002, heavily armed Chechen rebels stormed a theater in Moscow just after the start of the second half of a play. The group took 850 people hostage and demanded an end to the Russian military action in the breakaway republic of Chechnya. The terrorists claimed to be 'suicide attackers'; they had explosives strapped to their bodies, and they planted further devices around the theater, threatening to kill ten hostages for every one of their own group killed. Although they released about 100 women, children, and Muslims at the beginning of the standoff, 750 people were still held inside. After no activity for 24 hours, the Chechen terrorists threatened to start executing their hostages if their demand of Russian military withdrawal was not met. On October 26, Russian Special Forces stormed the theater, using a poisonous gas that was intended to stun the terrorists but that also harmed hundreds of hostages. The official Chechen rebel leadership denied any connection with the terrorists, and a Muslim leader appeared on Russian television condemning the attacks, declaring that 'terrorists have no nationality'. At least 129 of the hostages were killed during the rescue attempt, along with 39 of the terrorists. A memorial now stands at the site as a remembrance of the victims. Tens of thousands of Chechens had been killed in two wars with Russia since the predominantly Muslim area declared its independence in 1991.

> **'After no activity for 24 hours, the Chechen terrorists threatened to start executing their hostages if their demand of Russian military withdrawl was not met.'**

October 12
Bali Nightclub Bombings
Members of the violent Islamist group Jemaah Islamiyah detonate bombs in the tourist district of Kuta on the Indonesian island of Bali. The attack kills 182 people.

October 16
Iraq War Resolution
The U.S. Congress passes the Iraq War Resolution, authorizing the use of military force against Iraq.

November 18
Inspections in Iraq
United Nations weapons inspectors arrive in Iraq. They are searching for weapons of mass destruction, which Iraq has been banned from producing or possessing since the 1991 Gulf War.

S.A.R.S. SPREADS AROUND THE WORLD

In November 2002, a previously unknown infectious disease called S.A.R.S. (Severe Acute Respiratory Syndrome) broke out in the Guangdong province of China. The respiratory disease had a high fatality rate, and in the course of one year it killed 350 people in mainland China, 44 in Ontario, Canada, and around 400 elsewhere, including Singapore and Hong Kong. The disease managed to spread around the globe mostly by air travel. Its apparently selective infection puzzled health officials because the first man known to have contracted the disease infected four other people but did not infect his four grown-up children who lived with him. Eventually, the disease was traced back to civet cats, a Chinese wildcat that is seen as a delicacy, and the Chinese government ordered 10,000 of the animals to be slaughtered. In Canada, Ontario's healthcare system was overwhelmed with the severity of the crisis and did not cope well. Subsequent reports highlighted that more public health spending needed to be directed toward the early identification and control of infectious diseases.

ASTRONAUTS DIE IN SPACE SHUTTLE

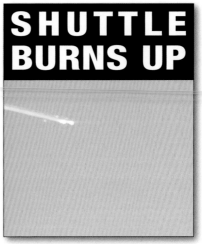

'It was the second space shuttle disaster in history, and it shocked and saddened the world as much as the destruction of the Challenger had in 1986.'

On February 1, 2003, the *Columbia* space shuttle broke up during re-entry into Earth's atmosphere. All seven crewmembers were killed. The *Columbia* crew had just completed a 16-day scientific research mission in space when the tragedy occurred. It was the second space shuttle disaster in history, and it shocked and saddened the world as much as the destruction of the *Challenger* had in 1986. The cause of the shuttle's disintegration was later found to have been sustained during launch. A piece of foam insulation had broken off and hit the left wing, damaging the thermal protection system that was designed to prevent overheating during re-entry. Although some N.A.S.A. officials suspected damage, nothing could be done about it once the shuttle had launched. Shuttle flights were stopped for two years while an investigation took place.

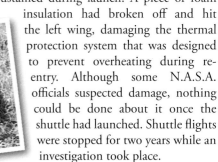

January 25
Human Shield
Volunteers travel to Iraq to act as human shields, hoping to prevent a U.S. invasion.

February 15
Millions Protest
In 800 cities around the world, millions protest against war on Iraq. Rome sees a crowd of 3 million in the largest anti-war rally in history.

March 13
Walking Tall
Some 350,000-year-old upright-walking human footprints are found in Italy.

March 17
No Resolution
U.S.-led efforts fail in securing a U.N. Security Council resolution supporting war on Iraq.

March 17
U.S. Ultimatum
U.S. President George Bush tells Saddam Hussein to leave Iraq or face military action.

COALITION FORCES INVADE IRAQ

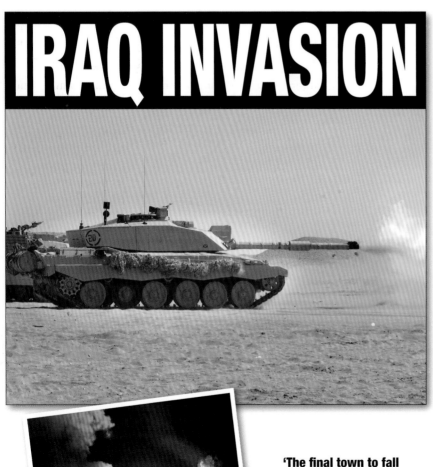

IRAQ INVASION

Above: The bombing of Baghdad.

'The final town to fall was Tikrit, the hometown of Saddam Hussein ... although coalition forces were to remain in Iraq for years to come.'

Above: American civil rights activist Jesse Jackson joins the anti-war protest in London.

British Prime Minister Tony Blair had enjoyed a strong relationship with U.S. President Clinton, with whom he shared a center-left political stance, so it was a surprise to many when he formed an even stronger bond with the right-wing U.S. President George W. Bush. The September 11 attacks in New York and Washington, D.C. in 2001 launched the U.S. into a 'War on Terror', which first brought down the Taliban regime in Afghanistan before moving on to Saddam Hussein's Iraq. By linking an invasion of Iraq with the 'War on Terror', President Bush managed to suggest to the American people that Saddam Hussein had some involvement in the 9/11 attacks. Bush

March 19
Baghdad Bombed
Saddam Hussein has not left Iraq. The first U.S. bombs fall on Baghdad.

March 20
Iraq is Invaded
U.S., U.K., Polish, and Australian troops invade Iraq.

April 9
Saddam's Regime is Over
U.S. troops take control of Baghdad, ending Saddam Hussein's 24-year rule.

April 14
Human Genome Sequenced
The Human Genome Project has mapped 99% of the human genome.

THE FALL OF SADDAM

immediately looked to Tony Blair for Great Britain's support in the war against Iraq, but Blair had much more difficulty convincing his people of the war's moral necessity. Blair took the stance that Great Britain and the rest of the world were at risk from Saddam Hussein's 'weapons of mass destruction' and that a 'regime change' was necessary both to liberate the Iraqi people and to remove the global threat of Saddam. United Nations inspectors continued to search for evidence of these weapons, and although Saddam Hussein obstructed their searches, which increased the world's suspicions, none was ever found, and the U.N. refused to support any war. There were several anti-war protests across the United States in January 2003, although the majority of the people still backed their President. On February 16, 2003, millions of British people took to the streets of London to protest against going to war. Despite the protests of the British people, Tony Blair committed Great Britain to an invasion of Iraq, sending tens of thousands of British troops to the aid of the United States. Together, on March 20, 2003, the coalition forces launched the first of many bombing campaigns on Baghdad, killing a number of Saddam's henchmen, as well as innocent civilians. On April 6, Basra became the first city to fall to coalition forces when it came under British control. On April 9, Baghdad itself fell to American forces, and the takeover was greeted by cheers from some Iraqis as the Americans pulled down a statue of Saddam Hussein. The final town to fall was Tikrit, the hometown of Saddam Hussein, and with this, President Bush declared the war effectively over, although coalition forces were to remain in Iraq for years to come.

Right: U.S. tankbuster planes let off anti-missile flares as they fire on Baghdad's presidential compound.

June 26
Landmark Ruling
The U.S. Supreme Court declares that laws against sodomy are unconstitutional.

August 1
Chechen Bomb
A Chechen suicide bomber strikes a Russian military hospital, killing 50 people.

December 13
Saddam Found in Tikrit
Saddam Hussein is captured by U.S. forces.

December 26
Earthquake in Iran
Southeastern Iran is hit by a massive earthquake, which kills 26,000 people.

N.A.S.A.'S SPIRIT LANDS ON MARS

PROBE EXPLORES MARS

Right: Spirit's airbag-protected landing craft on the Martian surface.

On January 4, 2004, N.A.S.A.'s first Mars exploration rover, known as *Spirit* or MER-A (Mars Exploration Rover A), landed safely on Mars. Since that day, the rover has been conducting geological analysis of the planet's surface and communicating effectively with its ground controllers to share invaluable information about the substance of the planet Mars. The specific aims of the MER-A mission are to identify evidence of water on the planet in the past and to determine what geological processes have shaped the current make-up of the terrain. The experiments were designed to add to the ongoing process of determining whether it is possible that life has ever existed on Mars. The *Spirit* rover landed on the site of a giant impact crater that is thought could possibly have been a former lake. The landing site was named 'Columbia Memorial Site' in honor of the seven astronauts killed in the 2003 *Columbia* disaster.

'The experiments were designed to add to the ongoing process of determining whether it is possible that life has ever existed on Mars.'

February 3
No Weapons
The C.I.A. admits there was no immediate threat from weapons of mass destruction before the 2003 invasion of Iraq.

February 4
Facebook Founded
Social networking website Facebook is launched by Harvard University students.

March 29
Smoking Ban
Ireland is the first country in the world to ban smoking in all enclosed workplaces.

May 1
Union Expands
Ten new member states join the European Union.

RUSH-HOUR TRAINS
BOMBED IN MADRID

On March 11, 2004, 191 people were killed when a series of explosions tore through three Madrid train stations during the morning rush hour. In simultaneous blasts, believed to have been remotely detonated by cell phone, the main commuter station of Atocha, in central Madrid, and two smaller suburban stations were targeted. Altogether, there were ten explosions, which ripped trains apart, killing many instantly, injuring thousands, and trapping others inside carriages. A field hospital was set up at Atocha station, and national appeals went out for people to donate blood. A temporary morgue was set up in an exhibition hall, although the busloads of relatives arriving to identify loved ones were warned that it was virtually impossible to match body parts. The attacks came three days before Spain's general election, and the Basque separatist terrorist group Eta was initially suspected to be responsible. However, political parties linked to Eta denied this and suggested that 'Arab resistance' groups could be responsible. Subsequent investigations have pointed toward the possibility of Al-Qaeda involvement. One Syrian-born Spanish citizen has since been extradited to Spain on a charge of recruiting bombers, and seven other suspects blew themselves up in an apartment in Leganés, Spain, to avoid arrest. In all, 27 people were tried regarding the attacks.

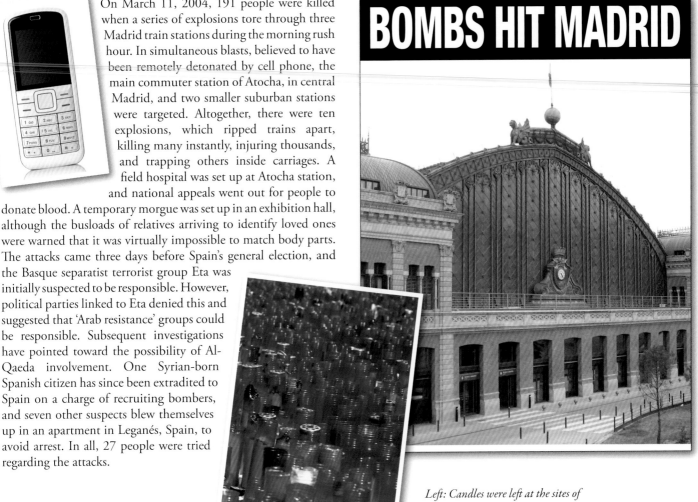

BOMBS HIT MADRID

Left: Candles were left at the sites of the attacks, while millions took to the streets to protest.

May 1
Beslan Massacre
At least 335 people are killed when Russian forces end the siege of a school in Beslan, Northern Ossetia, by Chechen terrorists.

November 2
Bush is Back
In the U.S. Presidential Election, President George Bush defeats Senator John Kerry.

December 26
Tsunami
More than 200,000 people die in Southeast Asia when an earthquake generates a devastating tsunami.

2005

SUICIDE BOMBERS SHAKE LONDON

TERRORISTS ATTACK LONDON

'The suicide attacks were the deadliest bombing in London since the Second World War.'

Above: Floral tributes were laid in Tavistock Square, where the fourth bomb exploded in a bus.

'The Underground bombs exploded when trains were crossing other trains, causing death, injury, and damage in two trains.'

January 16
Oldest Mother
Surrogate mother Adriana Iliescu becomes the oldest woman to give birth, at 66 years old.

January 30
Iraqi Elections
For the first time in 47 years, free parliamentary elections take place in Iraq.

February 16
Kyoto Protocol
The Kyoto Protocol international treaty to stabilize greenhouse gas emissions goes into effect.

March 3
Round-the-World Flight
Steve Fossett completes the first non-stop solo flight around the world.

March 4
H.I.V. Crisis
The U.N. warns that, without preventative action, around 90 million Africans could become infected by H.I.V.

During the commuter rush hour on the morning of July 7, 2005, three bombs exploded almost simultaneously on three separate trains in the London Underground, and an hour later a fourth explosion went off on a London bus. The suicide bombings, carried out by extremist British Muslims protesting against British involvement in the Iraq War, represented the first instance of suicide attacks on the London Transport system and the deadliest bombing in London since the Second World War. In total, 56 people were killed, including the four bombers. The force of the explosions, and therefore the number of fatalities, varied according to the tunnel construction within which each of the three trains was traveling. The two bombs on Circle Line trains were in shallow, wide tunnels, which sustained more of the brunt of the explosions, whereas the bomb on the Piccadilly Line train was in a deep, narrow tunnel, making the explosion more concentrated. In all cases, the Underground bombs exploded when trains were near other trains, thus causing death, injury, and damage in two trains. During the initial panic, London Underground thought that an unexpected power surge had caused the blasts, but within hours, the police issued a statement to say that a terrorist attack was the most likely explanation. Evidence found on the bodies of the bombers led the police to a bomb factory in Leeds. However, it is not clear whether the men had planned to commit suicide all along, due to inconsistent details, such as the fact that they bought return train tickets to London.

Right: In 2009, Prince Charles unveiled a memorial to the 52 victims.

April 9
Royal Wedding
Prince Charles, Prince of Wales marries Camilla Parker Bowles in Windsor, England.

April 19
New Pope Elected
Pope Benedict XVI succeeds Pope John Paul II, who died on April 2.

July 12
Attack in Israel
Members of Islamic Jihad kill five people in a shopping mall in Netanya, Israel.

July 28
Farewell to Arms
The Provisional Irish Republican Army (I.R.A.) formally ends its 36-year armed campaign.

October 8
Quake in Kashmir
A 7.6-magnitude earthquake in Kashmir kills more than 80,000 people.

2005

HURRICANE KATRINA STRIKES

HURRICANE SWAMPS CITY

'In New Orleans, the fierce hurricane completely destroyed the levee system, causing deadly floods all over the city'

Right: The hurricane totally destroyed many wooden houses in Louisiana.

In the summer of 2005, Hurricane Katrina became one of the deadliest storms in American history. It first hit the Bahamas then, on August 23, it crossed Florida as a relatively mild storm. But by the time it hit Louisiana on August 29, it had strengthened considerably, resulting in severe damage and loss of life. In New Orleans, the levee system is meant to act as protection against storms, but the fierce hurricane completely destroyed it, causing deadly floods all over the city. By the time Katrina had passed, 1,836 people had lost their lives, either as a result of the hurricane itself or during the floods. Although President Bush had issued a state-of-emergency warning two days before the hurricane hit, it did not include some of the most vulnerable areas on the Louisiana coast. Several evacuation orders went a little way toward saving lives, but it was estimated that around 80% of New Orleans residents were still in the city when the floodwaters broke. There was widespread criticism of the Bush administration, as well as the U.S. Federal Emergency Management Agency, in the aftermath of the New Orleans floods.

October 19
Saddam Tried
Saddam Hussein goes on trial in Iraq for crimes against humanity.

November 28
Climate Change Debated
The United Nations Climate Change Conference opens in Montreal.

November 30
First Face Transplant
Surgeons in Amiens, France, carry out the first human face transplant. The patient is Isabelle Dinoire, who had been mauled by her dog.

SADDAM HUSSEIN SENTENCED TO HANG

On November 5, 2006, Saddam Hussein was sentenced to death by an Iraqi court for the 1982 murder of 148 Shia Muslims in Dujail, Iraq. Saddam was due to be tried for further killings of the Kurd peoples, but the death penalty issued in November had to be carried out quickly, so it was never likely that subsequent trials would take place. Human rights groups criticized the inadequacies of the trial. However, the Iraqi court system insisted that no amount of international disapproval would change its decision. Appeals by Saddam's defense lawyers all failed. Iraq's new president, Jalal Talabani, had been an opponent of the death penalty in the past but had been known to have his deputies sign death sentences in his place. Saddam's trial had been beset by problems from the beginning due to the defendant's refusal to cooperate with the court on any level. He shouted abuse at anyone who dared to accuse him and refused to answer any questions. It had been a predictable conclusion, however, that the trial would result in the death penalty. The crime for which he was finally hanged on December 30, 2006 was one of many atrocities that had been committed during Saddam's rule. Video recordings of the noose being placed over his head and tightened were broadcast to the nation; he had refused to wear a black hood. Although the actual hanging was kept off-camera, images of Saddam's dead body in its shroud were also broadcast. It was reported that there was much celebration after his death, including cheering, chanting, and dancing around the dead body, although there were also pockets of protest, particularly in his hometown of Tikrit. The Prime Minister of Iraq, Nouri al-Maliki, said, 'Justice, in the name of the people, has carried out the death sentence against the criminal Saddam.'

'He shouted abuse at anyone who dared to accuse him and refused to answer any questions.'

SADDAM EXECUTED

January 15
Stardust Search
N.A.S.A.'s Stardust mission successfully returns dust from a comet.

February 3
Ferry Sinks
The sinking of Egyptian passenger ferry *al-Salam Boccaccio 98* kills over 1,034 people.

July 11
Mumbai Blasts
Rush-hour commuter trains are bombed in Mumbai, India, by Islamic terrorists. More than 200 people lose their lives.

July 12
Lebanon War
Israel invades Lebanon in response to attacks by Lebanon-based Hezbollah.

2006

YOUNGEST SURVIVOR OF OPEN HEART SURGERY

Owen Smith was born three months early, weighing just 1lb 8oz (0.68 kg), to Stephanie and Alan Smith of Southampton, England. Following his mother's strange premonition that he was about to be born, she went straight to the hospital, and her son was removed from her womb by an emergency caesarean section when it was discovered that he was shrinking rather than growing. In March 2006, still seven weeks before he was even due to have been born, it was found that he had a blood clot on his heart and that his only chance of survival was open-heart surgery. Although such an operation had never before been performed on such a small baby, surgeon Stephen Langley of the Southampton General Hospital knew that, despite the risks, there was no other choice. The operation was successful. Although Owen's heart was only the size of a marble, Dr. Langley managed to open it, remove the clot, sew him back up, and restart his heart.

'Seven weeks before he was even due to have been born, it was found that he had a blood clot on his heart'

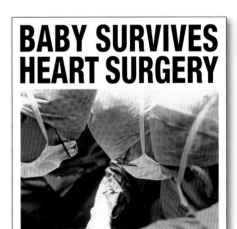

BABY SURVIVES HEART SURGERY

MASSIVE ROBBERY

40 MILLION STOLEN IN BIGGEST CASH ROBBERY EVER

On February 21, 2006, an armed gang managed to escape with £53 million (about $80 million) from a Securitas depot in Kent, England. They kidnapped a security manager as he was returning home from work by posing as police in an unmarked car. At the same time, other members of the gang went to his home and kidnapped his wife and son by also posing as police. The security manager was then bundled into a white van and driven at gunpoint to the depot, with threats that his wife and son would be hurt if he did not cooperate. At the depot, where cash is stored to be loaded into A.T.M.s, they tied up staff and spent an hour loading banknotes into the van.

August 23
Kidnapped
Austrian Natascha Kampusch escapes after being held by Wolfgang Priklopil for eight years.

August 24
Pluto Downgraded
Pluto is officially demoted to the status of dwarf planet.

October 15
North Korea Sanctioned
The U.N. sanctions North Korea over its nuclear testing.

November 23
Death Toll in Iraq Mounts
Bombs and mortar attacks kill more than 200 in Baghdad, Iraq.

218

GUN MASSACRE AT UNIVERSITY IN VIRGINIA

On April 16, 2007, a student at Virginia Tech killed a total of 32 students and professors in the deadliest shooting incident by a single gunman in U.S. history. Seung-Hui Cho, who was from South Korea but had been in America for 15 years, had received therapy for severe anxiety disorder in high school and continued to suffer from mental health problems, including severe depression and selective mutism. His mental illness was not reported to staff at Virginia Tech because of privacy laws, and by then Cho had discontinued his treatment. At the university, staff had first been alerted to his problems when he stalked female students and wrote a hate-fueled essay. Campus police were notified, but the only action taken was to remove Cho from class and teach him separately. Cho's professor described him as the 'loneliest person in the world'. In the early morning of April 16, Cho went to the dormitory of Emily Hilscher, a freshman with whom he may have been infatuated, and shot her dead, along with another student, Ryan Clark. While police and emergency services dealt with the initial shootings, Cho returned to his own dorm room, changed his clothes, logged on to his email, and removed his hard drive. Two hours later, after mailing a package of documents and recordings to N.B.C. News, Cho entered the university building that housed the engineering and mechanics faculty, chained the doors closed, and began shooting into the classrooms. He fired single controlled shots that were apparently random in their intended targets. It was around 15 minutes before police responding to 911 calls were able to break into the building. By then, Cho had killed five professors and 27 students. He then shot himself dead. Inquiries into the massacre found fault with the gun laws that had allowed a psychiatric patient to buy weapons and ammunition. Later that year, a law was passed that allowed educational institutions to ban guns on campus.

'By the time police were able to break into the buildings, Cho had killed five professors and 27 students.'

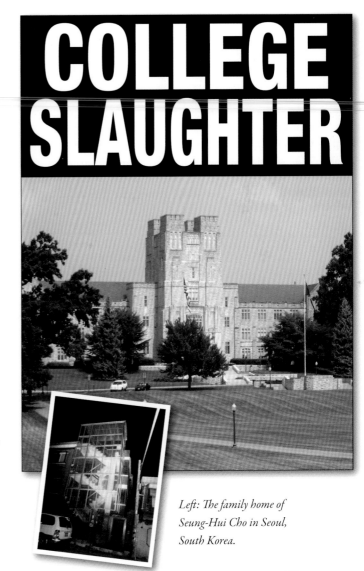

COLLEGE SLAUGHTER

Left: The family home of Seung-Hui Cho in Seoul, South Korea.

February 2
War in Somalia
In the Somalian civil war, eight people are killed in a mortar attack in the capital, Mogadishu.

May 15
Gaza Fighting
Fighting breaks out in the Gaza Strip as the Palestinian National Authority government falls.

June 5
Messenger Mission
N.A.S.A.'s *Messenger* spacecraft makes a fly-by of Venus en route to Mercury.

June 24
Brown for P.M.
Gordon Brown is elected leader of the U.K. Labour Party. He becomes Prime Minister three days later.

2007

BLOW FOR DEMOCRACY IN PAKISTAN

On October 18, 2007, two Al-Qaeda suicide bombers killed 136 people in Karachi, Pakistan, in an assassination attempt on Pakistan's former Prime Minister Benazir Bhutto. Bhutto's truck was sufficiently armored to save her life. She had been aware of the threats that greeted her return from self-imposed exile. Nevertheless, she was determined that extremist terrorists should not destroy the path to democracy in Pakistan, declaring, 'Democracy alone can save Pakistan from disintegration and militant takeover.'

'Benazir Bhutto's support of America in the "War on Terror" made her a constant target of extremist groups.'

Her return to Pakistan signaled a possible power-share between her own Pakistan People's Party and President General Pervez Musharraf, who had seized power in 1999, as a step towards restoring democracy. Benazir Bhutto's support of America in the 'War on Terror' had forced her into exile in Dubai and made her a constant target of extremist groups. On December 26, 2007, just over two months after the failed assassination attempt, Benazir Bhutto was shot dead in another suicide attack, which also killed 14 of her supporters. Al-Qaeda's main commander in Afghanistan claimed responsibility, saying, 'We terminated the most precious American asset.' A U.S. Senator unintentionally upheld this notion with the statement, 'Our foreign policy had relied on her presence as a stabilizing force.'

BHUTTO ASSASSINATED

Left: General Pervez Musharraf, who seized power in a coup in 1999.

June 29
Bombs Defused
Two car bombs are made safe in central London. The plot is linked to extremist Islamist groups.

June 30
Glasgow Terror Alert
In an attack linked to the previous day's London car bombs, a jeep loaded with propane is driven into Glasgow Airport. The attack is foiled.

August 14
Iraq Horror
Suicide bombs in northern Iraq kill 796 people, in the Iraq War's worst car bomb attack.

August 25
Greek Wild Fires
Heatwaves, drought, arson, and negligence cause a series of devastating forest fires in Greece.

September 26
Burma Protests
In Burma (also known as Myanmar), the military cracks down on anti-government protests.

BLIND PATIENTS FITTED WITH ELECTRONIC EYES

In April 2008, surgeons at Moorfields Eye Hospital in London successfully implanted bionic eyes into two blind patients during a four-hour operation. The electronic devices consist of miniature cameras that are mounted in a pair of glasses, which themselves transmit wireless signals into a receiver attached to the patient's retina. The patients are not expected to have clear sight, but they should be able to distinguish light and dark and recognize shapes, as well as being able to navigate sufficiently to walk unaided. Second Sight's Argus II retinal implant works by imitating the eye's action, with the signals received from the camera stimulating the existing nerve endings in the patient's eye. The first patients both had an inherited condition called retinitis pigmentosa, but it is thought that the bionic eye could eventually also by used on people with non-inherited blindness.

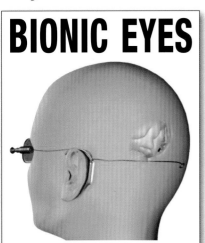

STORM DEVASTATES BURMA

On May 3, 2008, a tropical cyclone hit Burma (also known as Myanmar), leaving around 50,000 people dead and millions homeless. In several townships in the Irrawaddy region, 90–95% of buildings were destroyed and survivors were unable to get food or clean drinking water. As Cyclone Nagris tore through the rice-growing region of the country, winds reached 120 mph (200 kph), sweeping away roads, trees, and buildings. In the main city of Yangon (previously Rangoon), power was lost. The ruling military junta had refused aid in the aftermath of the 2004 tsunami, but the scale of the wreckage from Cyclone Nagris meant that foreign aid was essential. Aid agencies found it difficult to operate in the restricted conditions brought about by the collapsed infrastructure, and many areas were totally cut off.

January 21
Stock Plunge
Fueled by fears of a U.S. recession, stock markets around the world take a plunge.

February 17
Kosovo Declaration
In the Balkans, Kosovo declares its independence from Serbia.

February 22
Rock Falls
In the U.K., Northern Rock is the first bank in Europe to be taken into state control.

March 1
Gaza Strikes
In the ongoing Israeli-Palestinian conflict, Israeli air strikes kill 50 in the Gaza Strip.

March 6
Israeli Dead
Eight Israelis are killed when a Palestinian gunman opens fire in a seminary in Jerusalem.

2008

CREDIT CRUNCH BEGINS

The global financial crisis had been brewing for some time when it began to show its effects in the middle of 2007. Many large financial institutions collapsed when they were unable to call in massive debts, and stock markets fell across the world. After years of economic boom, the financial bubble finally burst at the end of 2007. The first noticeable collapse involved the sub-prime mortgage market in the U.S., in which high-risk individuals had been lent money at high rates of interest. As soon as problems emerged, confidence plummeted, and assets began to drop dramatically in value. Governments poured public money into the banks to prevent them from collapsing, but nothing was sufficient to fill the credit hole. The 'credit crunch' followed, and businesses that relied on credit from failing banks also collapsed. It is estimated that, in the U.S. alone, taxpayers will have paid out $9.7 trillion (£6.5 trillion) to bail out their banks. By the start of 2008, the industrialized world had entered an economic recession.

May 25
Phoenix Lands
N.A.S.A.'s *Phoenix* robotic spacecraft is the first to land on the northern polar region of Mars.

June 27
Elections in Zimbabwe
President Robert Mugabe retains power in a disputed election in Zimbabwe.

August 7
War in South Ossetia
Russia and Georgia launch offensives in the South Ossetia region.

September 9
Thailand Crisis
The Constitutional Court of Thailand orders Prime Minister Samak to resign.

September 15
Mugabe Shares Power
In Zimbabwe, Robert Mugabe signs a power-sharing deal.

FIRST BLACK PRESIDENT OF THE UNITED STATES

OBAMA ELECTED PRESIDENT

Right: Obama supporters celebrate his election in Washington, D.C.

On November 4, 2008, Illinois Senator and Democrat candidate Barack Obama was elected 44th President of the United States of America. He is the first African American in U.S. history to become president, defeating Republican John McCain. At Harvard Law School, Obama had been the first black president of the Harvard Law Review, and he practiced as a civil rights attorney in Chicago before being elected to the Illinois State Senate in 1997. In 2004, he was elected as a Democratic Senator to the U.S. Senate, and in 2008, he beat his rival Hillary Clinton to become the Democratic candidate for the 2008 presidential elections. Then, just 45 years after racial segregation in the United States had come to an end, Barack Obama ascended to the highest office in the land. He came to power during a difficult time in U.S. history, in the middle of a world economic crisis and while the United States military was still tangled in problematic operations in Iraq and Afghanistan. In his acceptance speech, Obama, whose rhetorical powers had been compared to civil rights leader Dr. Martin Luther King, echoed King's speeches by referring to the 'arc of history' that had led to his election. His words, spoken to an audience of 240,000 supporters in Chicago, were broadcast live across the world.

'Just 45 years after racial segregation in the United States had come to an end, Barack Obama ascended to the highest office in the land.'

Left: Michelle Obama, Barack's wife.

September 20
Pakistan Bomb
A suicide truck bomb destroys a hotel in Pakistan, killing at least 60 people.

October 7
Iceland in Trouble
Russia and Iceland begin discussions of a Russian financial bail-out.

October 21
Hadron On
The world's largest particle accelerator, the Large Hadron Collider, is officially inaugurated near Geneva, Switzerland. It will test various propositions of high-energy physics.

November 26
Mumbai Terror
Terrorist attacks by Islamic militants in Mumbai, India, kill 173 people and injure over 300.

Acknowledgements

The publishers would like to thank the following people for their kind permission to reproduce their photographs

Key: a-above; b-bottom/below; c-center; l-left; r-right

All images supplied by Mirrorpix – archives of the Daily Mirror, © Mirrorpix (MGN LTD), except:

1 NASA, 3b Dirck Halstead/Getty Images, 5tr NASA, 5br istockphoto.com/geopaul, 6r WILLIAM BETSCH/AFP/Getty Images, 7 MPI/Getty Images, 8 NASA, 9 JEAN-PIERRE PREVEL/AFP/Getty Images, 10tl istockphoto.com/duncan1890, 10bc istockphoto.com/Anthony Baggett, 10br istockphoto.com/Peter Spiro, 11cr istokphoto.com/Rob Friedman, 15bc istockphoto.com/Igor Marx, 16bl MPI/Getty Images, 18b istockphoto.com/james steidl, 21b H. F. Davis/Topical Press Agency/Getty Images, 22tr istockphoto.com/John Cairns, 25b FPG/Hulton Archive/Getty Images, 27b Paul Popper/Popperfoto/Getty Images, 28b Time Life Pictures/National Archives/Time Life Pictures/Getty Images, 29bc istockphoto.com/Duncan Walker, 30b Hulton Archive/Getty Images, 31b istockphoto.com/Brent Bossom, 34b Popperfoto/Getty Images, 37c istockphoto.com/Amanda Udlinek, 40cr Popperfoto/Getty Images, 48tr Monty Fresco/Topical Press Agency/Getty Images, 49cr Yale Joel//Time Life Pictures/Getty Images, 50br istockphoto.com/ayzek, 59bl istockphoto.com/Denis Babenko, 63bl istockphoto.com/clu, 68b Paul Schutzer/Time Life Pictures/Getty Images, 73b NASA, 74tr Loomis Dean/Time Life Pictures/Getty Images, 76b Howard Sochurek/Time Life Pictures/Getty Images, 77bc istockphoto.com/lara seregni, 79b istockphoto.com/sx70, 81tr istockphoto.com/Steven Allan, 82bl Getty images, 83c istockphoto.com/Alexander Fediachov, 83bl istockphoto.com/jaynemccarthy, 84bl istockphoto.com/woodstock, 84cb istockphoto.com/elmvilla, 85br istockphoto.com/Dave Long, 86l NASA, 86bl istockphoto.com/petestopher, 86bc istockphoto.com/EuToch, 87br istockphoto.com/Dmitry Nikolaev, 88bc istockphoto.com/Kamyshko, 88tc NASA, 89bc istockphoto.com/Chris Reed Photography, 91bc istockphoto.com/infospeed, 91br istockphoto.com/Kaufmann Visual Arts, 92l Time & Life Pictures/Getty Images, 92bc istockphoto.com/joebobbubba, 93r Getty Images, 93br istockphoto.com/Kapstadt, 94b istockphoto.com/Torsten Ståhlberg, 95tr NASA, 95cr istockphoto.com/RFStock, 96tr Time & Life Pictures/Getty Images, 98 istockphoto.com/gprentice, 101tl Time & Life Pictures/Getty Images, 101bl istockphoto.com/stevenallan, 102 Time & Life Pictures/Getty Images, 106l, 107 all NASA, 109bl istockphoto.com/naes, 110l NASA, 112tr Getty Images, 115br istockphoto.com/Robert Mayne, 117br istockphoto.com/Thomas Hottner, 118l AFP/Getty Images, 119l and cr NASA, 119br istockphoto.com/RUDI TAPPER, 120r istockphoto.com/Richard Gunion, 123br istockphoto.com/Hendrik De Bruyne, 123bc istockphoto.com/Alex de groot, 125cl istockphoto.com/SERDAR YAGCI, 125bc istockphoto.com/alandj, 125br istockphoto.com/alandj, 125tr Getty Images North America, 126tl Getty Images, 128tl Getty Images, 128bc istockphoto.com/Cliff Parnell, 129l courtesy of U.S. Government, 129r Keystone/Hulton Archive/Getty Images, 130cr AFP PHOTO/Getty Images, 130bl abd br NASA, 134tl and bl Getty Images, 135br Time & Life Pictures, 136l AFP/Getty Images, 136bc istockphoto.com/Guillaume Dubé, 138br Getty Images, 140bc istockphoto.com/Scorpion_PL, 141tr istockphoto.com/creativephoto, 142br istockphoto.com/Steven Allan, 143br itsockphoto.com/Jeremy Voisey, 145bc istockphoto.com/Johan Ramberg, 147tl istockphoto.com/ivan mateev, 147bl AFP/Getty Images, 149tl Time & Life Pictures, 149bc istockphoto.com/SlidePix, 150tl istockphoto.com/dan_prat, 150tr NASA, 150bc istockphoto.com/Mooneydriver, 151 Peter Jordan/Time & Life Pictures/Getty Images, 154tl and cb NASA, 156tl AFP/Getty Images, 156br Code Red, 157r Getty Images, 157bl istockphoto.com/Mateusz Skalski, 158bc istockphoto.com/Sergey Kamshylin, 159r Getty Images, 159bc NASA, 160tr Holger Ellgaard, 160bl Wayne Eastep, 161tl istockphoto.com/Pierre Janssen, 162bl istockphoto.com, 165tl Time & Life Pictures/Getty Images, 167r Michael Chow//Time Life Pictures/Getty Images, 173 Time & Life Pictures/Getty Images, 175tr Time & Life Pictures/Getty Images, 177tr Ed Pritchard, 177cr istockphoto.com/abbesses, 177br Time & Life Pictures/Getty Images, 180tl Hulton Archive, 180tr Getty Images, 182l AFP/Getty Images, 184tl AFP/Getty Images, 184tr AFP/Getty Images, 184c istockphoto.com/Alan Tobey, 185bc istockphoto.com/John Barnett, 186tl AFP/Getty Images, 186bl Time & Life Pictures/Getty Images, 187bc istockphoto.com/Denis Smith, 189 AFP/AFP/Getty Images, 189tr and bc NASA, 190bl AFP/Getty Images, 191tl istockphoto.com/Scott Orr, 196tl AFP/Getty Images, 197 Getty Images, 198tl istockphoto.com/Àlex Culla i Viñals, 199br istockphoto.com/Simon Podgorsek, 201tr istockphoto.com/bluestocking, 201bl istockphoto.com/geopaul, 202tr istockphoto.com/nathan winter, 202bl AFP/Getty Images, 204tr istockphoto.com/Terraxplorer, 204bl istockphoto.com/Markus Seidel, 287tr Getty Images, 208l Getty Images, 209ll istockphoto.com/Tomaz Levstek, 209tr CNN/Getty Images, 209bc CNN/Getty Images, 212 all NASA, 213tl istockphoto.com/Jakub Semeniuk, 213r istockphoto.com/harryfn, 213bc istockphoto.com/kelvin wakefield, 216l istockphoto.com/Joseph Nickischer, 216tr istockphoto.com/Parker Deen, 216br istockphoto.com/Joseph Nickischer, 217 Chris Hondros/Getty Images, 218tr Ben Edwards, 219r istockphoto.com/Brian Adams, 221l Mohammed Sawan, 221tr and bc istockphoto.com/Grace Tan, 222l istockphoto.com/JoeClemson, 222r istockphoto.com/Kirby Hamilton, 223tr istockphoto,com/Dan Moore endpapers: front – Getty Images, back – AFP/Getty Images

Page 3: Journalists and South Vietnamese flee Saigon as communist North Vietnamese troops enter the city in April 1975.

Page 5
Top: Skylab was launched in 1973 and was America's first space station. It remained in orbit until 1979, when it burned up on reentry.

Middle: Concorde made its first supersonic flight on October 1, 1969, and remained in service until October 2003.

Bottom: On June 26, 2000, scientists declared that they had decoded most of the chemical instructions that made up human D.N.A.

Endpapers
Front: The space shuttle Challenger explodes just 73 seconds after launch from Cape Canaveral, Florida, on January 28, 1986, killing all seven astronauts on board.

Back: Rescue workers sort through the wreckage of a building in Nairobi, Kenya, following a terrorist attack on the U.S. embassy on August 7, 1998.